IMAGES
of America

WAYNESVILLE AND WAYNE TOWNSHIP

On the Cover: An oil strike along the Little Miami River bottoms between Waynesville and Corwin in October 1897 turned out to be natural gas. Pictured here are some unidentified workmen and investors. The man in the straw hat at the right is possibly Walter Kilbon of Corwin. The Waynesville Gas Company was incorporated by subscription. Mamie Chandler was the first woman to invest. Only the one well was drilled and successful, although 3,000 acres of land were leased by December 23, 1897, for future drilling. (Courtesy of Mary L. Cook Public Library.)

IMAGES
of America

WAYNESVILLE AND WAYNE TOWNSHIP

Dennis E. Dalton

ARCADIA
PUBLISHING

ISBN 978-0-7385-9444-6

Published by Arcadia Publishing
Charleston, South Carolina

Printed in the United States of America

Library of Congress Control Number: 2012940165

For all general information, please contact Arcadia Publishing:
Telephone 843-853-2070
Fax 843-853-0044
E-mail sales@arcadiapublishing.com
For customer service and orders:
Toll-Free 1-888-313-2665

Visit us on the Internet at www.arcadiapublishing.com

To Charles Dickens, Waynesville's most colorful tourist, on the 200th anniversary of his birth and to all readers who have ever called a small town home.

CONTENTS

ACKNOWLEDGMENTS

Thank you to the following who gave unselfishly of their professional time, talent, and friendship: Victoria Van Harlingen, executive director of the Warren County History Center; Lynley Dunham, Warren County History Center archivist and assistant curator; Linda Swartzel, director of Mary L. Cook Public Library; Prof. Michael Coyan; Wilma Surface Coyan; Suzanne Harlan Andrews; Marilyn Lamb Thompson; Lucille Lamb Henry; and Don McLaughlin. Special thanks go to Bob and Penny Haas and Larry Tobias for their gifts of technical equipment.

And many thanks to Scott Davis, Gerald Miller, and all others who generously gave of their unselfish and kind assistance.

INTRODUCTION

Waynesville, Ohio, has hosted the curious and famous throughout its history. Among its influential visitors have been politicians, US presidents, actors, and oddities. Samuel Heighway, the English mastermind and founder of Waynesville on March 8, 1797, expected his projected new "plantation" to become the legislative capital of the Northwest Territory. He went as far as providing a site on the map of the village for a courthouse on the public square.

He and his partners, Francis Baily, a young scientist; Dr. Evan Banes, MD; and Rev. John Smith, expected their 30,000-acre joint investment to become a prosperous agricultural and business center. Heighway negotiated the $1.25-per-acre purchase from Judge John Cleves Symmes between the Little and Great Miami Rivers.

The settlement party purchased over 10 tons of supplies and tools and shipped them from Philadelphia aboard a 12-by-36-foot Kentucky ark flatboat in the fall of 1796. The cargo was moved on the Allegheny and Monongahela Rivers to where they form the Ohio River at Pittsburgh. These half-dozen pioneers suffered the rigors of the Ohio River until they arrived near the Little Miami River close to Cincinnati in early March 1797.

After transporting their possessions by wagon to the site of Waynesville on March 8, the settlers dug in with primitive log shelters. Heighway's layout of the village was on a rectangular plan facing the Little Miami River. An arrangement of formal parks and squares was proposed around a central public square. The design was accented with plans for a serpentine walk, groves of ornamental trees, and fishponds. Heighway's map of the village also included spots for fountains and a tree-shaded esplanade.

Heighway's dream of Waynesville becoming the capital of the Northwest never came true, but the village did develop into what would become one of the most important trade centers in the new state of Ohio.

One

THE BEGINNING

By using discarded mussel shells, a subordinate business was created. Piles of shells along the riverbanks of the Little Miami led to the 1865 opening of a pearl button factory in Waynesville. If Louisa Stetson Larrick had not grubstaked her younger brother John B. Stetson the $60 to open a one-man hat factory in Philadelphia, his world-recognized hat empire would have been lost. Regaining his health at Louisa's home on South Main Street in Waynesville in 1865, Stetson devised plans for his factory for manufacturing the famous American cowboy headgear, the "Boss of the Plains" 10-gallon hat. Patent medicine wizards made Waynesville the proprietary medicine capital of Warren County. Dr. J.M. Robb and two other dentists concocted Dr. Robb's Hippodrome Liniment in 1848.

In 1850, Dr. William Anderson introduced his gastric neutralizer, a cough syrup, and a liniment. Another cough remedy of vegetable composition was made in 1851 by a Dr. Borton. Dr. Haines Golden Specific, a cure for drunkenness was sold worldwide. Developed by Dr. James Haines, a Quaker, in 1876, it was prepared from catalpa tree buds. Waynesville National Bank, now Lebanon Citizen's National Bank, ventured into branch banking in 1877, just two years after its founding. The bank extended services to nearby Lebanon, Warren County. Lebanon's banks had closed in 1873 and 1877. Waynesville's branch was opened in Lebanon's Boake and Hunt Building on March 28, 1877. The *National Bankers* magazine scooped the story in its August issue. This was the "first instance on record of the establishment of a branch by a national bank." The Lebanon branch was closed on October 18 because there was "no authority in law" providing for branch banks.

An official of the National Cash Register Company at Dayton, Ohio, tried to locate a factory branch in Waynesville in 1894. The representative, named Briedenbaugh, was unable to close the deal. Waynesville Village Council did not want a smoky factory "stinking up its village." The C.W. Lamar Cracker Factory was opened at 258 Miami Street in July 1894. The factory baked crackers from flour ground by LaMar's Telegraph Mill on the Little Miami River. The cracker factory was leased to its head baker, Hinsman of Reading, Ohio, in 1898 for five years. A Waynesville farmer named Palmer was credited with growing the first commercial chewing tobacco in the United States in 1825. Wayne Township farmers experimented with growing cotton, rice, pecans, and grapes from 1816 until 1860. The silk industry was attempted in the early 1830s.

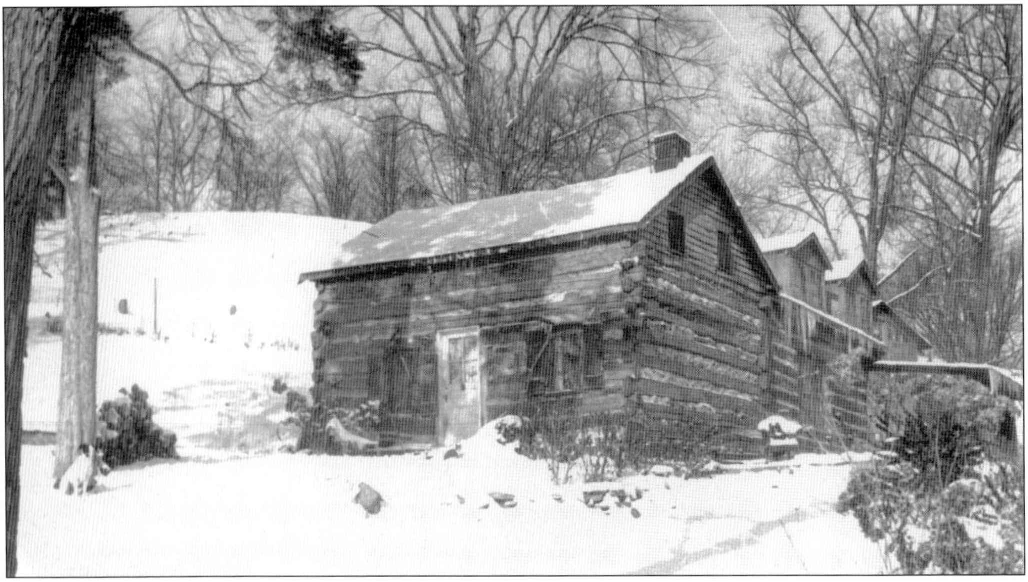

This log cabin was built by Samuel Heighway, Waynesville's founder, on Newman's Run about 1792 while he surveyed the area. It also served as the miller's house; the miller's gristmill was also built on Newman's Run by Heighway in 1802. The cabin was purchased in 1946 by John J. and Martha Nichols Edmiston, noted journalists, and later enlarged. The Edmistons served as undercover agents for the FBI from 1939 to 1941. This photograph was taken in 1970. (Author's.)

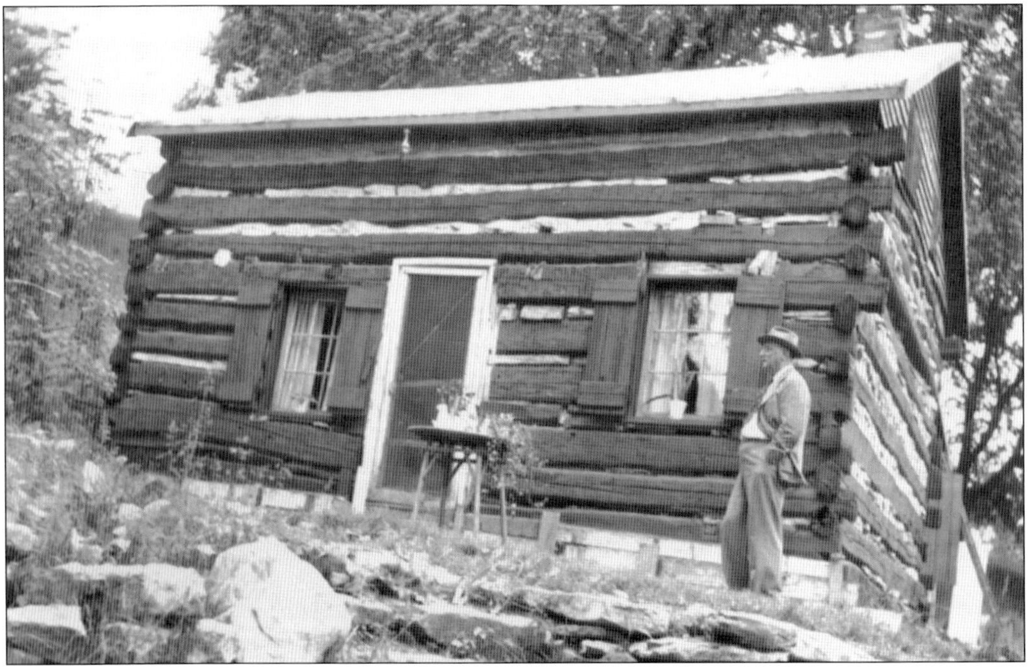

The Heighway-Edmiston log cabin was the first home of Lewis and Jane McClelland Edwards after they were married on October 13, 1833. The cabin was mostly destroyed by fire in 1971, when it was the home of Martha Edmiston. Logs were salvaged for a surveyor's log cabin at Caesar's Creek Pioneer Village, located southeast of Waynesville. (Courtesy of Warren County Historical Society [WCHS] Museum.)

William H. Heighway, Samuel Heighway's grandson, married Julia Von Salis, daughter of Baron Ullyses Von Salis. Baron Von Salis's wife had died prior to the time this photograph was taken in 1869. From left to right are Baron Von Salis and daughters Charlotte and Julia Von Salis. (Author's.)

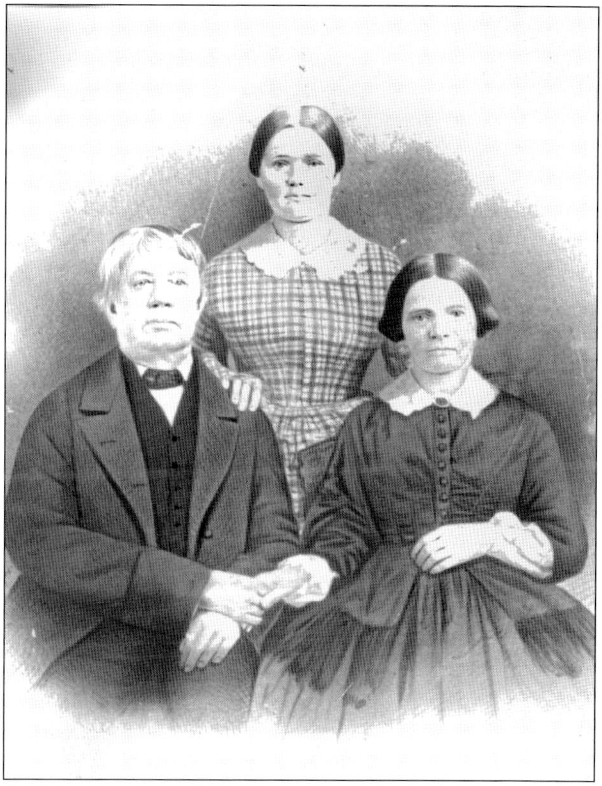

Early Waynesville was built around this public square at High and Main Streets. This winter scene, photographed in 1950, shows the Church of Christ, which was built in 1877 on the site of the old McKay Hall. The original Siamese twins, Cheng and Eng Bunker, were exhibited in McKay Hall in 1833. Tom Thumb appeared there in 1865. The earliest shows on the square included an African elephant and lion in 1818. The village's first circus was performed there in 1832. (Courtesy of WCHS Museum.)

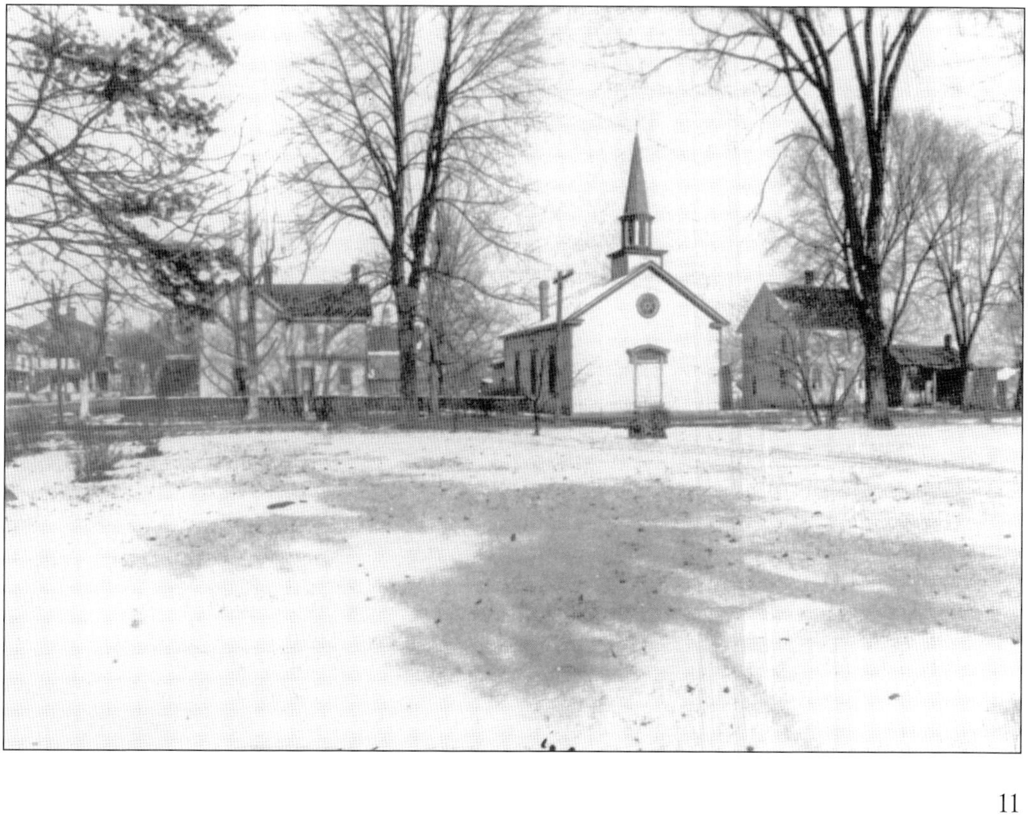

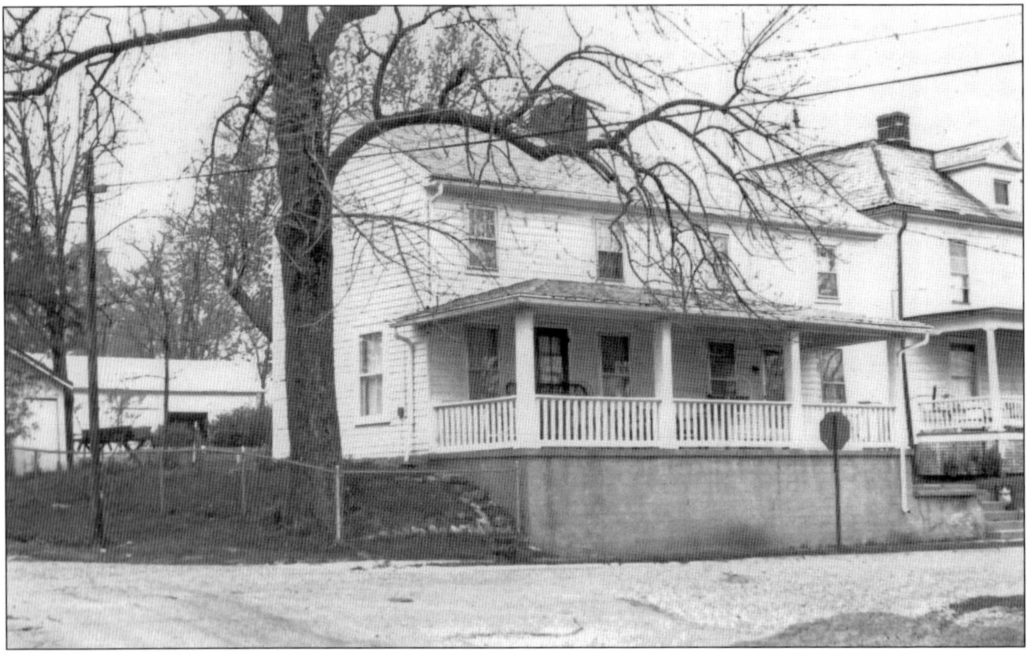

The Holloway House Inn, shown above in 1970, hosted the famous English author Charles Dickens on April 21, 1842. Expecting brandy, Dickens was served plain cold water. On April 22, 1999, Dickens's great-great-grandson, English actor Gerald Charles Dickens, visited the house, which was then the home of Laura Brown. (Courtesy of Mary L. Cook Public Library.)

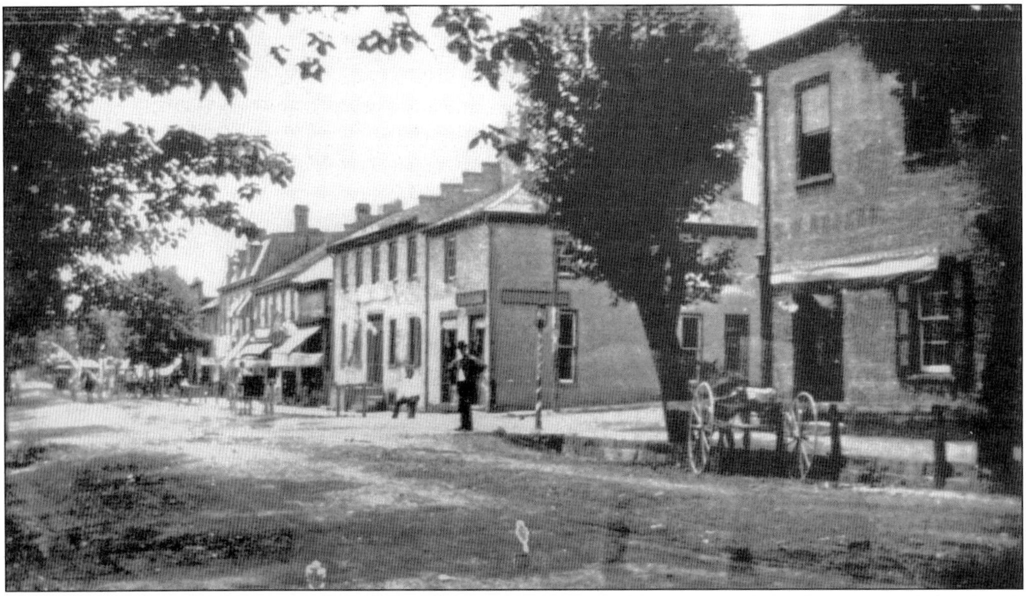

This photograph, taken in 1875, shows the intersection of Main and North Streets. The brick building with the stair-step gable on the left is the Wright-Scanlon home, built in 1814. The addition to it on the corner is the old drugstore, constructed in 1860. It was the second location of the Waynesville National Bank in 1880. From 1926 through the early 1940s, it housed the Burton and Satterthwaite Restaurants. At the right corner is the S.W. Rogers store, which was originally built in 1847 by John Haddon. (Courtesy of WCHS Museum.)

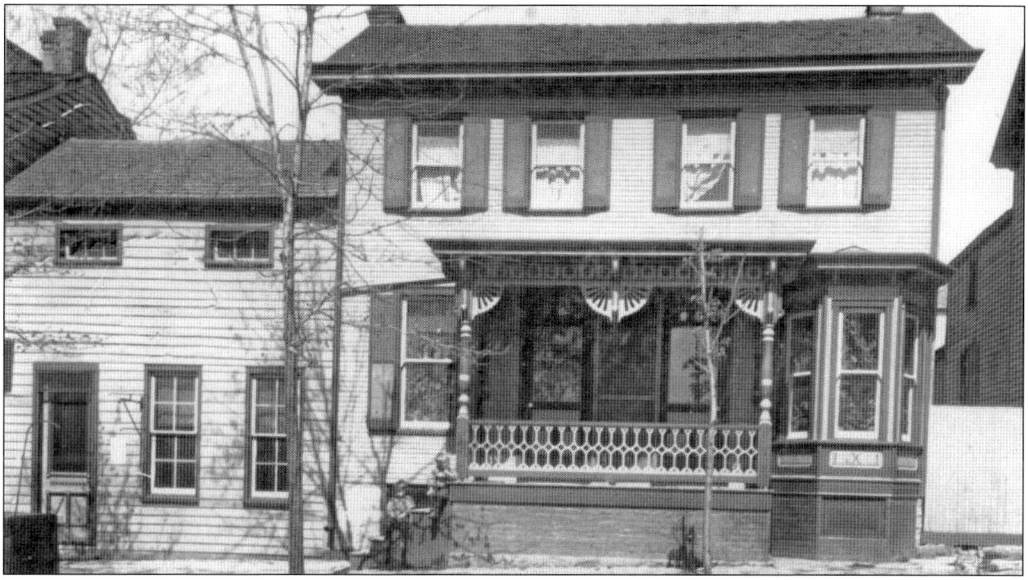

This 1879 photograph shows the Samuel Smothers Barbershop on the left and the Mahlon Ridge home on the right. When it was taken, Ridge operated a barbershop in the Smothers Building. The Smothers barbershop was built in the 1840s. Smothers had a barbershop in the building in 1853 and hid fugitive slaves there as well as in his home at Crosswicks. African American Smothers was a free man. He was followed by African American barber Henry Foster. (Courtesy of WCHS Museum.)

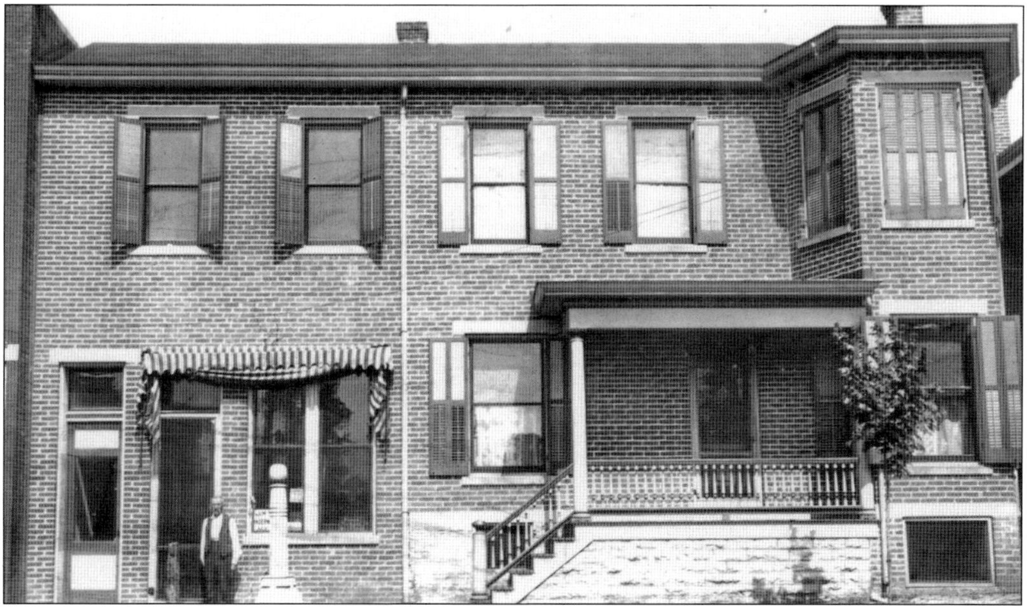

Mahlon Ridge stands in front of his new barbershop and home on the northwest side of Main Street in 1901. The frame buildings that previously stood on the same site in 1879 were destroyed by Waynesville's great fire of April 7, 1900. The buildings were the barbershop and residence of Orville Gray, whose partner was Chester Carey. They were demolished for the entrance to the drive-in banking window and the office expansion of the Waynesville National Bank. (Courtesy of Mary L. Cook Public Library.)

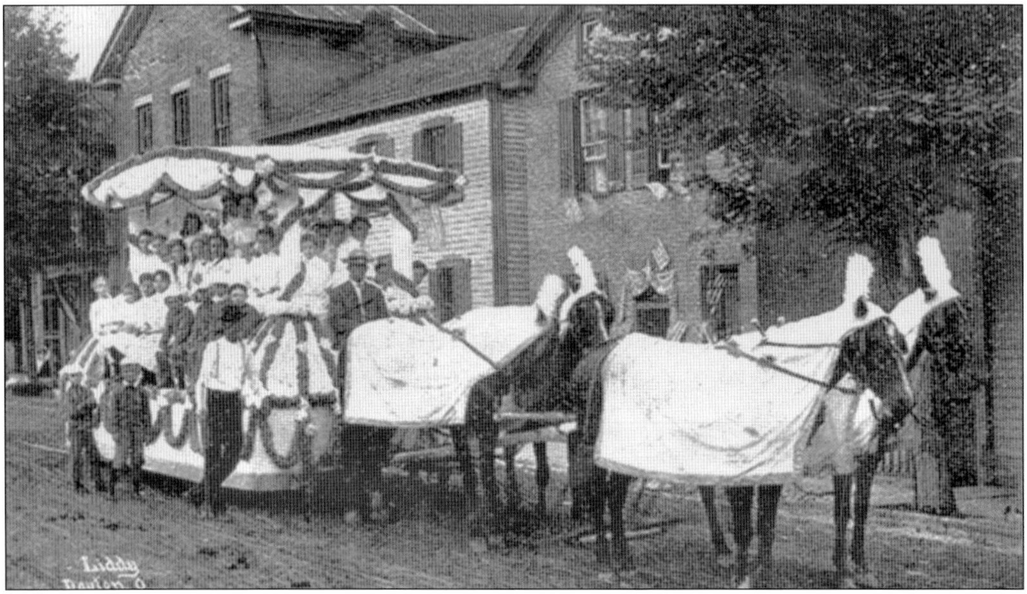

A float in the 1905 Waynesville Homecoming parade is shown on North Main Street. In the background are, from left to right, the Wayne Township House, the Morris Cook home and tailor's shop, and the Holland Building. The Holland Building, at 50 North Main Street, was erected in 1837 by Reeve Holland. The first floor was originally a carpenter's shop. Upstairs on the second story was a weaving shop. A room on the first floor served as the village jail in 1871. (Courtesy of Mary L. Cook Public Library.)

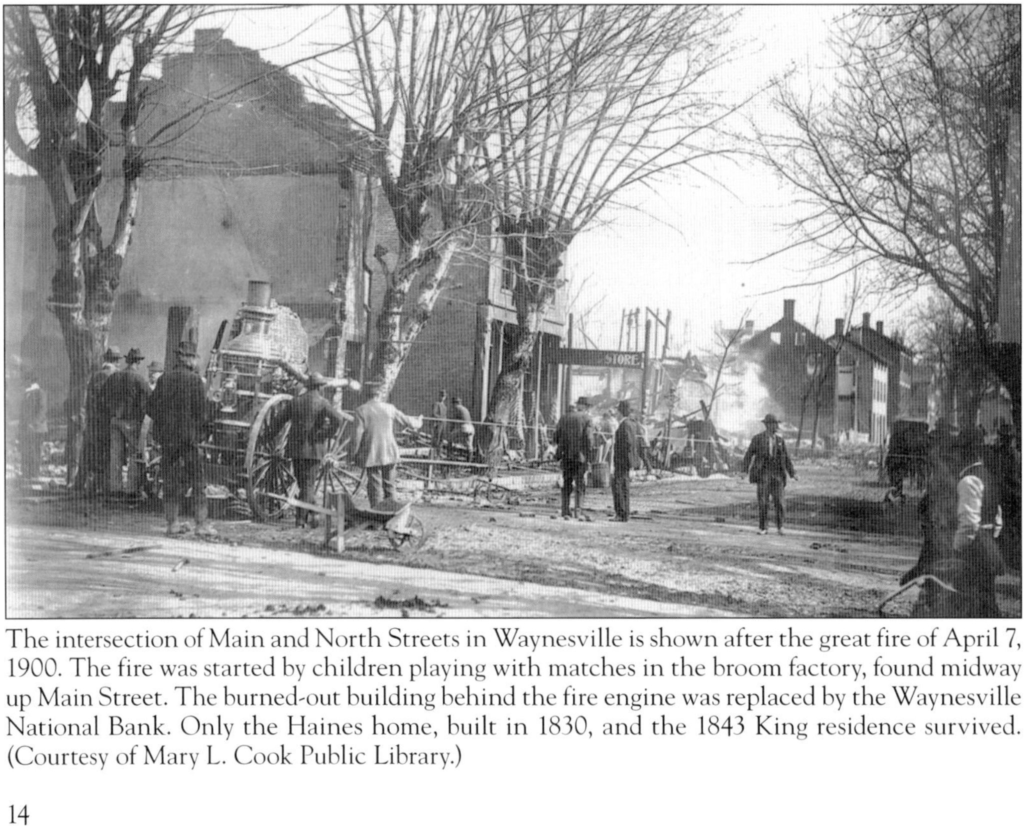

The intersection of Main and North Streets in Waynesville is shown after the great fire of April 7, 1900. The fire was started by children playing with matches in the broom factory, found midway up Main Street. The burned-out building behind the fire engine was replaced by the Waynesville National Bank. Only the Haines home, built in 1830, and the 1843 King residence survived. (Courtesy of Mary L. Cook Public Library.)

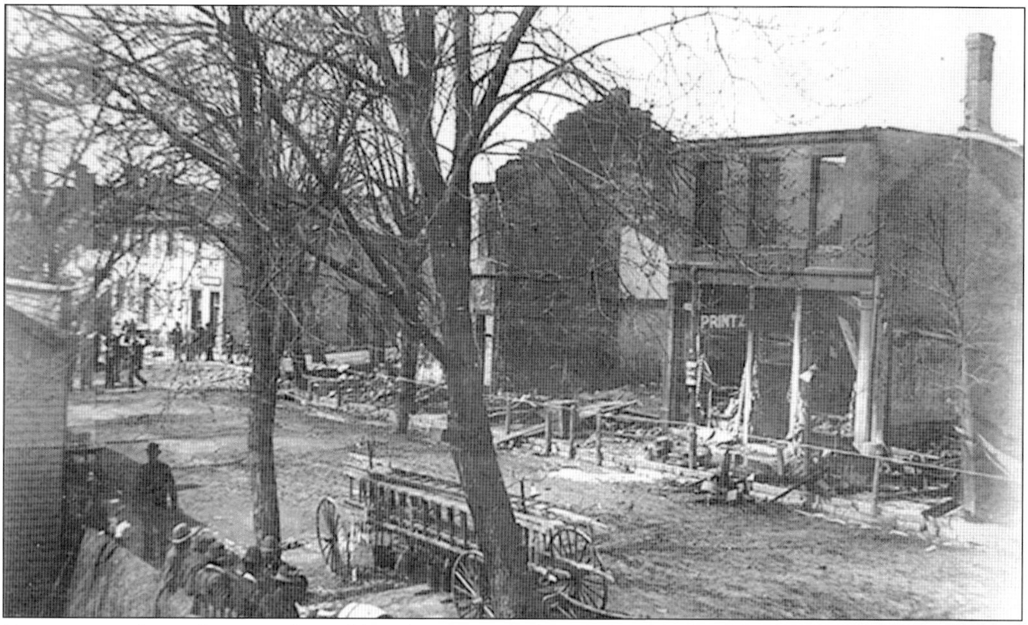

Destruction from the great fire of April 7, 1900, is shown from the east side of North Main Street. The Lebanon Citizens National Bank is located on that site now. On the left is the intersection of North and Main Streets. The buildings on the corner were demolished for a bank parking lot. The Printz Grocery Store sign is visible on the building on the right. (Courtesy of Mary L. Cook Public Library.)

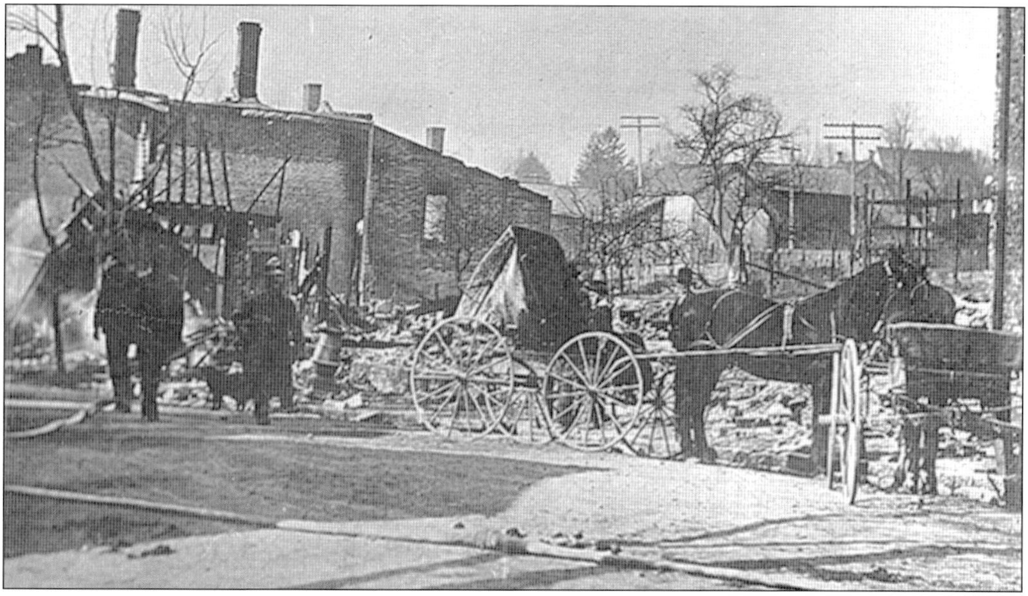

Two unidentified buggies of sightseers are shown on Waynesville's North Main Street looking over the destruction from the great fire of April 7, 1900, which almost leveled the entire business block. Women formed bucket brigades to assist the local firemen as well as fire companies from Harveysburg and Morrow. Morrow's fire engine was brought on a flatcar on the Pennsylvania Railroad by special arrangements and pulled from Corwin across the "Avenue." (Courtesy of Mary L. Cook Public Library.)

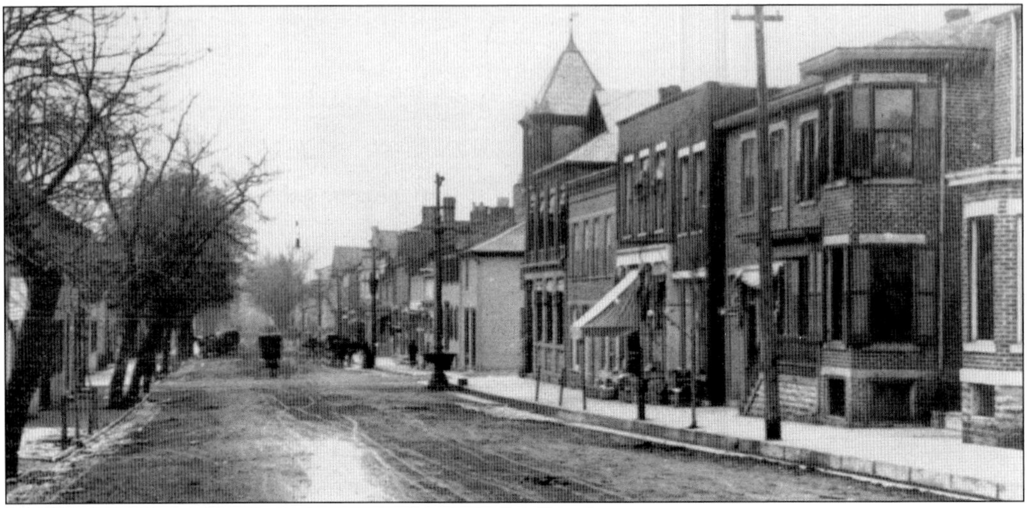

The North Main Street business block is shown here in 1905, after reconstruction took place in 1901. An ornamental fountain, which doubled as horse-watering trough, is shown in front of Waynesville National Bank in the background. The building with the store awning, which was constructed in 1881, was not entirely destroyed by the fire, and so it was refurbished. A cigar factory in this building manufactured Star Cigars from 1895 until after 1905. The *Miami Gazette* was located on the second floor during the 1900 fire. (Courtesy of Mary L. Cook Public Library.)

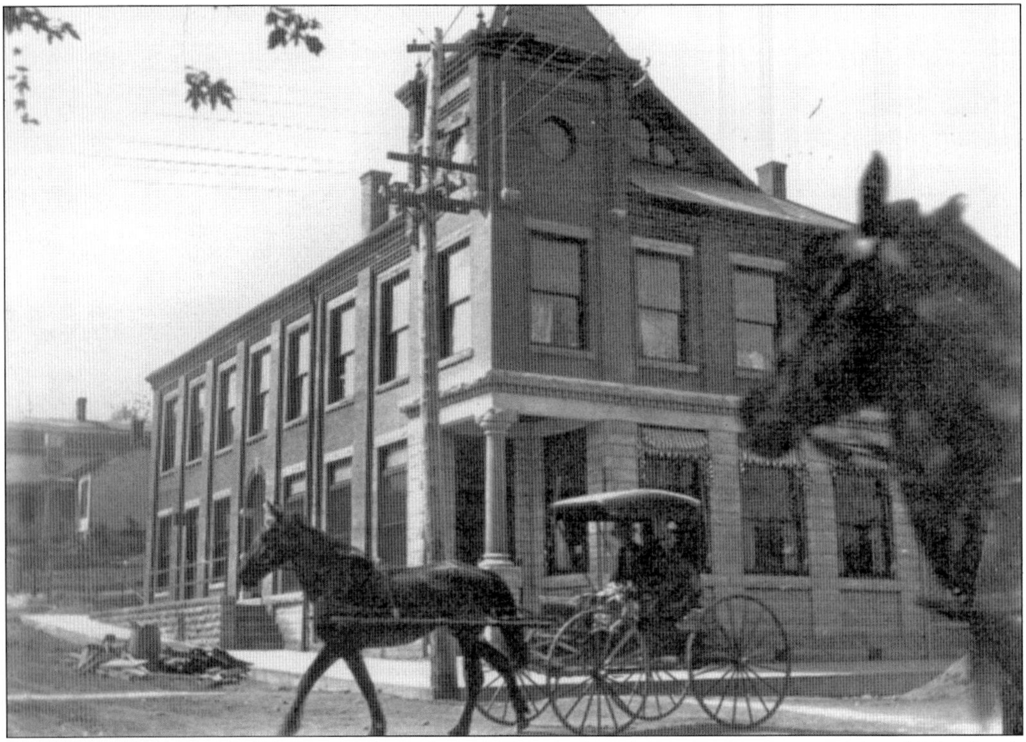

The Waynesville National Bank is shown in 1901, just after construction was completed. The bank is now a branch of the Lebanon Citizens National Bank. Waynesville National made banking history in 1877 by opening a short-lived branch at Lebanon, whose bank had closed. (Courtesy of Mary L. Cook Public Library.)

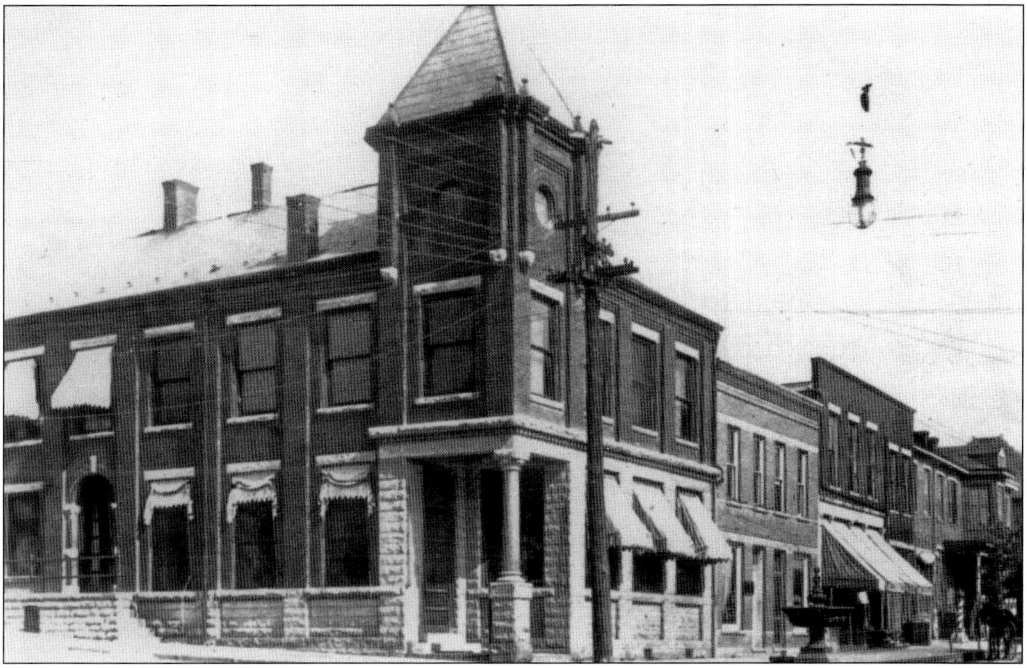

The ornamental fountain, which was also a horse-watering trough, was installed in front of the Waynesville National Bank in 1905. In 1917, it was moved to Miami Cemetery at Corwin and converted into a flower urn. The fountain was replaced by a public drinking fountain, which still exists. The first floor of the building adjacent the bank was Emmor Baily's Meat Market. The second floor housed the offices of village mayor and council. (Courtesy of Mary L. Cook Public Library.)

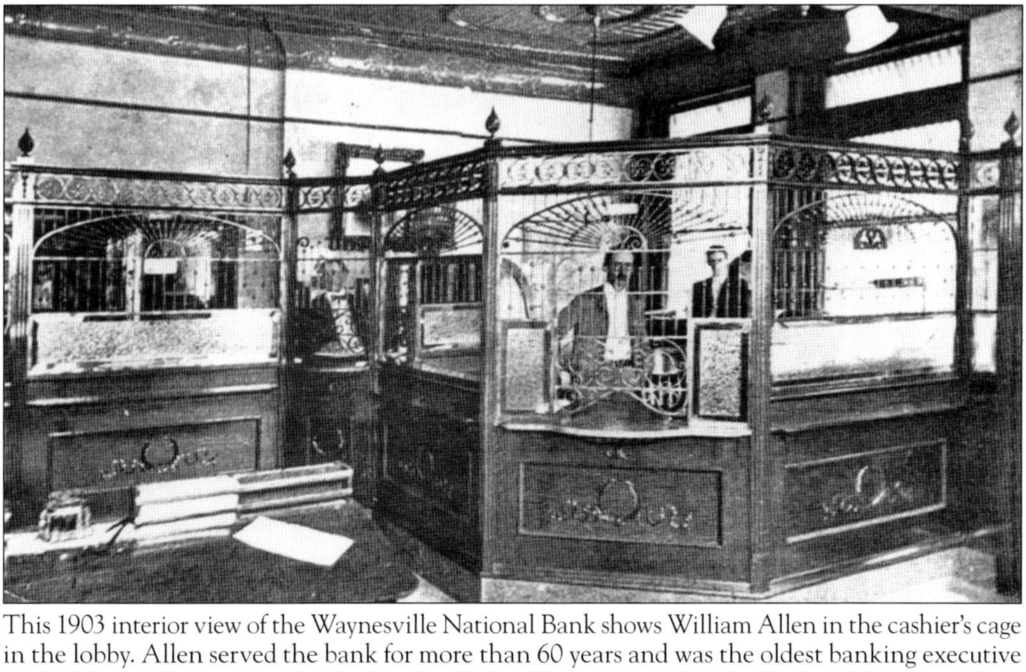

This 1903 interior view of the Waynesville National Bank shows William Allen in the cashier's cage in the lobby. Allen served the bank for more than 60 years and was the oldest banking executive in the United States when he died in the 1940s. (Courtesy of Mary L. Cook Public Library.)

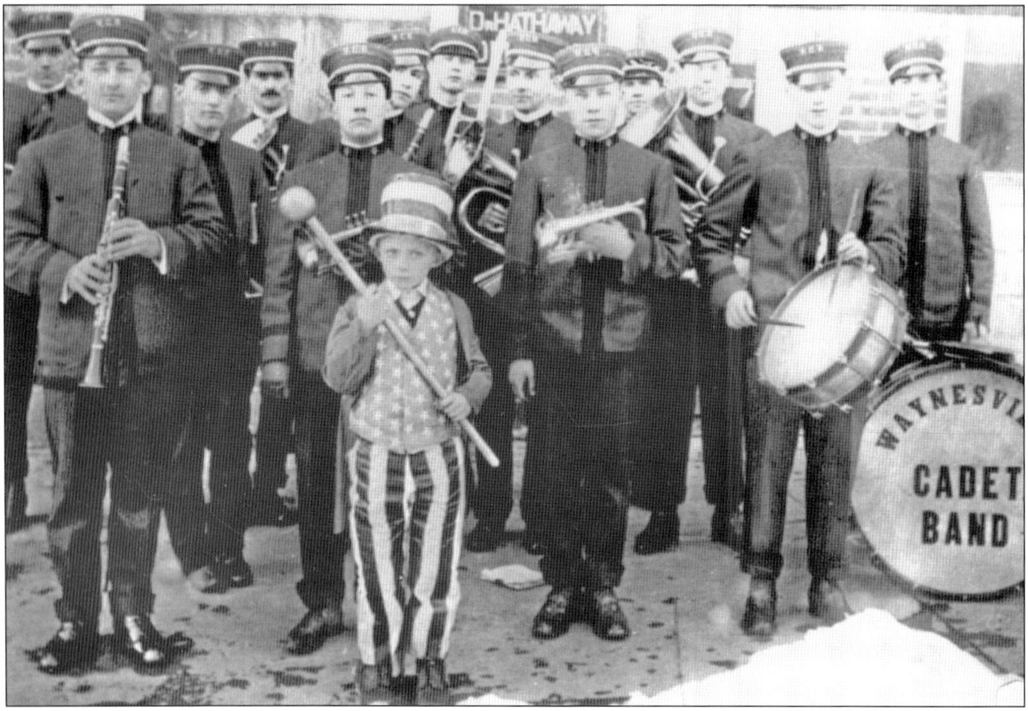

The Waynesville Cadet Band is shown on the North Street side of the Waynesville National Bank in 1902. The sign of Dr. Hathaway, dentist, can be seen in the background. The office of Dr. Mary L. Cook, MD, was located there in 1908. (Courtesy of Mary L. Cook Public Library.)

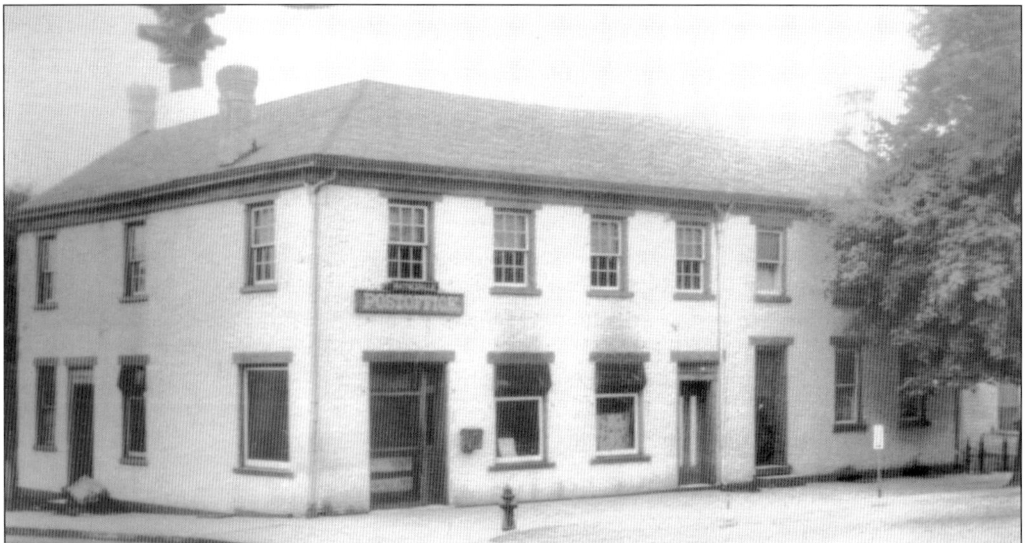

The I.H. Harris business and residence building is shown in this 1930 photograph. It was then the location of the Waynesville Post Office. The building was constructed on the southeast corner of Main and North Streets in 1844. It once housed Harris's famous collection of freshwater pearls when it was the Exchange Bank. Harris sold the pearls to Tiffany & Co. in New York on September 15, 1885. In 1889, they won a gold medal at the Paris World Exposition. (Courtesy of Mary L. Cook Public Library.)

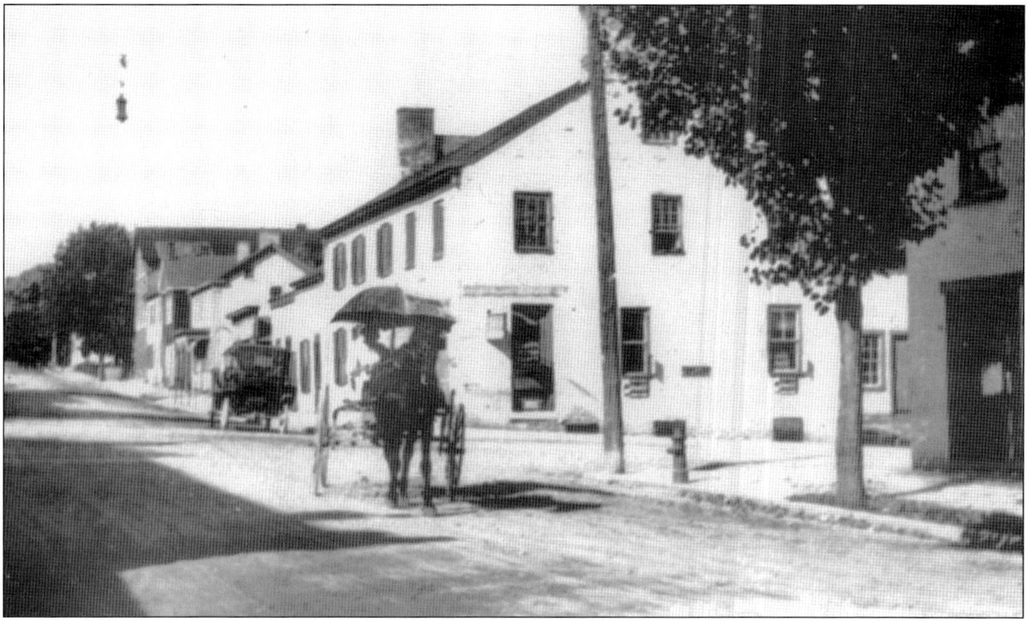

The intersection of Main and North Streets is shown in this 1901 photograph. The Miami House Inn at the center was built in 1826. The Little Miami Railroad was organized here in 1835. The Waynesville inn was a station on the Underground Railroad. A secret tunnel lead from the Little Miami River to the cellar, and fugitive slaves were hidden in a concealed room over the kitchen. (Courtesy of Mary L. Cook Public Library.)

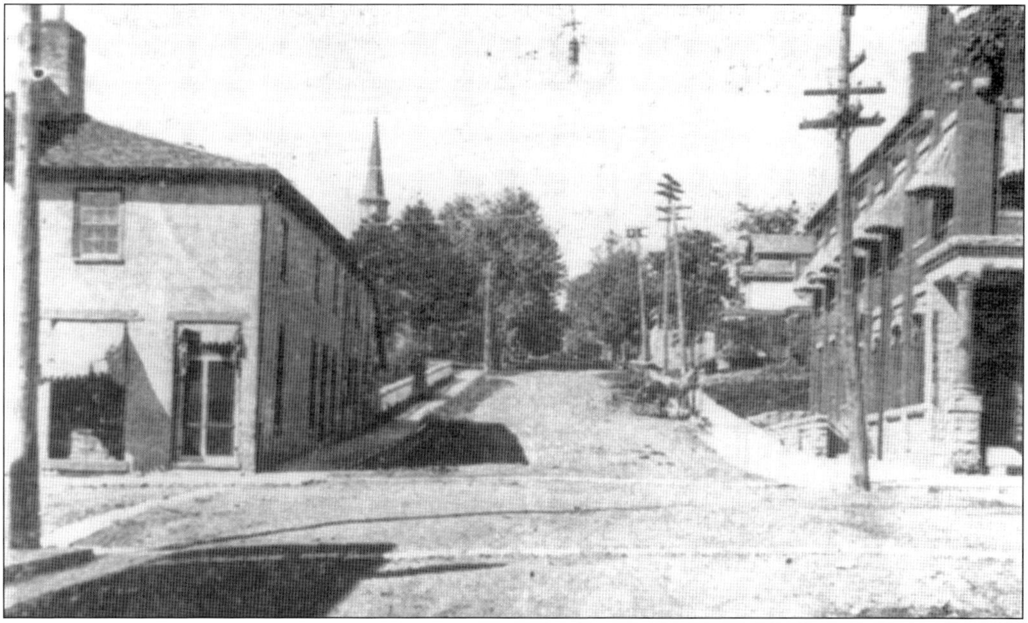

Looking up the hill on North Street, this 1901 photograph shows the intersection of Main and North Streets. On the left is the Asa Trahern Drugstore. Part of the entrance of the Waynesville National Bank is visible on the right. At left, up the hill, is the steeple of the 1840 Methodist church. Across the street is the house where Dr. William Anderson made patent medicines in 1852. (Courtesy of Mary L. Cook Public Library.)

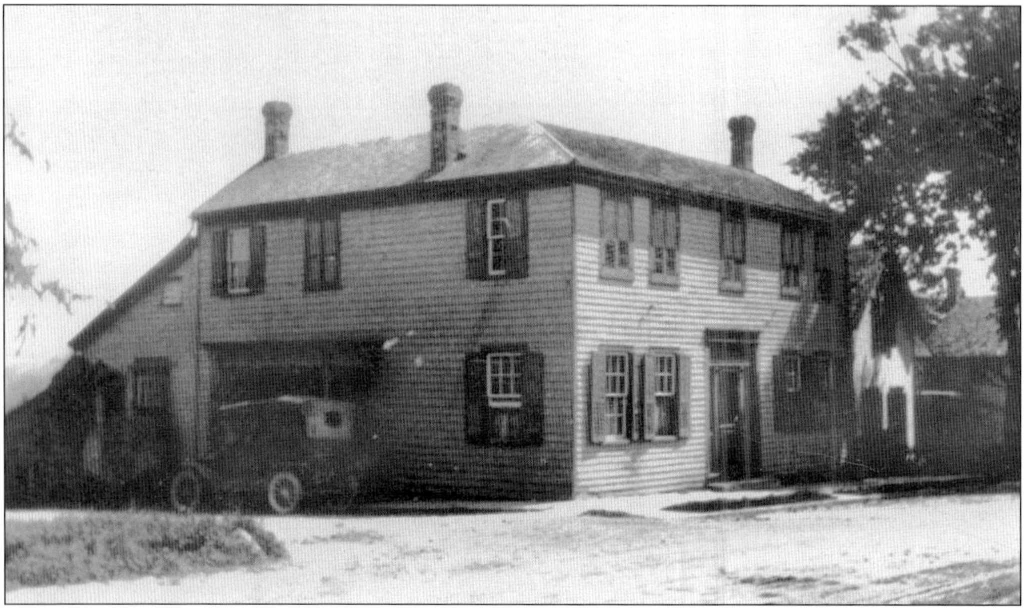

The Thomas residence, on the northeast corner of Main and Mill Streets, was built about 1860. This 1917 photograph shows its Greek Revival doorway and an early automobile at the side. During its history as a private residence, it was also the home of the Henry Upp family. (Courtesy of Mary L. Cook Public Library.)

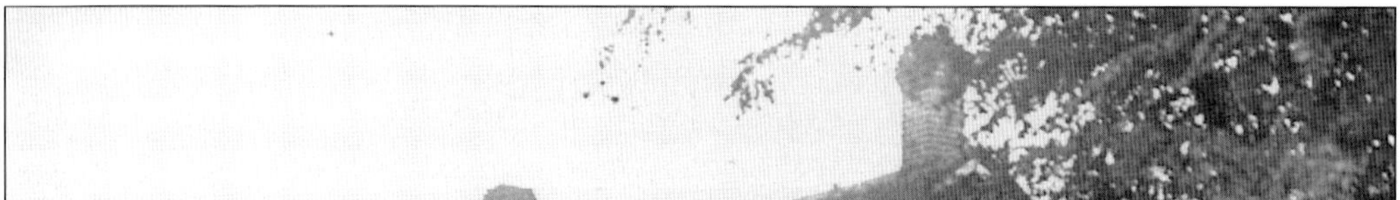

The Mark and Sue Satterthwaite Davis residence is shown in this 1905 photograph. It was constructed in the 1840s on the northeast corner of Main and Mill Streets. The last two Native American women in the Little Miami Valley lived on the back of the lot and made herbal medicines. At left is part of a poured-concrete house built in 1860. The rear section is the original brick dwelling, constructed in 1815. (Courtesy of Mary L. Cook Library.)

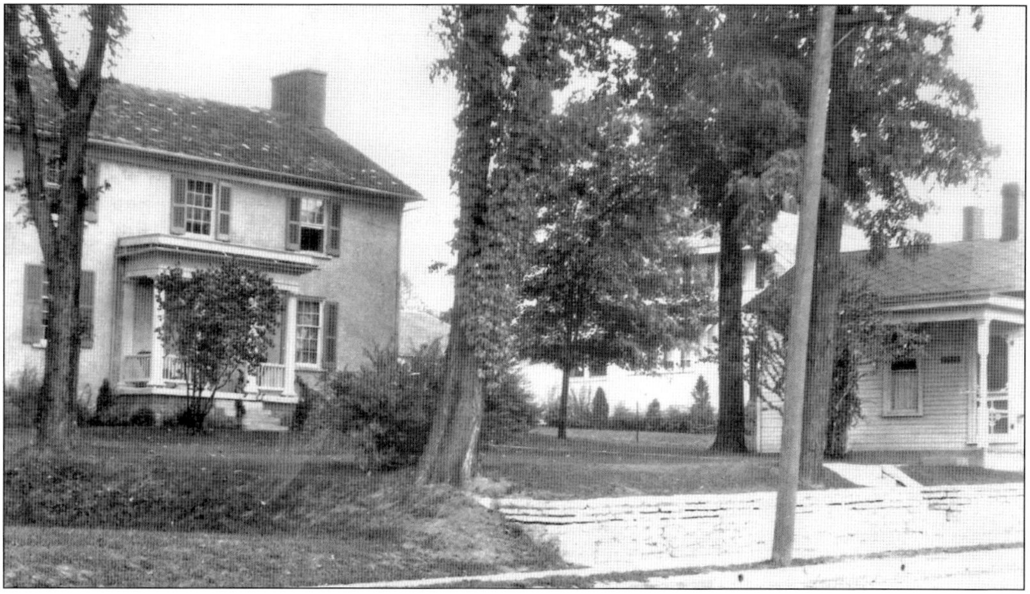

The David and Rachal Burnet Evans house on North Main Street in Waynesville was built by them in 1836. Their son Dr. John Evans was appointed the second territorial governor of Colorado in 1862 by Pres. Abraham Lincoln. Evans also founded Northwestern University at Evanston, Illinois, and the University of Denver, Colorado. His brother Joel, Warren County surveyor, built the cabin at the right in 1845. This photograph was taken in 1940. (Courtesy of Mary L. Cook Public Library.)

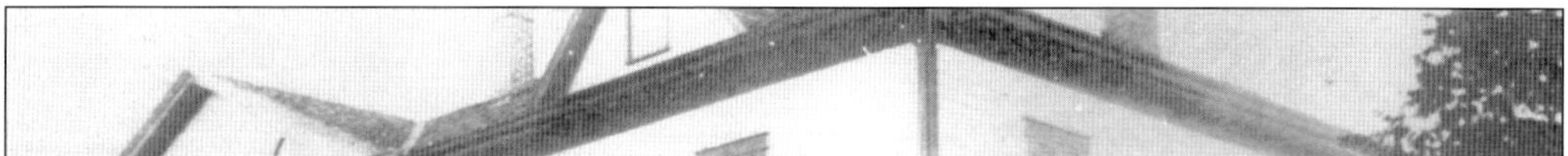

The A.B. Sides Agricultural Implements Warehouse on East North Street at the alley is shown in this 1905 photograph. The warehouse was originally a pork-packing house built in 1845 by James Harris. The c. 1860 building on the left housed Waynesville's Odd Fellows lodge, a theater, and a concert hall. George Sides linked the buildings in 1873 when he founded the Sides business. (Courtesy of Mary L. Cook Public Library.)

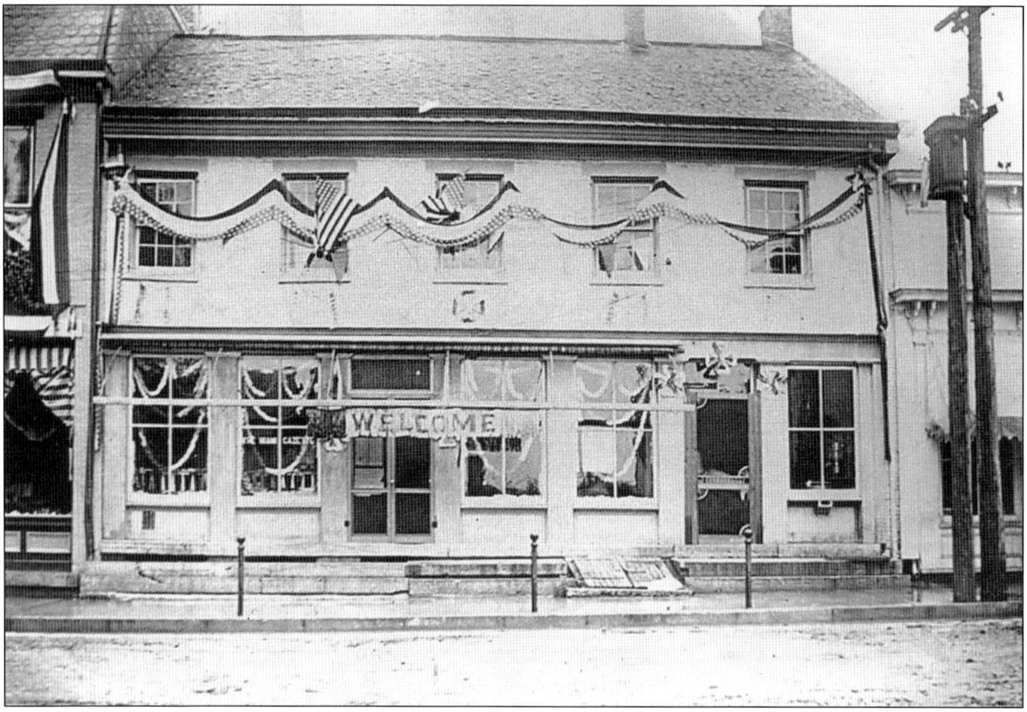

The building that housed the *Miami Visitor* is shown in this 1905 Waynesville homecoming photograph. It was built in 1820 by John Satterthwaite, a prominent Quaker businessman. The *Visitor*, which changed its name to *Miami Gazette* in 1865, was founded on the second floor in January 1850. It closed on the first floor in 1955. In 1850, the first floor was Allen's General Merchandise, also known as the Sign of the Golden Ball. (Courtesy of Mary L. Cook Public Library.)

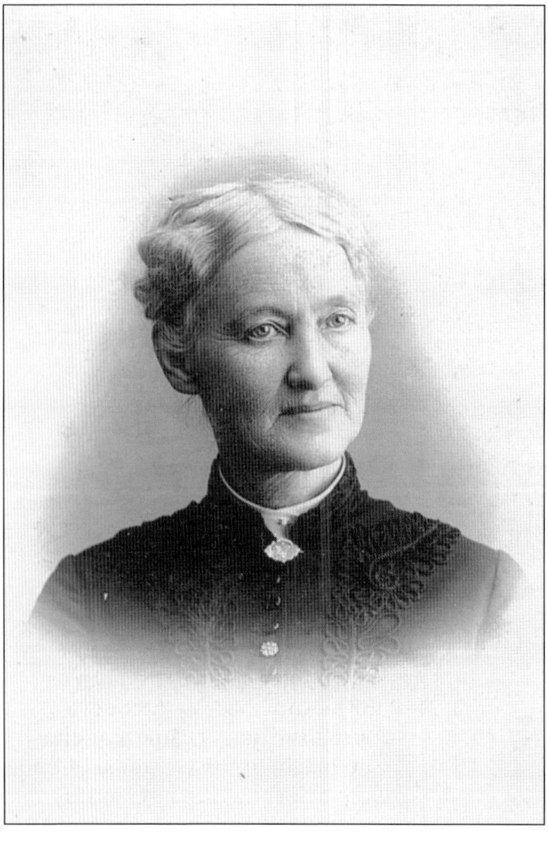

Mary Brown, shown in this 1905 photograph, was co-owner and publisher of the *Miami Gazette* in partnership with her husband, Thomas, from 1881 to 1906. She was the newspaper's literary editor and was fond of the works of Charles Dickens. She and James Drew Sweet, who owned and published the *Gazette* from 1865 to 1881, were cofounders of St. Mary's Episcopal Church. (Courtesy of Mary L. Cook Public Library.)

Thomas Brown purchased the *Miami Gazette* from James Drew Sweet in 1881. He was the *Gazette*'s editor until 1906, when he and his wife, Mary, retired. Brown is shown here in 1905. (Courtesy of Mary L. Cook Public Library.)

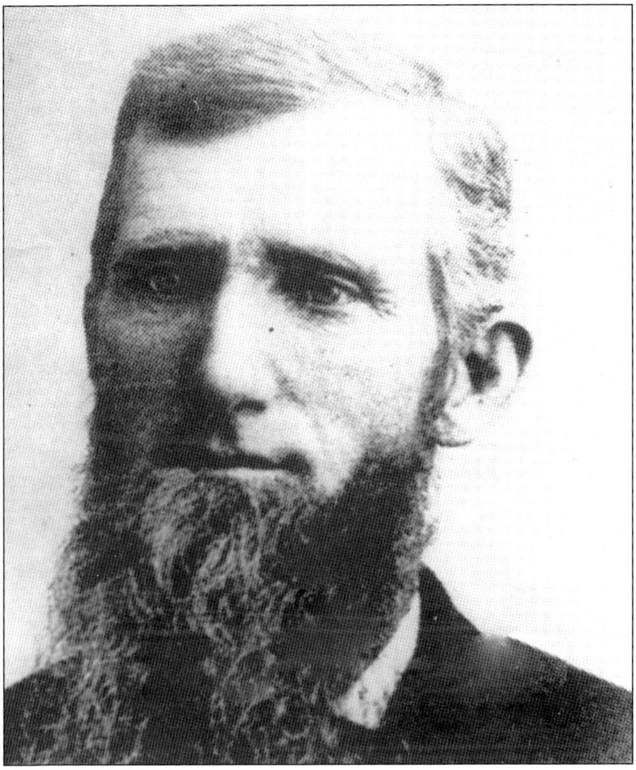

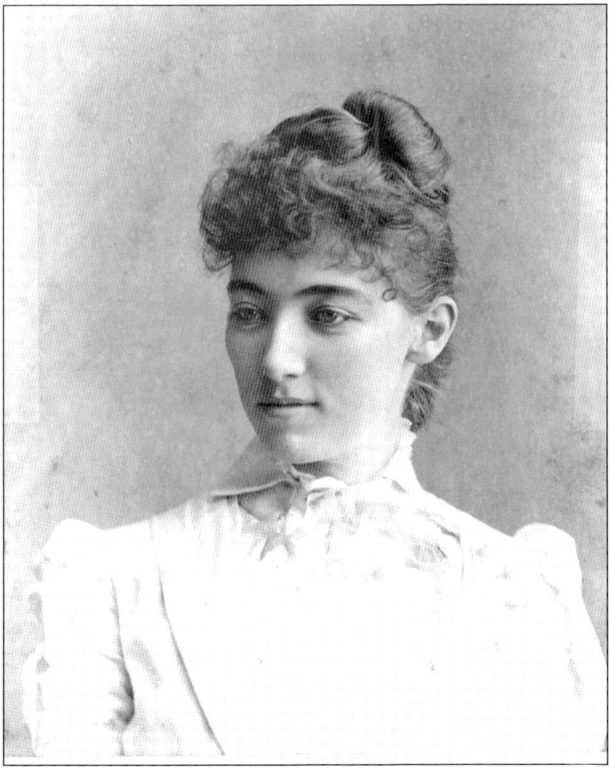

Anna U. Brown, daughter of Thomas and Mary Brown, is shown in a photograph taken in 1883. Anna had no interest in journalism and became a teacher. She taught at the Columbus, Ohio, School for the Blind. (Courtesy of Mary L. Cook Public Library.)

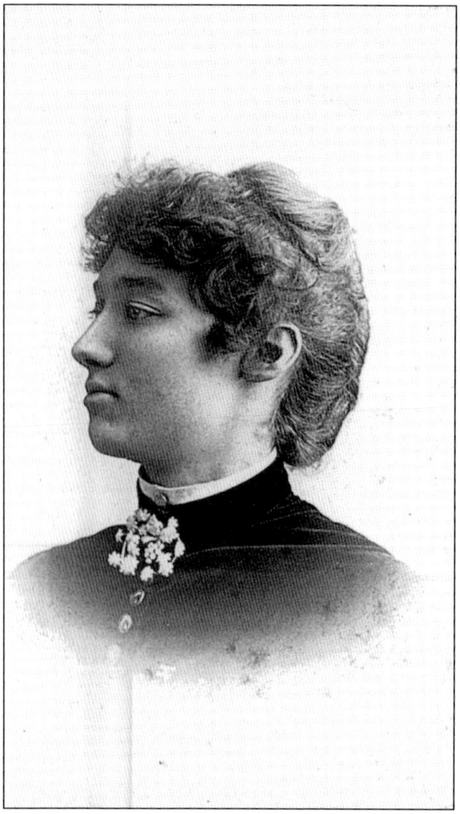

Mary Thomas Brown followed in the footsteps of her parents, Thomas and Mary Brown. She is shown in this 1883 photograph when she assisted with the operation of the *Miami Gazette*. The *Miami Gazette* was inherited by her in 1906. Mary "Mame" Brown continued her mother's women's liberation example throughout her life. (Courtesy of Mary L. Cook Public Library.)

Wooley and Son Harness and Saddles was the first business to move into the new Seller's Building on Main Street in Waynesville when construction was finished in 1879. Some of the Wooley leather craftsmen, including the owners in the center, are shown behind a hitching rack in this 1880s photograph. (Courtesy of Mary L. Cook Public Library.)

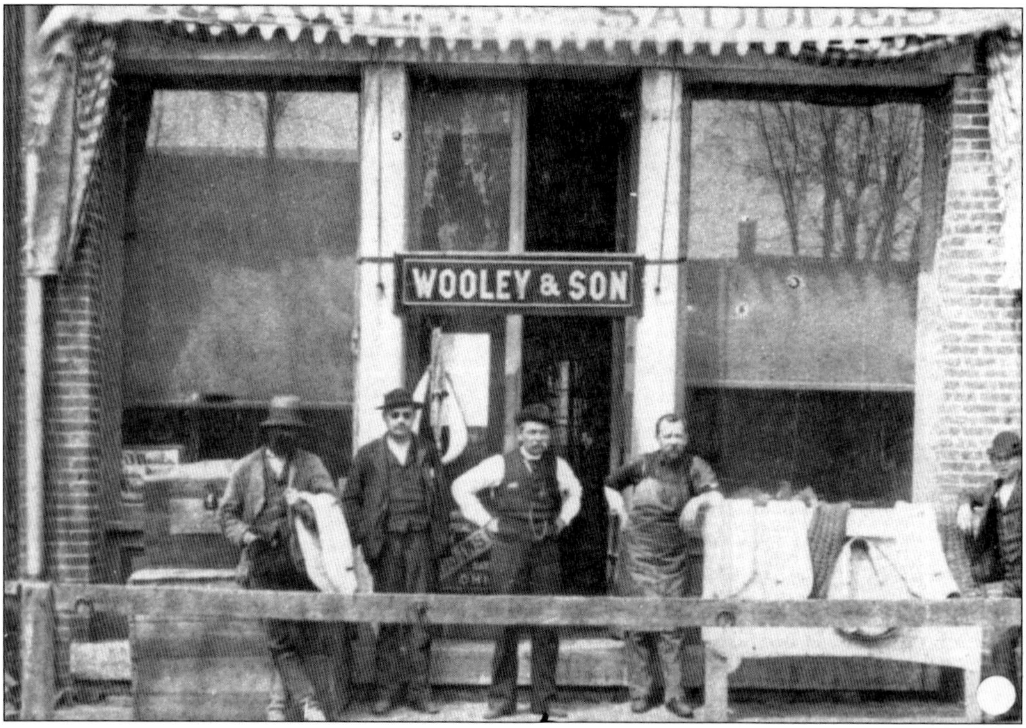

Oil was struck on the Wright Mill property between Waynesville and Corwin, as shown in this 1895 photograph. Although the excitement was short lived when the oil fizzled out, local investors were bolstered by the discovery of natural gas. Stock was issued, and natural gas was piped up the hill to Waynesville. Enough gas was pumped to light businesses along Main Street until 1899. (Courtesy of Mary L. Cook Public Library.)

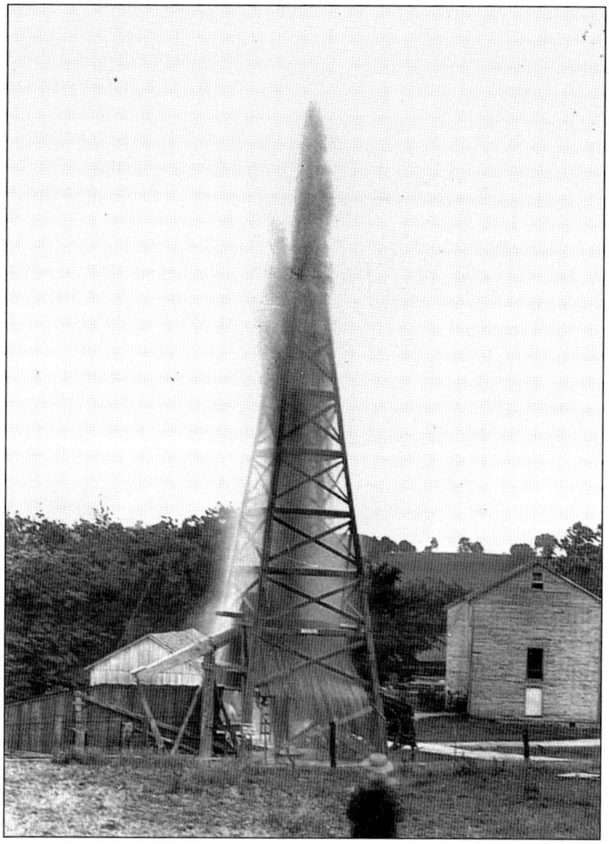

No one got rich over the oil strike between Waynesville and Corwin in 1897. The rig crew is shown in this 1897 photograph of the derrick. Natural gas was discovered along with the oil and turned out to be more plentiful. (Courtesy of Mary L. Cook Public Library.)

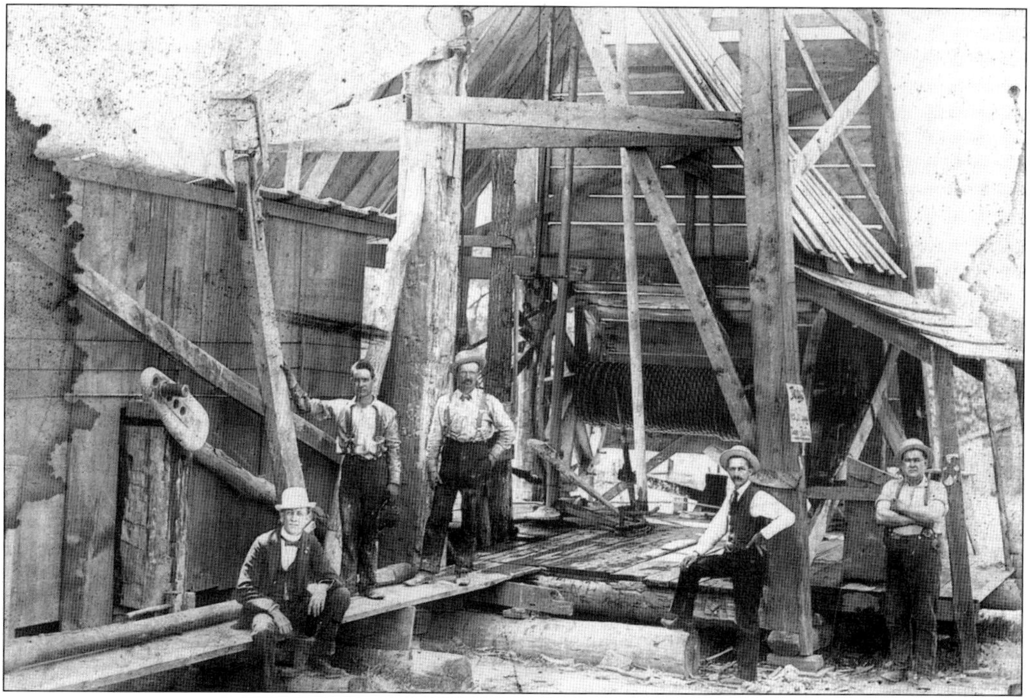

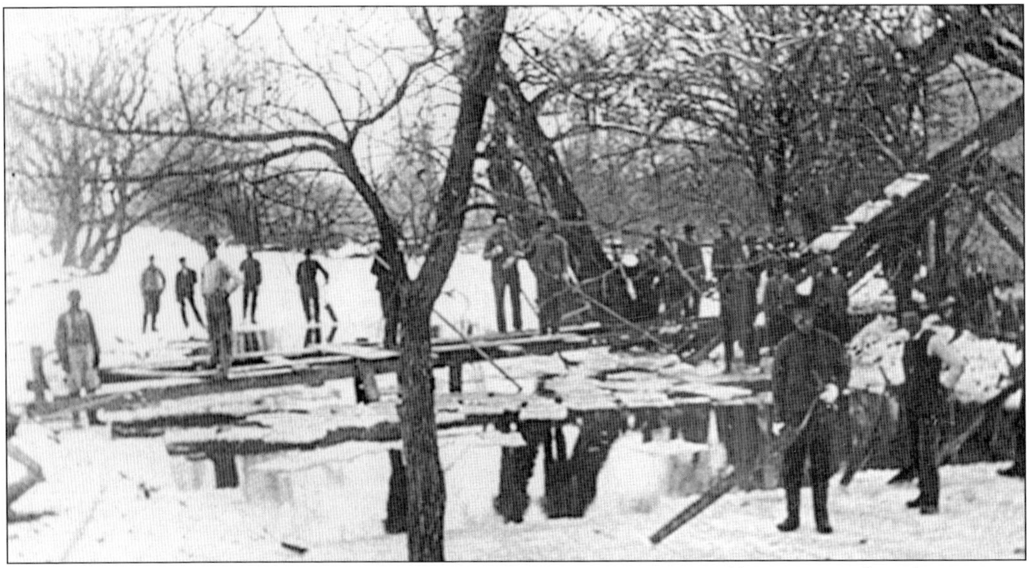

This 1900 photograph of Waynesville and Corwin men cutting ice illustrates early refrigeration. In this scene, the group is cutting ice from the ponds of Waynesville Mills. The mills' storage buildings included a large icehouse where the blocks were stored, layered in sawdust. The supply usually lasted the village consumers a year. (Courtesy of Mary L. Cook Public Library.)

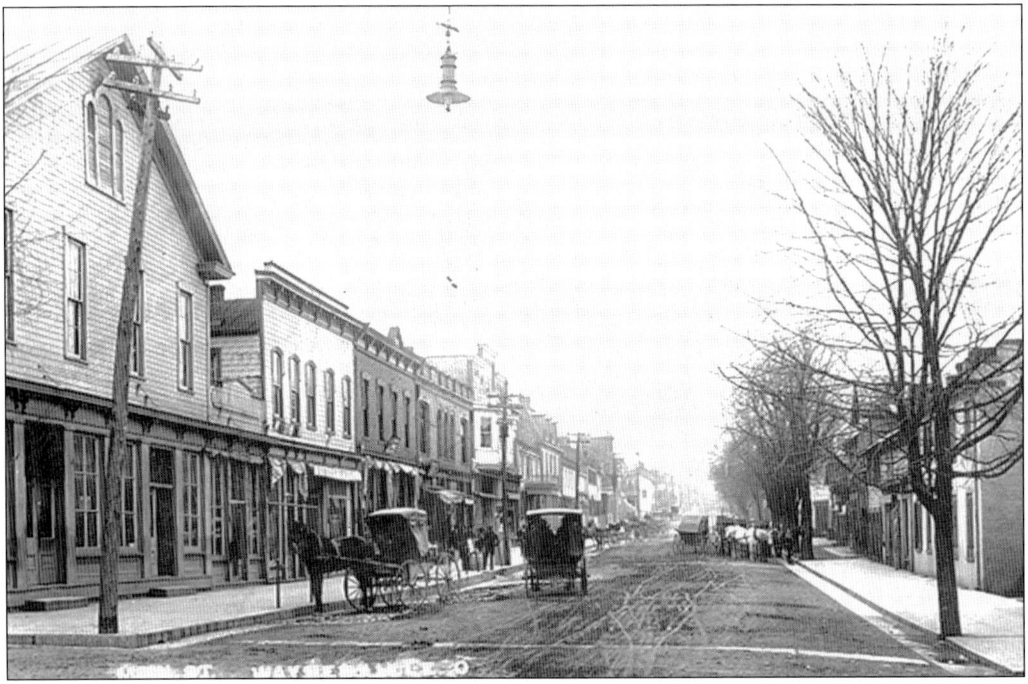

Looking north on Main Street from the intersection of Miami Street, this 1901 photograph shows Cadwallader Hall, Waynesville's town hall, on the left. The hall, built in 1868, facilitated a 300-seat theater on the second floor. In 1869, a dozen Shakers visiting from Union Village near Lebanon demonstrated their church services before a packed house. The Shakers, who were on a goodwill mission, also investigated the Sunday schools of the Methodist and St. Mary's Episcopal Churches. (Courtesy of Mary L. Cook Public Library.)

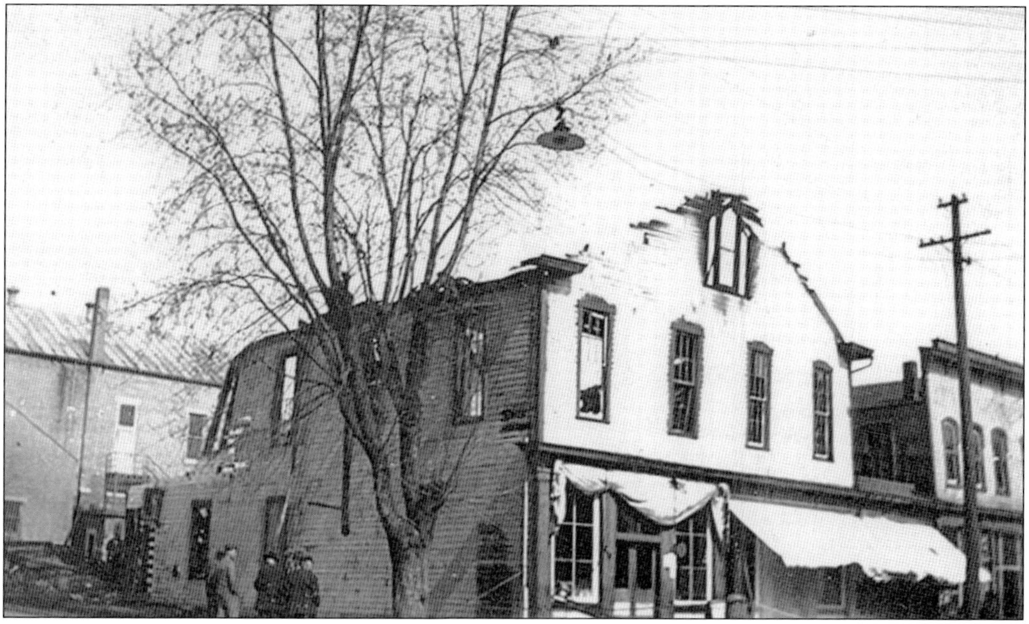

Cadwallader Hall is shown in this 1929 photograph; it was partially destroyed by fire on April 1. The building was remodeled into a single-story structure. Visible behind the hall is the Miami Valley Baptist Church. Constructed in 1874, the church closed in 1896 and was bought by Waynesville Masonic Lodge No. 163 F&AM. The building was converted to the lodge's temple in 1900. (Courtesy of Mary L. Cook Public Library.)

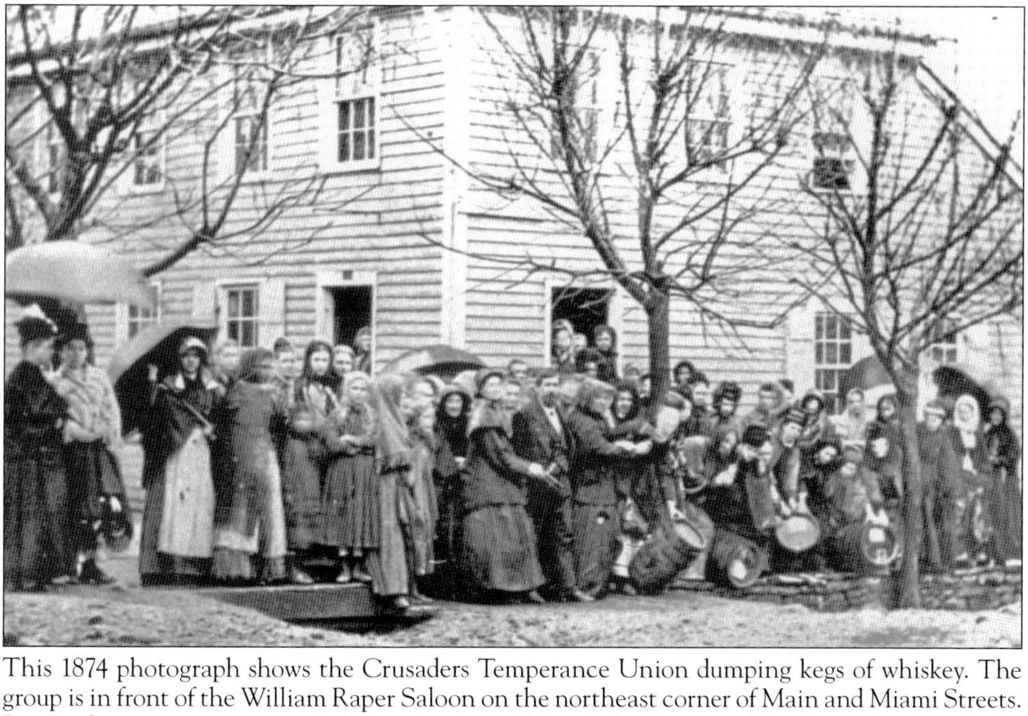

This 1874 photograph shows the Crusaders Temperance Union dumping kegs of whiskey. The group is in front of the William Raper Saloon on the northeast corner of Main and Miami Streets. Raper, the repentant owner, is shown in the middle of the first row. The Crusaders hit all the saloons in town and in Corwin. (Courtesy of Mary L. Cook Public Library.)

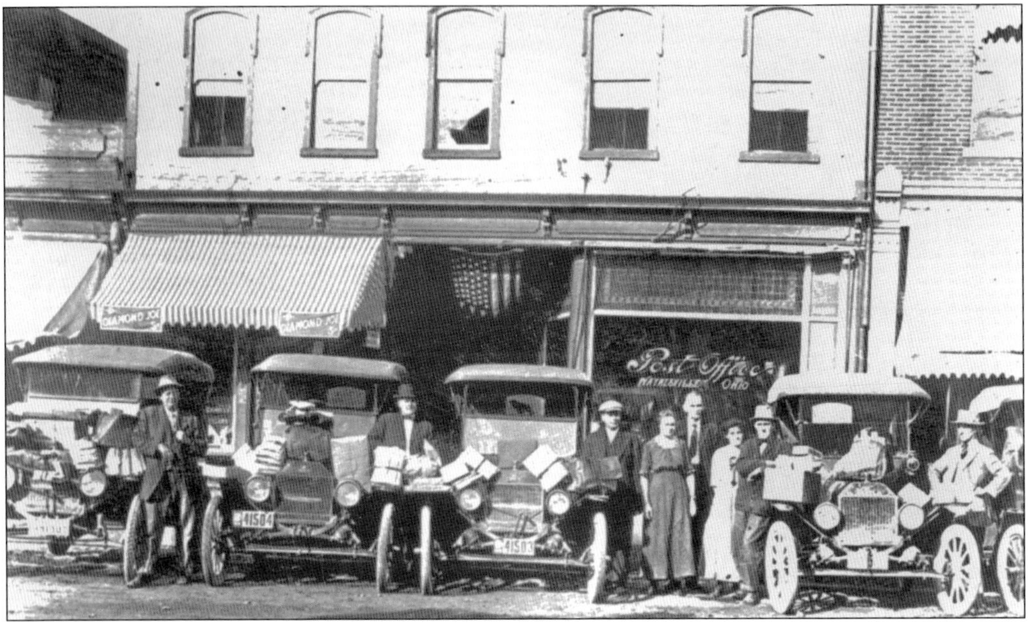

The staff and delivery vehicles of the Waynesville Post Office are shown in front of the building on Main Street in 1906. The building was demolished in 1960 and replaced by the new Fairley's Hardware Store. Waynesville's first post office was opened in 1804 in the log store of Samuel Heighway, the village founder. Samuel Heighway Jr. was the first postmaster. (Courtesy of Mary L. Cook Public Library.)

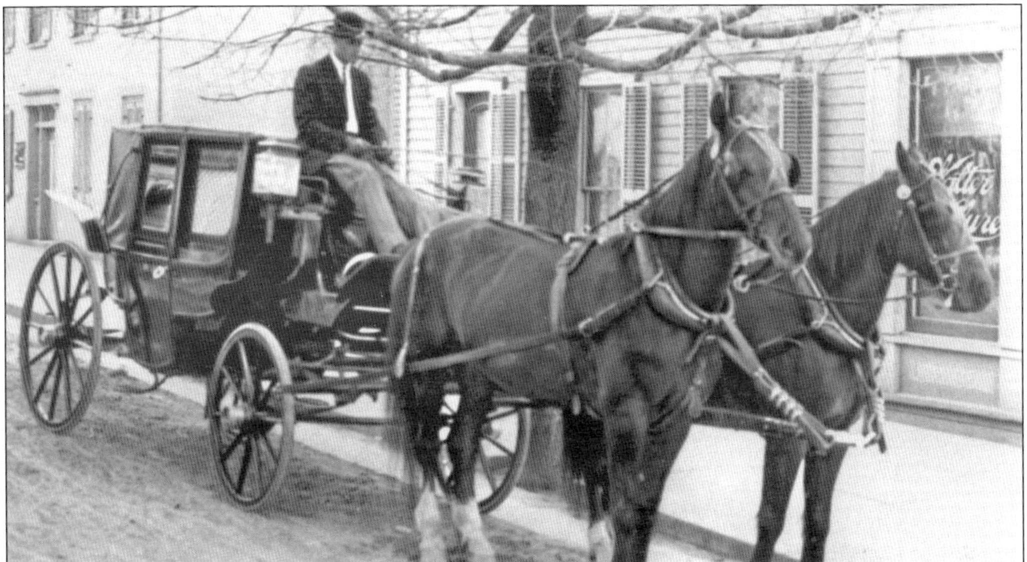

Earl Conner is shown in the driver's seat of the Walter McClure Funeral Home family carriage on the northeast corner of Main and Miami Streets. Dr. Francis and Miriam Williams's building, which housed Farmer's Grange No. 13 from 1874 to 1920, is shown behind the carriage. (Courtesy of Mary L. Cook Public Library.)

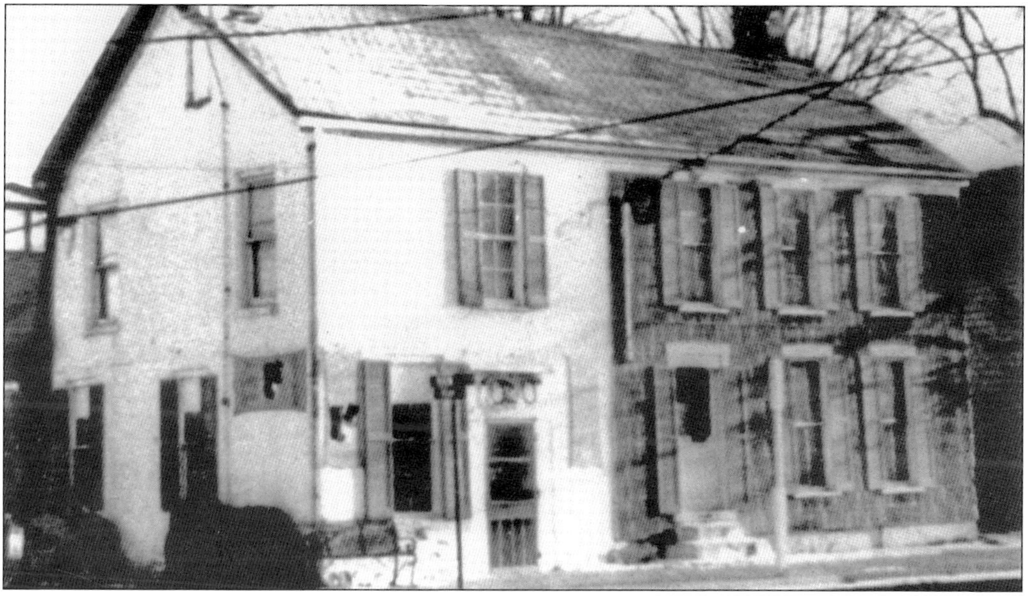

The William and Clara Mills Phillips ice cream parlor and residence are show in this 1974 photograph. The brick half, where the ice cream parlor was located, was built in 1806. The adjoining residence was added about 1830. The ice cream parlor was the Michael Liddy Exchange Saloon in 1875. The ice cream parlor operated from 1900 to 1926. In the winter of 1901, Phillips introduced moving pictures here with his Phillips's Electric Theater. (Courtesy of Mary L. Cook Public Library.)

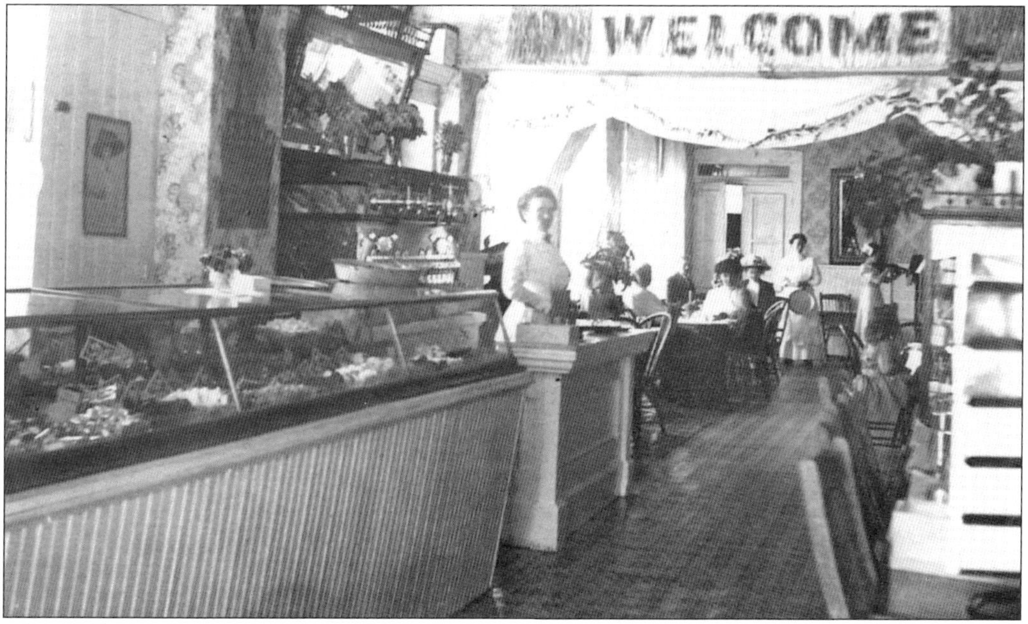

The Phillips Ice Cream Parlor is shown in this 1905 photograph. The building was located on the southeastern corner of Main and Miami Streets. Ice cream that was manufactured in the rear of the building sold for a penny a scoop. The first ice cream made and sold in Waynesville was introduced by Biddle B. Hay at his ice cream parlor in the Haddon Building on North Main Street. (Courtesy of Mary L. Cook Public Library.)

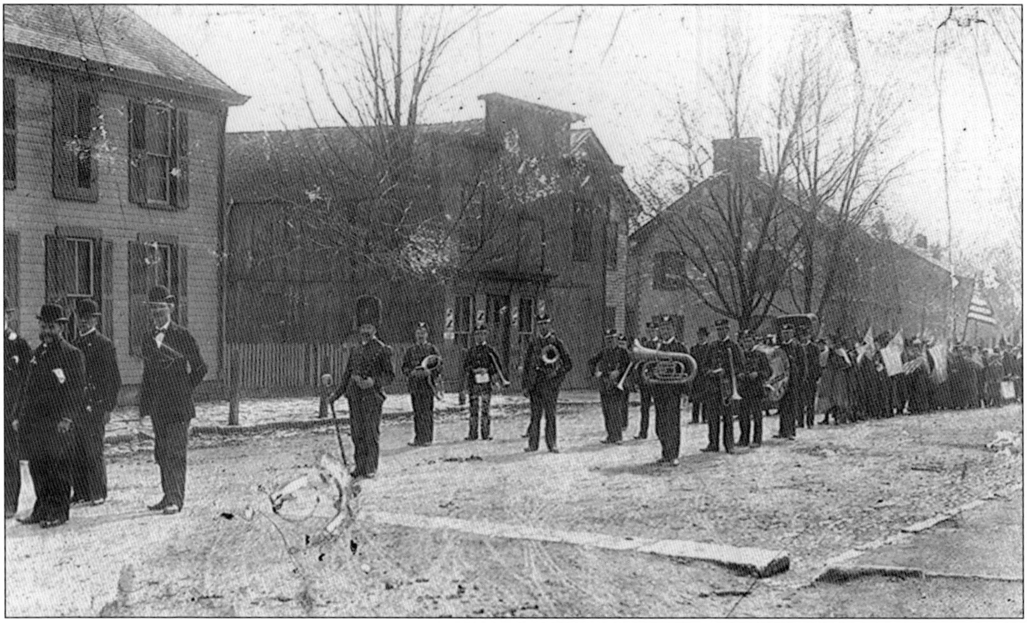

The Waynesville Band leads a political parade up Main Street in this 1900 photograph. The photograph was taken from the intersection of Miami Street looking south on Main Street. The south end of the Phillips home is on the left. The center building is a livery stable with the corner of the next building showing. The building with the large chimney on the left was built by Josiah Craft, an early Quaker builder, in 1815. (Courtesy of Mary L. Cook Public Library.)

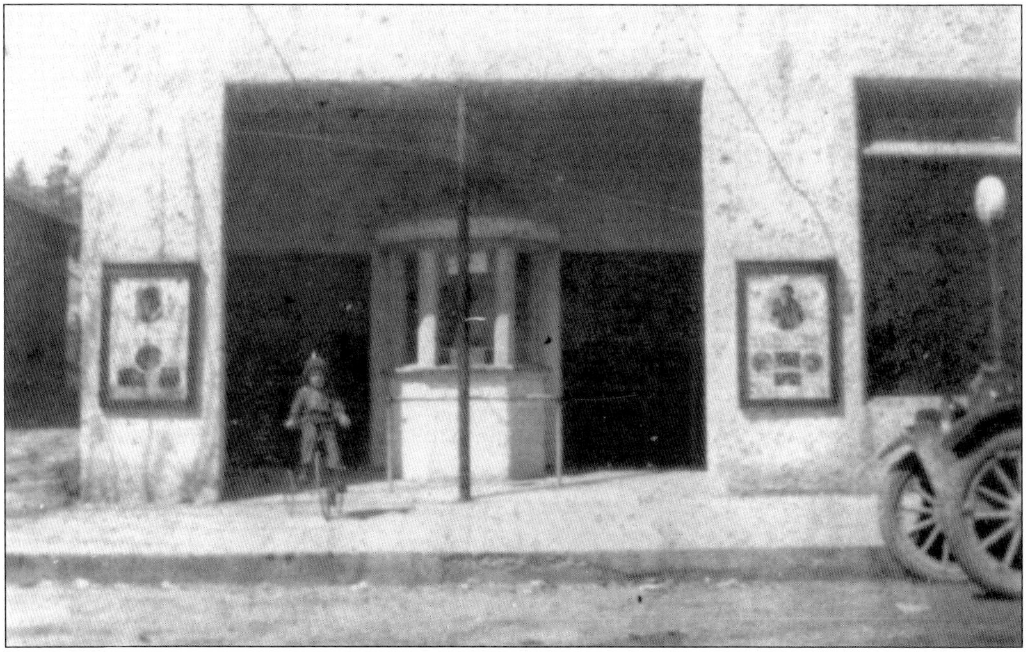

The Miami Theater was added to the south end of Kilpatrick Garage in 1919. The building was located on the southwest corner of Main and Miami Streets. In the 1940s, the theater's name was changed to the Twin Theater by a new owner. The unidentified child in front is riding a tricycle. (Courtesy of Mary L. Cook Public Library.)

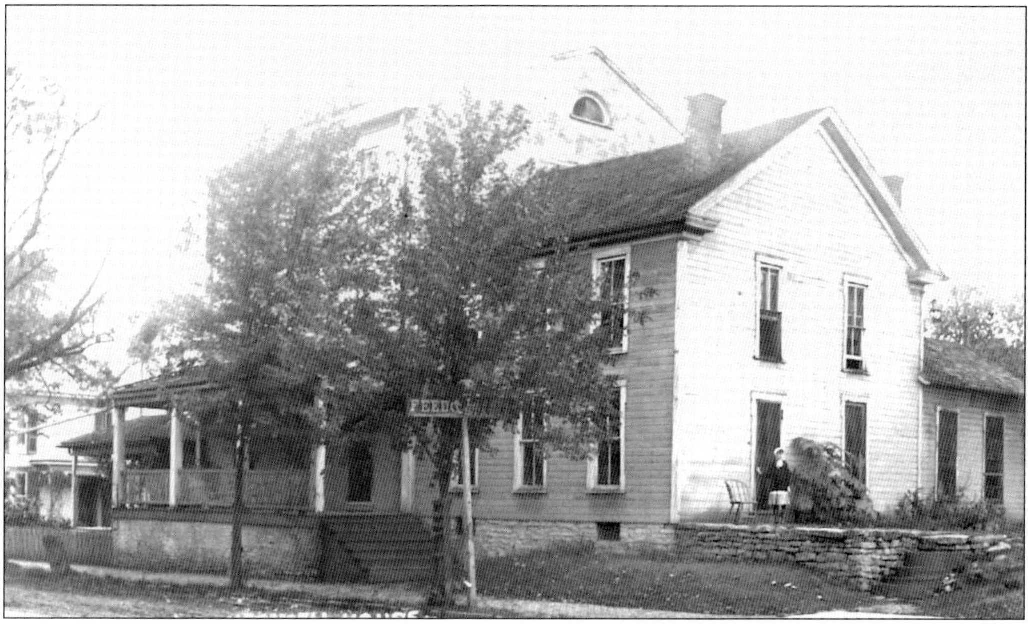

The Hammell House Inn, on South Main Street, occupies a 1799 log tavern site. The frame half on the right was built in 1817. The brick addition on the left was made in 1822 by John Worrell. Enoch Hammell added a third-floor ballroom in 1843. This photograph, taken in 1911, shows Mildred Gustin standing on the stone wall. Mildred's father, William, bought the hotel in 1901 and changed the name to Gustin House. (Courtesy of Mary L. Cook Public Library.)

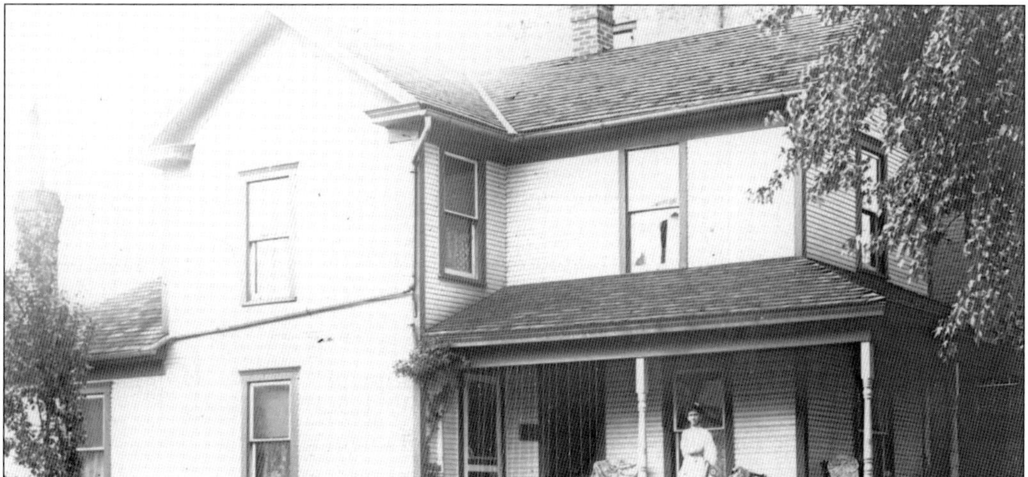

Olive Casey Gustin is shown on the veranda of her South Main Street home in this 1905 photograph. Her husband, William, had the house built in 1905 at a cost of $946.92. In 1905, Gustin also built a show barn adjacent the north side of the house behind the hotel for his purebred racehorses. His account book shows that the barn cost $1,007.24. (Courtesy of Mary L. Cook Public Library.)

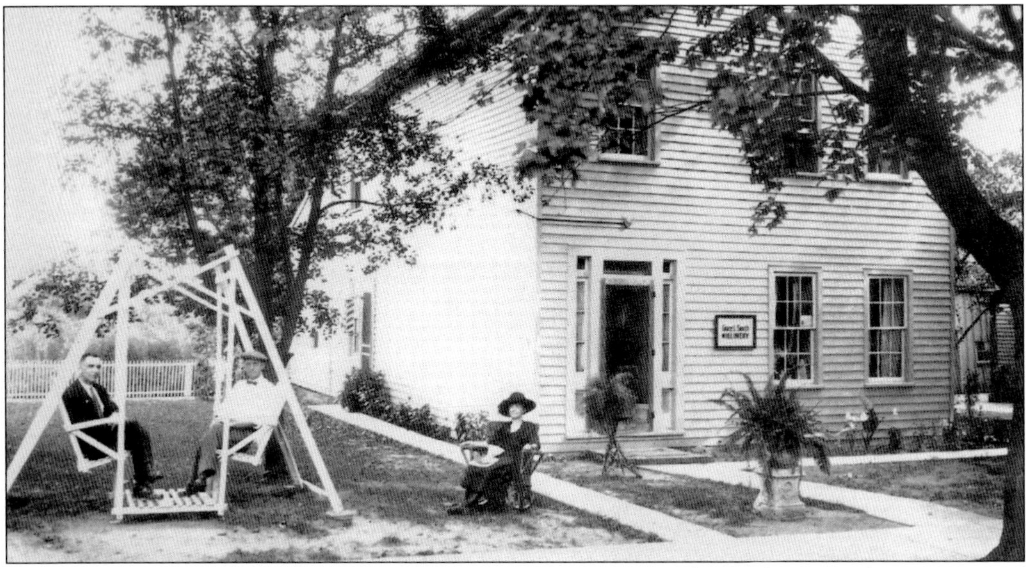

The Grace Lincoln Smith Millinery Shop and residence was located on South Main Street by 1930, which was when this photograph was taken. Grace opened her first shop in the King Building on the northwest corner of Main and Chapman (then Tyler) Streets in 1902. She moved to the Dr. S.J. Way Building and made hats there until after 1916. Grace was a cousin of Pres. Abraham Lincoln. Shown in this 1930 photograph are, from left to right, an unidentified man, William Smith (in swing), and Grace. The building was constructed in 1857. (Courtesy of Mary L. Cook Public Library.)

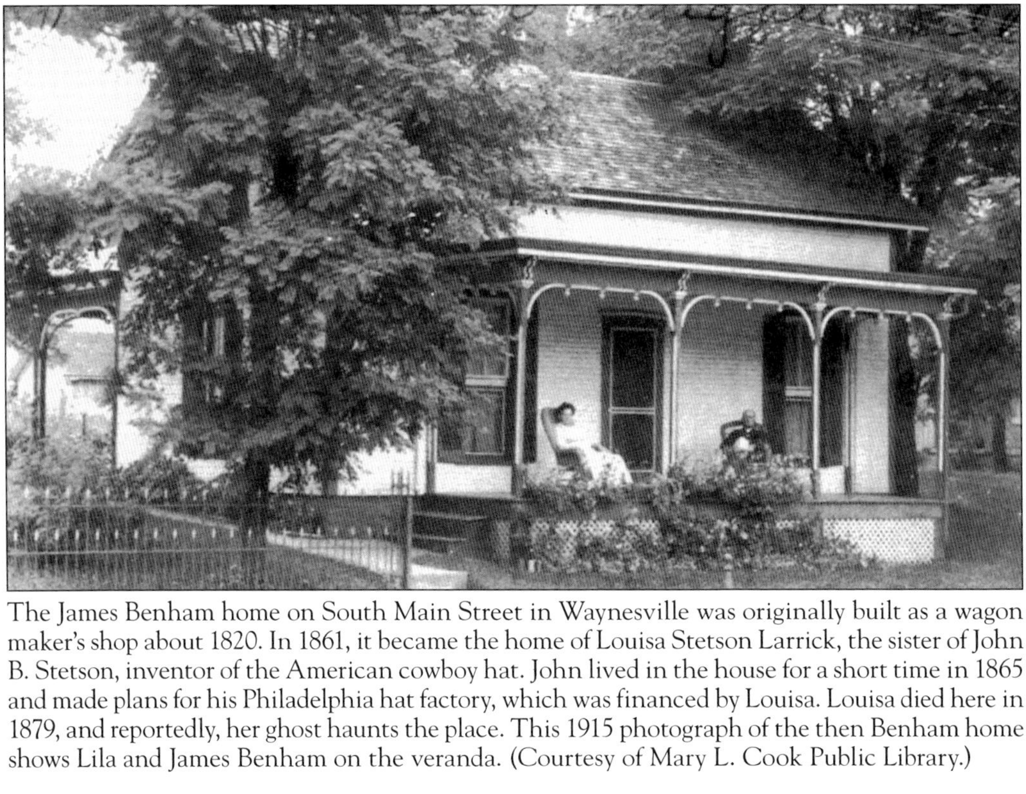

The James Benham home on South Main Street in Waynesville was originally built as a wagon maker's shop about 1820. In 1861, it became the home of Louisa Stetson Larrick, the sister of John B. Stetson, inventor of the American cowboy hat. John lived in the house for a short time in 1865 and made plans for his Philadelphia hat factory, which was financed by Louisa. Louisa died here in 1879, and reportedly, her ghost haunts the place. This 1915 photograph of the then Benham home shows Lila and James Benham on the veranda. (Courtesy of Mary L. Cook Public Library.)

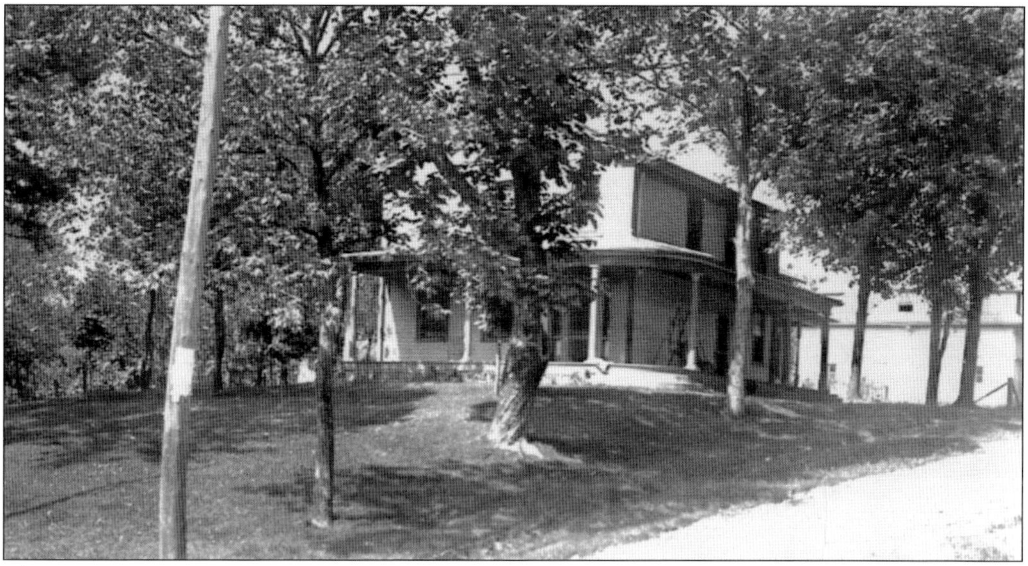

The residence of Achilles Pugh was built in 1876 on the southwest corner of Main and South Streets. Pugh, a Quaker abolitionist, published an antislavery newspaper in Cincinnati and assisted with the Underground Railroad. He provided church facilities in a converted stable known as Pugh's Chapel to help St. Mary's Episcopal and St. Augustine's Roman Catholic Churches to get established in 1869. (Courtesy of Mary L. Cook Public Library.)

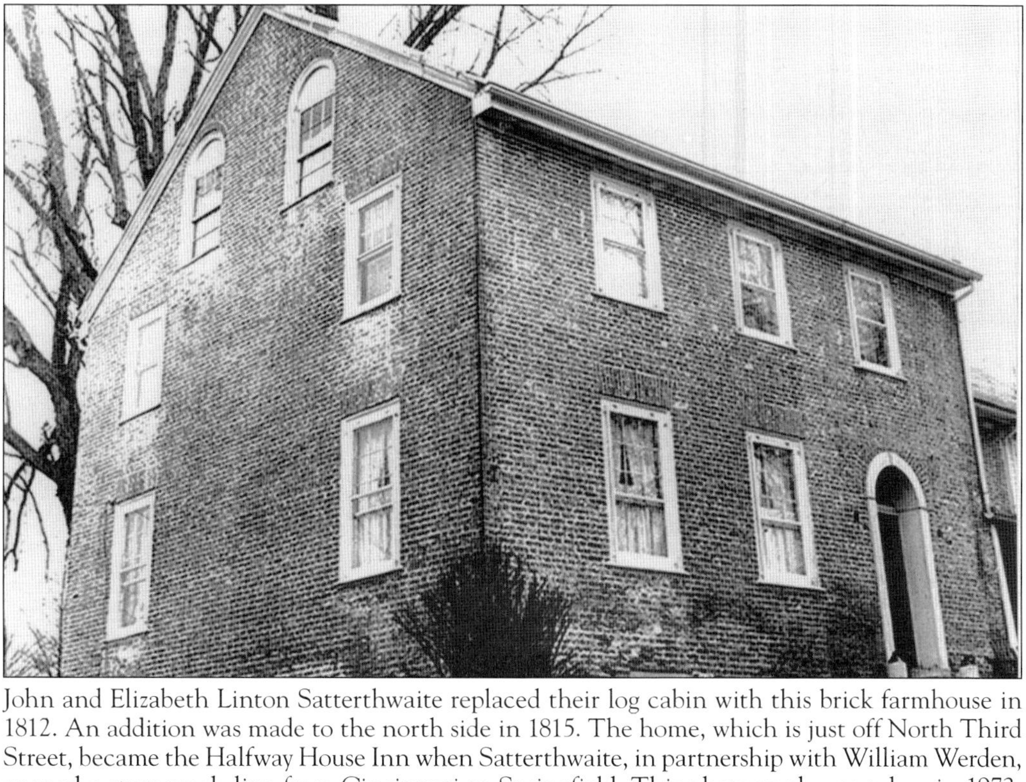

John and Elizabeth Linton Satterthwaite replaced their log cabin with this brick farmhouse in 1812. An addition was made to the north side in 1815. The home, which is just off North Third Street, became the Halfway House Inn when Satterthwaite, in partnership with William Werden, opened a stagecoach line from Cincinnati to Springfield. This photograph was taken in 1972. (Courtesy of Mary L. Cook Public Library.)

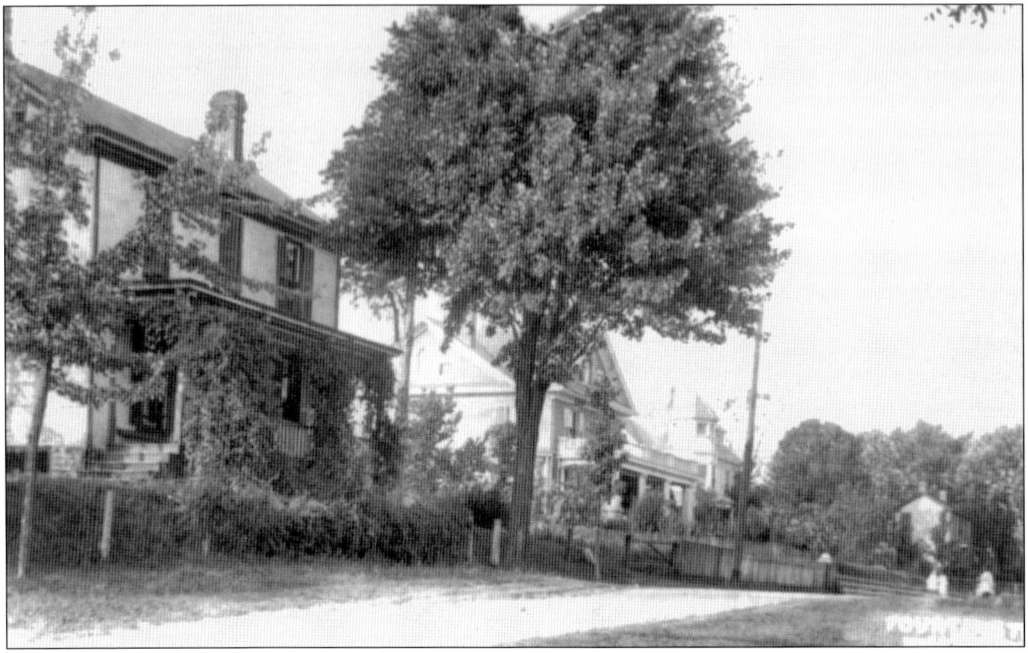

The Haines-Borton house, on Fourth Street in Waynesville, was built in 1823 by Quaker Noah Haines. Beginning in the 1850s, the Borton family manufactured Borton's Cough Syrup, a popular Waynesville patent medicine until the 1880s. This photograph was taken around 1902, when Fourth Street was still dirt and gravel and there were no sidewalks. (Courtesy of Mary L. Cook Public Library.)

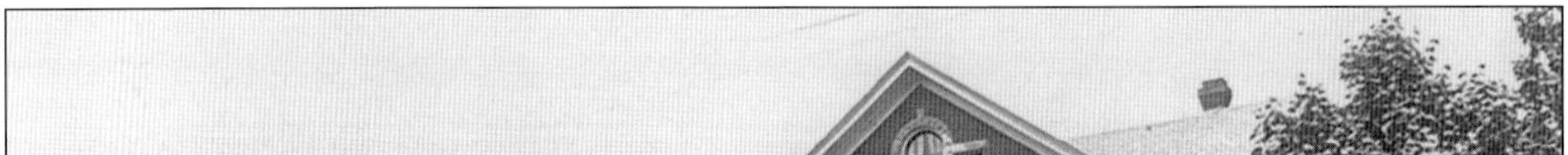

The William H. Allen residence, on the southwest corner of North and Fourth Streets, was constructed in 1902–1903. Allen worked at the Waynesville National Bank for 69 years. When he died on February 24, 1944, he had the longest continuous banking career of anyone in the nation. This photograph was taken in 1905. (Courtesy of Mary L. Cook Public Library.)

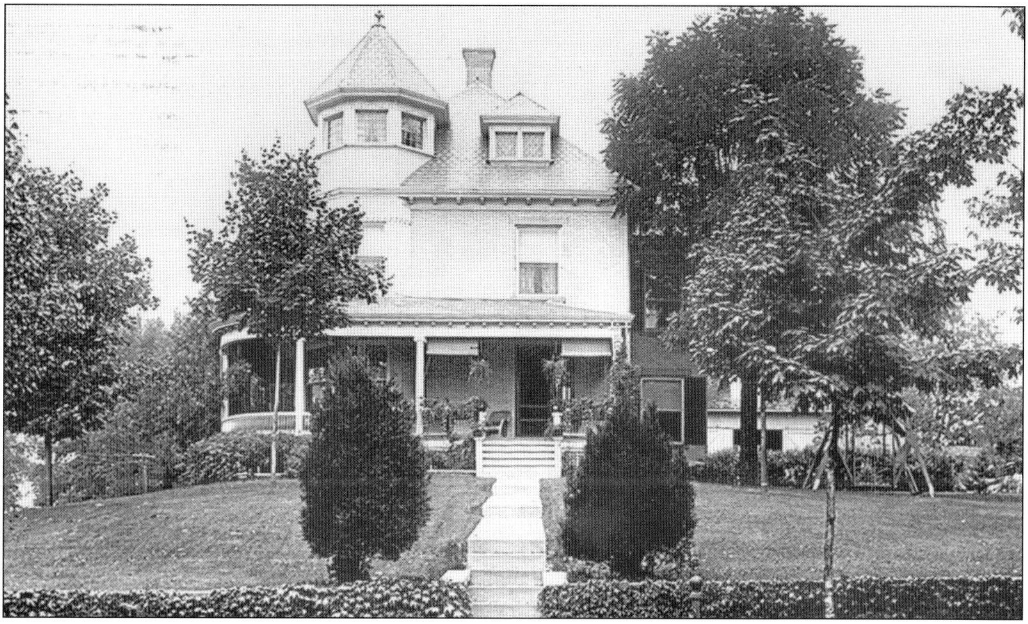

The John W. and Amelia Farr White residence, on the northwest corner of North and Fourth Streets, was built in 1901 and was still new when this view was photographed in 1904. White and his father-in-law, Frank Farr, operated Farr and White Grocery. They constructed a new building at 75 South Main Street in Waynesville in 1886.

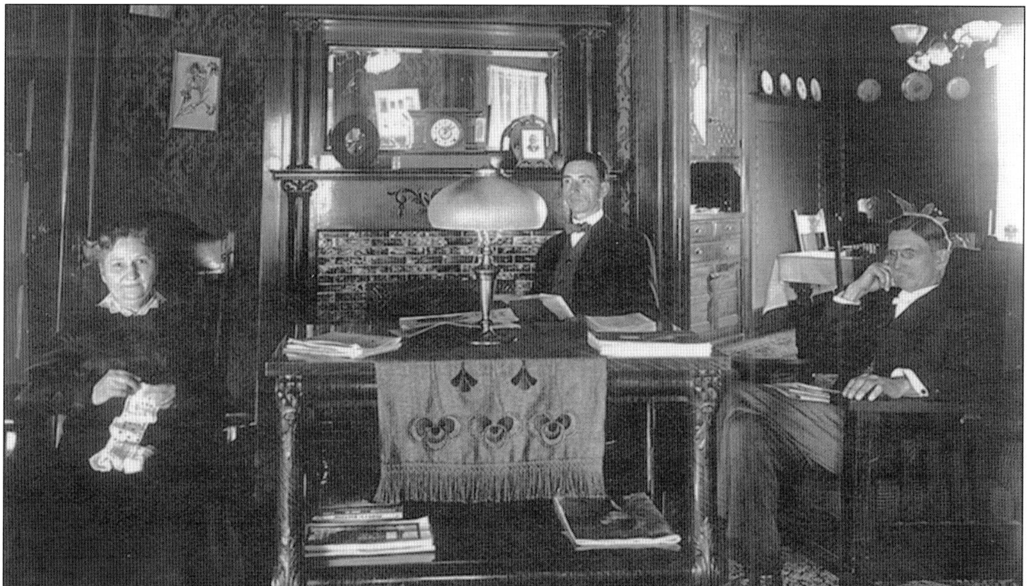

Shown in the parlor of their home in this 1904 photograph are, from left to right, Amelia Farr White; Horace F. White, son; and John W. White. The Waynesville YMCA was organized in 1886 and located on the second floor of the Farr and White Grocery. It functioned only a few months before the National YMCA closed it for being too small. (Courtesy of Mary L. Cook Public Library.)

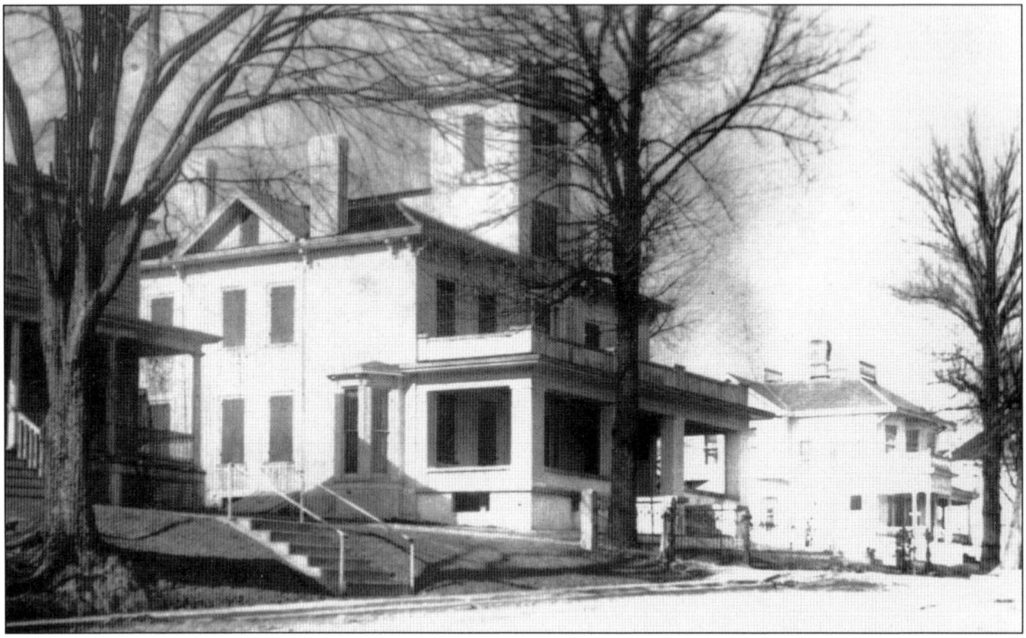

Seth S. Haines built this Gothic Victorian mansion, photographed in 1915, on South Third Street in 1855. Haines, a former Waynesville and Cincinnati businessman, was the first president of the Waynesville National Bank in 1875. The Haineses were Quakers, and the house was once a station on the Underground Railroad. Sister Ruth Webster, a Union Village Shaker, recuperated here in 1869 after having fainted during a Shaker religious ritual at Cadwallader Hall. (Courtesy of Mary L. Cook Public Library.)

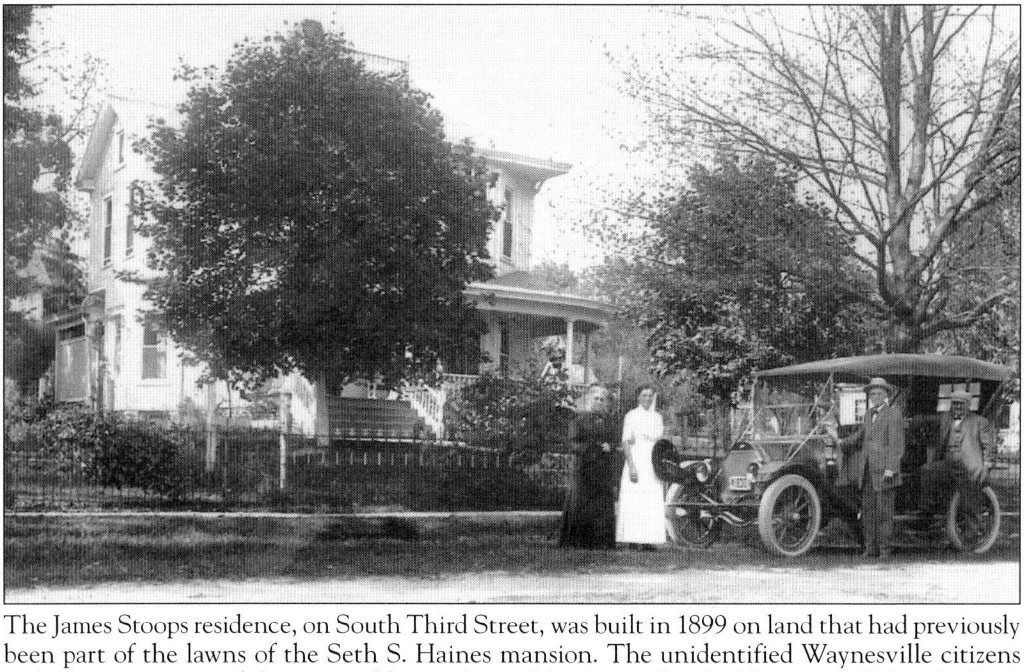

The James Stoops residence, on South Third Street, was built in 1899 on land that had previously been part of the lawns of the Seth S. Haines mansion. The unidentified Waynesville citizens with their new automobile are possibly members of the Stoops family. (Courtesy of Mary L. Cook Public Library.)

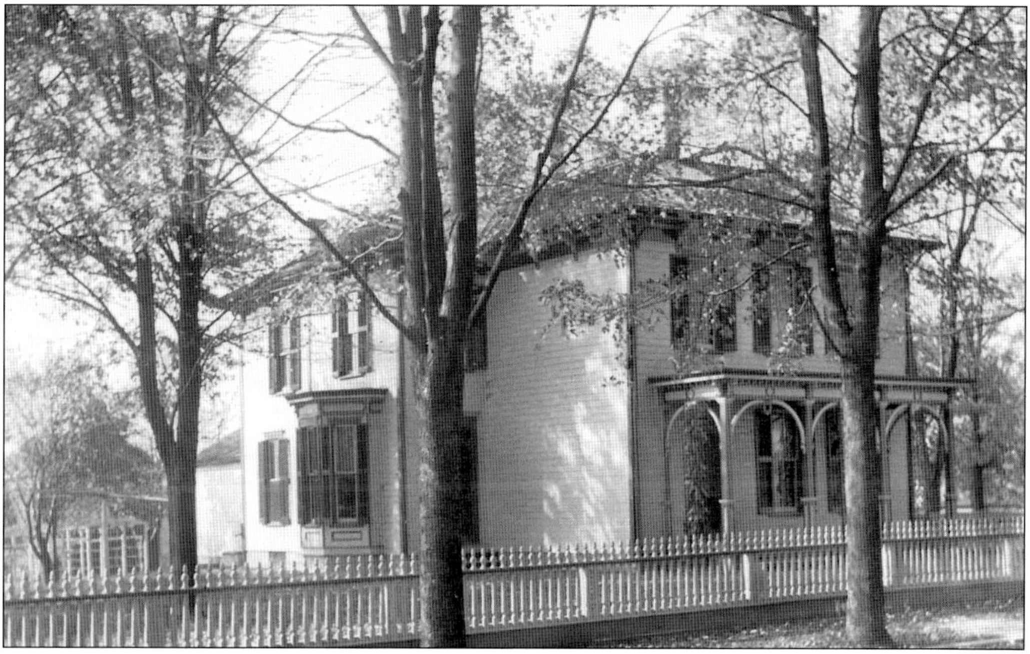

The Frank Farr residence, on the southeast corner of Chapman and Fifth Streets, was built around 1890. Farr, in partnership with his son-in-law John W. White, owned the Farr and White Grocery. This Waynesville photograph was taken in 1916. This house was for many years the home of Mark and Laura Shepherd. (Courtesy of Mary L. Cook Public Library.)

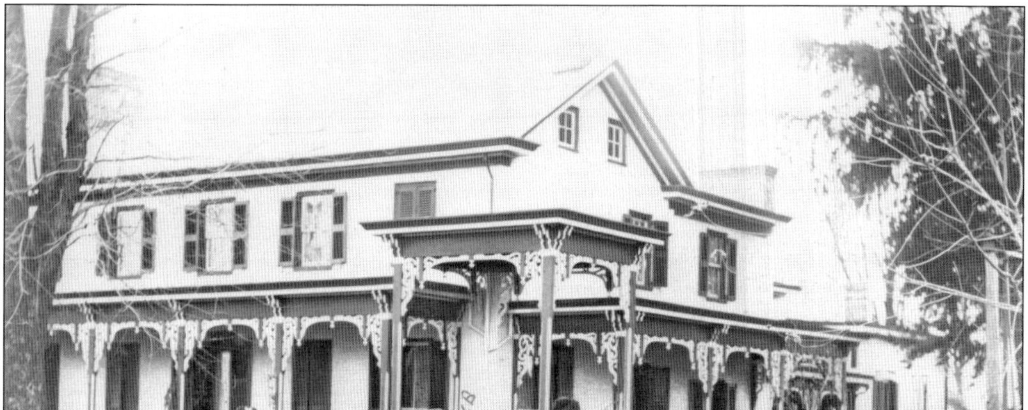

The Waynesville Cornet Band is posed in this 1899 photograph in front of the Greer-Heighway residence on East High Street. Dr. John Greer built the brick house in 1831 on the site of a two-room brick house built by Samuel Heighway in 1801. The west lawn, which bordered the Waynesville Public Square, once accommodated Samuel Heighway's log store and hop field. (Courtesy of Mary L. Cook Public Library.)

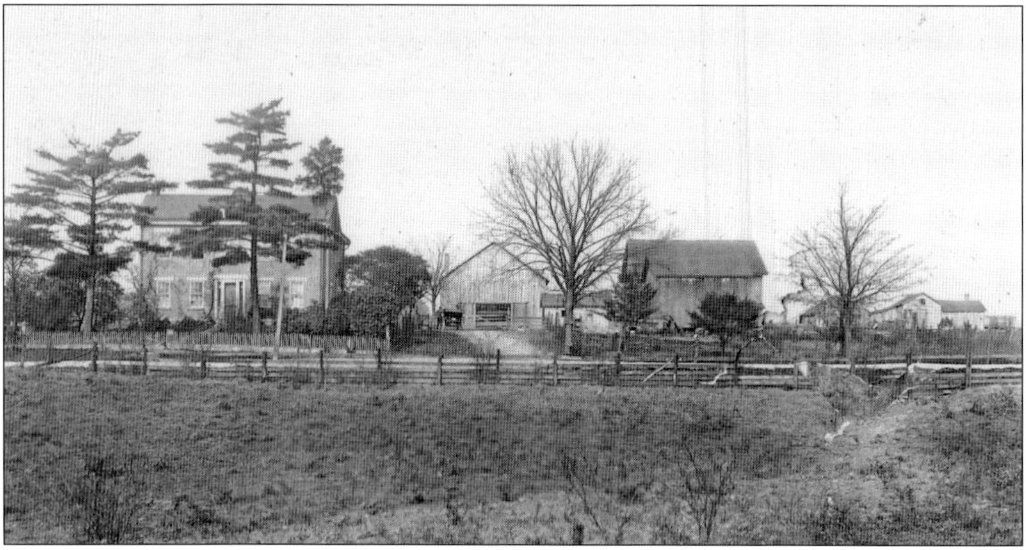

This 1910 photograph is of the Emmor and Mary Satterthwaite Baily farmhouse, built on the Waynesville-Bellbrook Road in 1857. Mary Baily was a cousin of American flag maker Betsy Ross. A prosperous Quaker farmer, the Bailys' son Emmor was the first student to enroll in Ohio State University. The farm became a major sightseeing attraction in 1914 when one of the Wright brothers' airplanes landed in its wheat field. (Courtesy of Douglas and Pamela Campbell.)

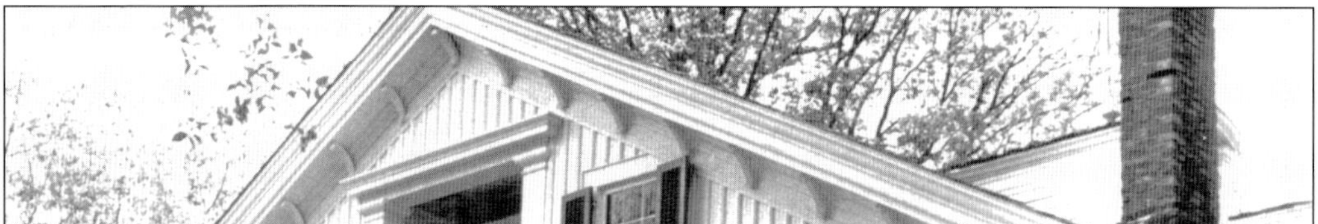

The Greek Revival home of Dr. Mary L. Cook, MD, on Wilkerson Lane at the southern edge of Waynesville was built about 1849. Dr. Cook practiced medicine in Wayne Township from 1908 to 1955. She was the founder of the Wayne Township Public Library in 1917. The library took her name in 1961. The house was previously the home of Patrick and Sophia Apjohn Kearney and Hatton family members, who constructed it. (Courtesy of Mary L. Cook Public Library.)

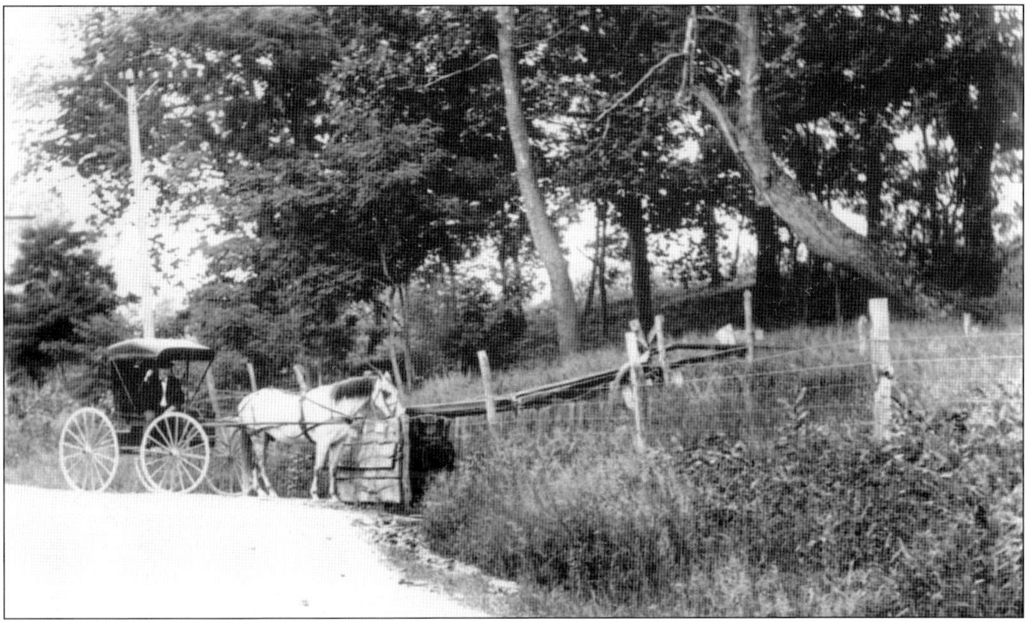

Mason Spring was an important watering hole along the Cincinnati-Columbus Road (old Ohio Route 42) on the Mason farm. Owner David Mason is shown in his buggy in this 1905 photograph while watering his horse. In 1877, the freight wagon delivering a vault to the new Citizens National Bank at Lebanon was bogged down to the axles here and a near catastrophe. (Courtesy of Mary L. Cook Public Library.)

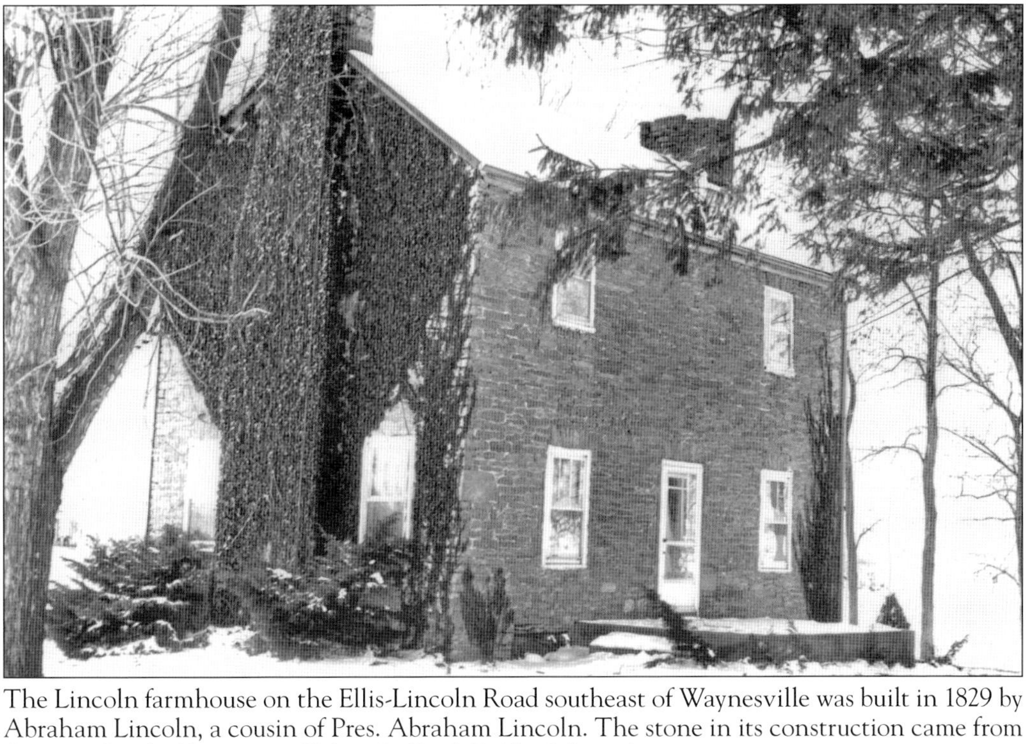

The Lincoln farmhouse on the Ellis-Lincoln Road southeast of Waynesville was built in 1829 by Abraham Lincoln, a cousin of Pres. Abraham Lincoln. The stone in its construction came from Caesar's Creek. (Courtesy of Mary L. Cook Public Library.)

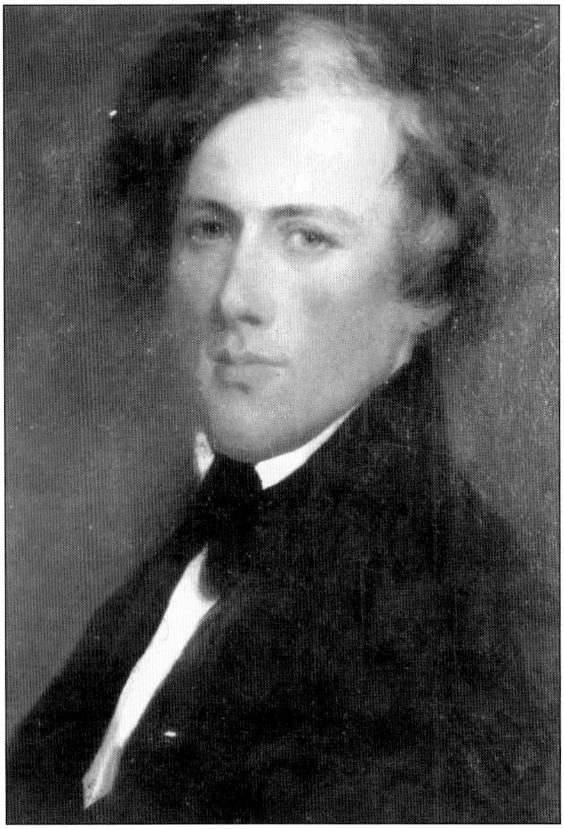

This oil portrait of John Heighway, son of Samuel Heighway, was painted in 1803 in Cincinnati, Ohio. John was born in England in 1785 and came to Waynesville, Ohio, in 1797. John married Eliza Mercer at Cincinnati in 1810. He became a leading Cincinnati businessman and built the city's first bank vault. His portrait hangs in the Ohioana Room of Mary L. Cook Public Library in Waynesville. (Courtesy of Mary L. Cook Public Library.)

Waynesville, Ohio, settlers built one-room log cabins like the one in this photograph, taken in the 1920s. This unidentified cabin squats in a field of wildflowers in Wayne Township as a reminder of pioneer homes of the early 1800s. (Courtesy of Mary L. Cook Public Library.)

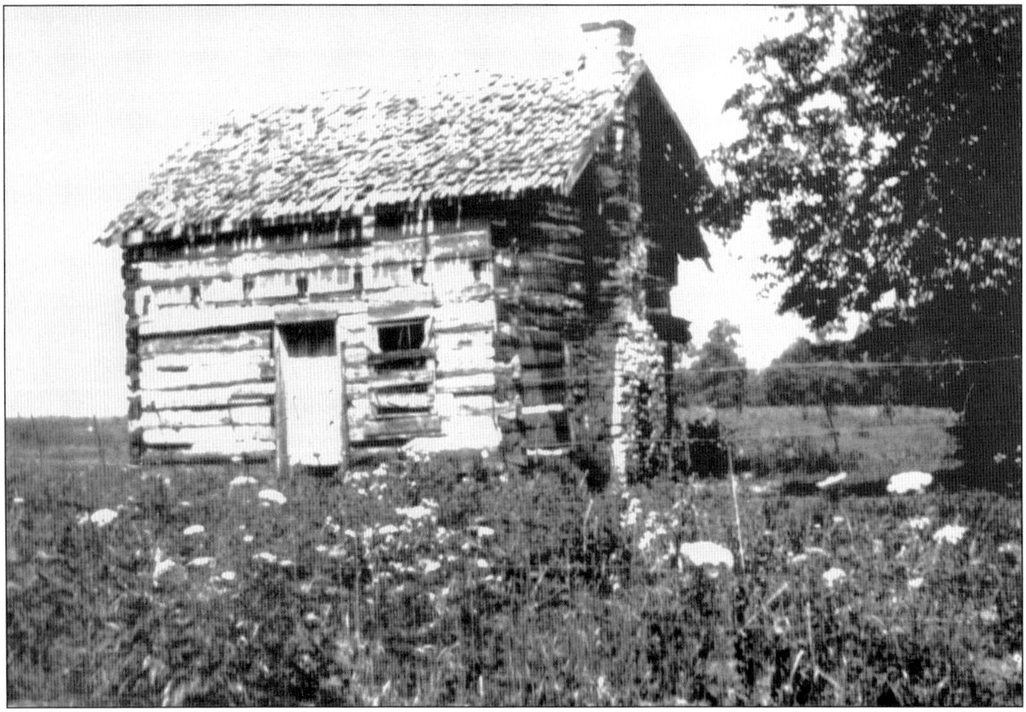

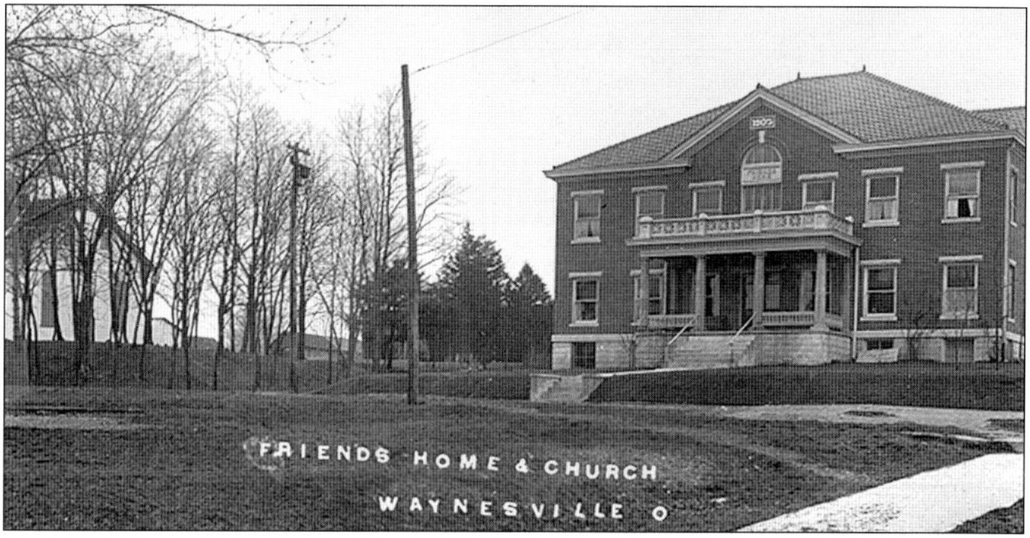

The Friends Boarding Home, shown at the right in this 1905 photograph, was built in 1905 for the care of elderly Quakers. Originally, each bedroom had its own parlor adjacent. The Home was constructed by Indiana Yearly Meeting of the Religious Society of Friends (Quakers). The Miami Friends "White Brick" Meetinghouse can be seen at left. The building, which is at Miami and Fourth Streets, is now the Friends Home Museum, showcasing Wayne Township history. (Courtesy of Mary L. Cook Public Library.)

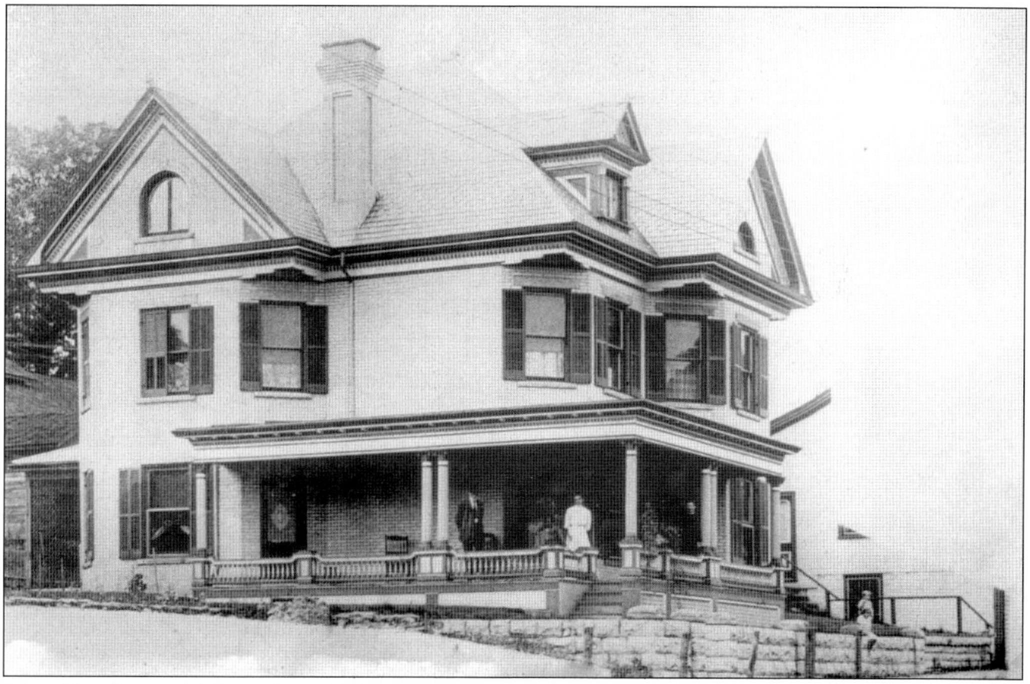

The Charles and Mary Cornell Home, at 71 North Main Street in Waynesville, was built by them in 1901. The house was designed and constructed by Stacey Kindall. Mary Cornell is shown in this 1905 photograph in the center of the veranda with Charles Cornell on the right. Charles was a cousin of Ezra Cornell, founder of Cornell University. (Courtesy of Mary L. Cook Public Library.)

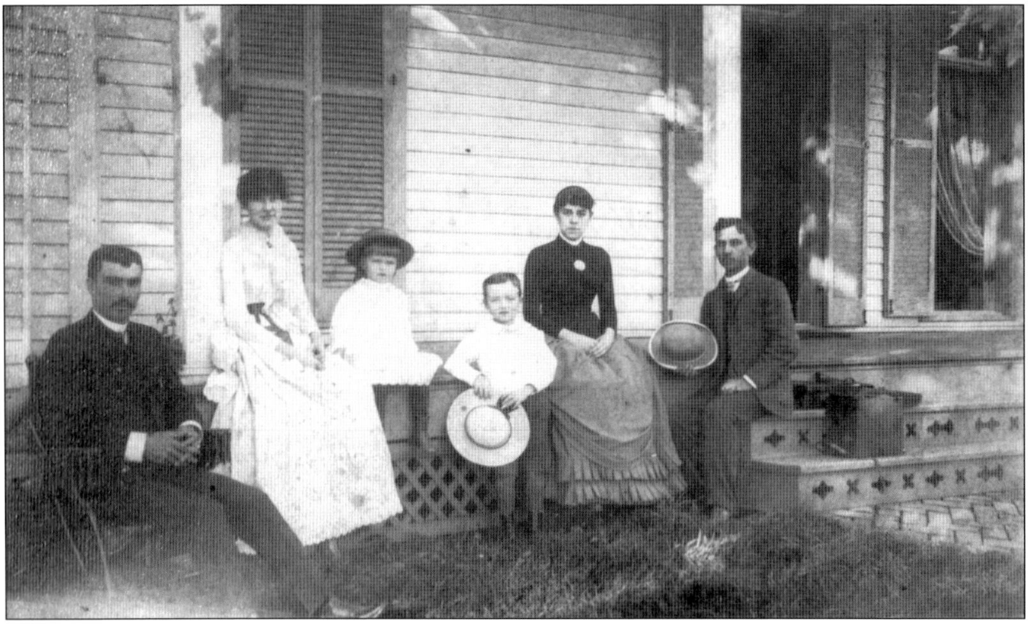

A group of Tennessee Williams's Dakin relatives is shown in this 1882 photograph on the veranda of the Gordon Wright home, at 460 West Miami Street in Waynesville. From left to right are Warren Dakin; May Wright, Wayne Township Public Library's first librarian in 1917; unidentified Dakin children; Nan Wright Dakin, wife of Warren and May Wright's sister; and an unidentified man. Tennessee Williams's mother was Edwina Dakin Williams, daughter of the Reverend Walter Edwin Dakin of St. Mary's Episcopal Church. (Courtesy of Mary L. Cook Public Library.)

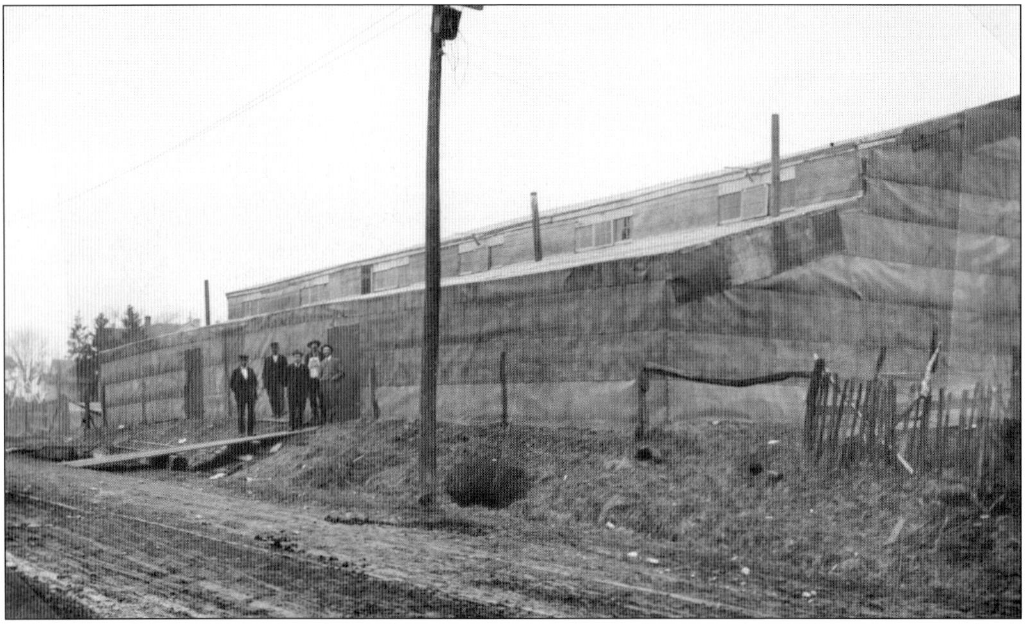

The Waynesville Tabernacle is shown here just after its construction was finished in 1904. It was built on the northwest corner of North Main Street and Franklin Road to facilitate interdenominational religious meetings and revivals. An unidentified group of its promoters is shown at the entrance on Franklin Road. (Courtesy of Mary L. Cook Public Library.)

Judge John W. Keys, Warren County probate judge in the 1870s, was Waynesville's first mayor in 1849. He was a cabinetmaker from 1836 until 1876, when he was elected probate judge. He was also the Waynesville justice of peace in 1842. Judge Keys brought national attention to Waynesville in 1882 when he headed the hunt for the "Crosswicks Monster," now known to be an allosaurus but described in the *Miami Gazette* at the time as "Snaix." (Courtesy of Mary L. Cook Public Library.)

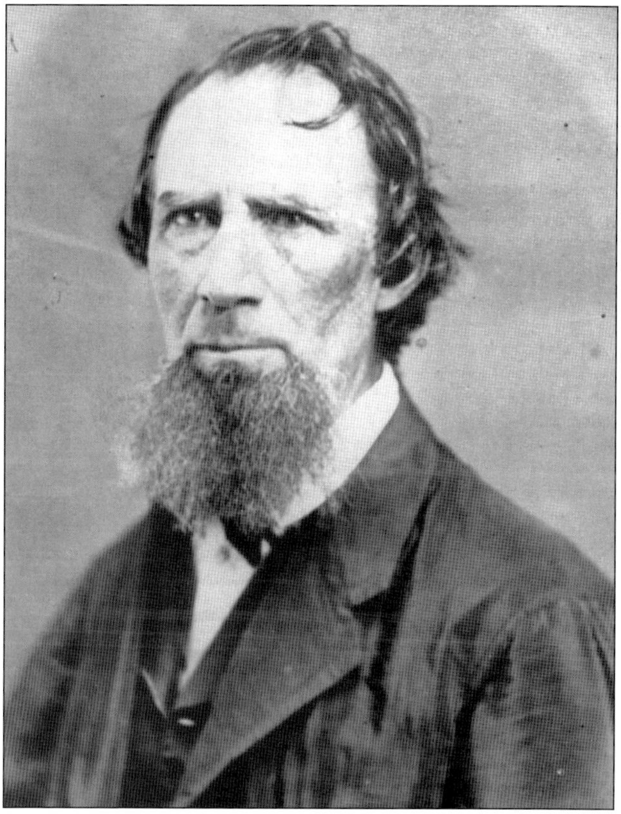

The Wayne Novelty Ironworks began manufacturing iron garden ornaments and doorstops in 1879. The ironworks operated in a building on North Main Street adjacent what is now the Lebanon Citizens National Bank. The cast-iron frog shown in this 2011 photograph was one of its most popular sellers. The ironworks closed in 1885. (Courtesy of Mary L. Cook Public Library.)

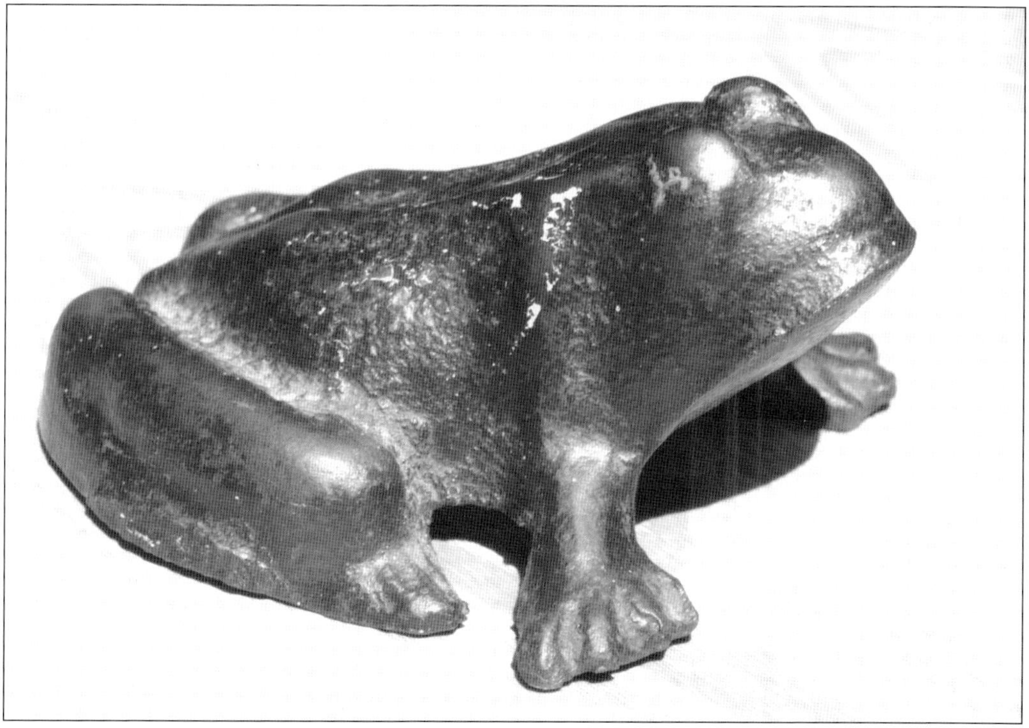

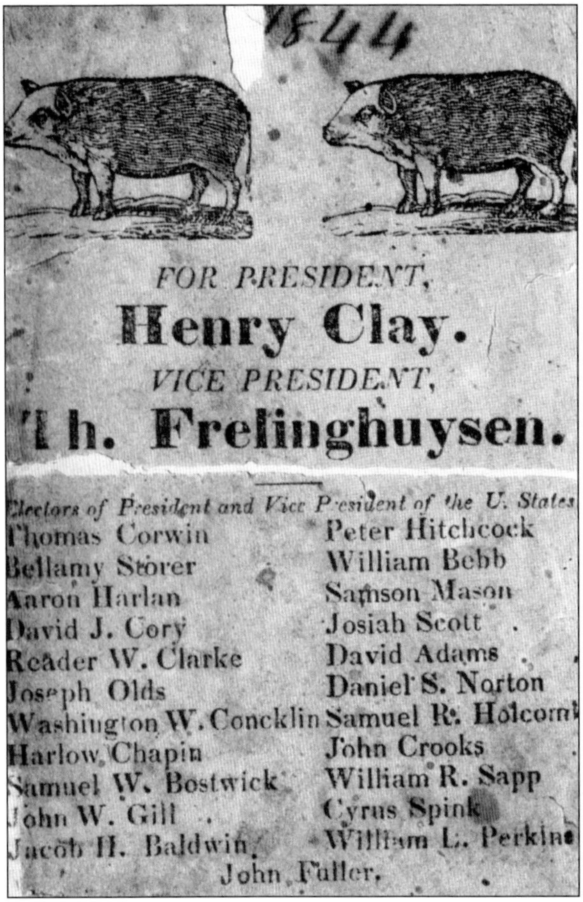

1844

FOR PRESIDENT,

Henry Clay.

VICE PRESIDENT,

Th. Frelinghuysen.

Electors of President and Vice President of the U. States

Thomas Corwin	Peter Hitchcock
Bellamy Storer	William Bebb
Aaron Harlan	Samson Mason
David J. Cory	Josiah Scott
Reader W. Clarke	David Adams
Joseph Olds	Daniel S. Norton
Washington W. Concklin	Samuel R. Holcomb
Harlow Chapin	John Crooks
Samuel W. Bostwick	William R. Sapp
John W. Gill	Cyrus Spink
Jacob H. Baldwin	William L. Perkins

John Fuller.

Wayne Township citizens were almost equally divided in their political views. This "Henry Clay for president" handout is dated 1844. Clay often lodged at Satterthwaite's Halfway House Inn during the 1820s when his political travel took him through Wayne Township. Many Waynesville voters were members of the Whig Party, the forerunner of the Republican Party. In 1850, Waynesville was also the location of a major Democrat convention. (Courtesy of Mary L. Cook Public Library.)

Waynesville citizens were health conscious, as shown in this photograph taken in 1920. This group of young men is shown during a sleep out in front of the Miami Friends "White Brick" Meetinghouse, at Fourth and High Streets. The man on the right wrapped in quilts is Edward Burton. (Courtesy of Mary L. Cook Public Library.)

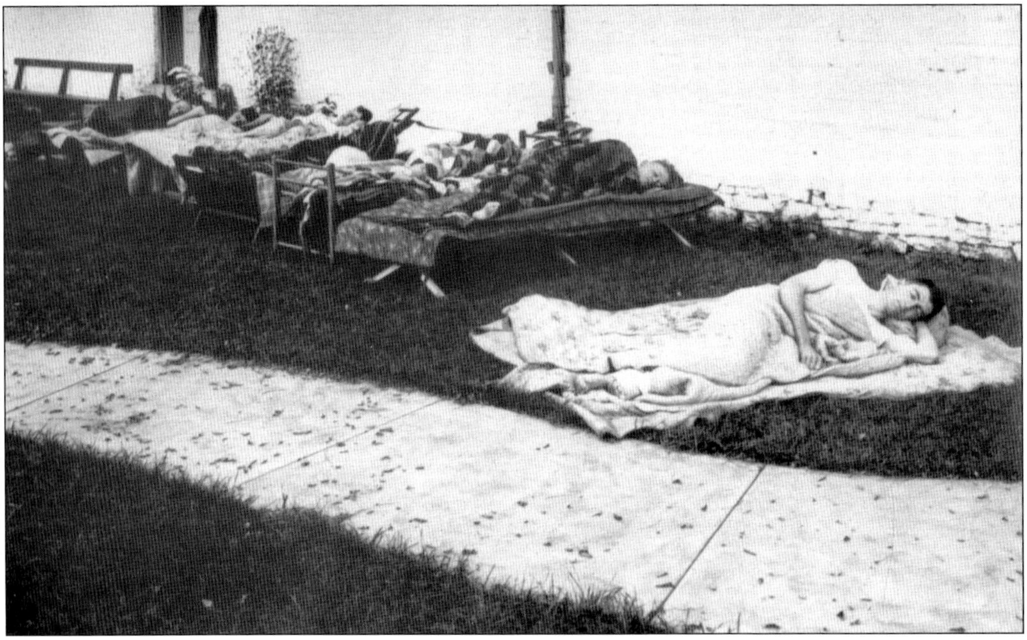

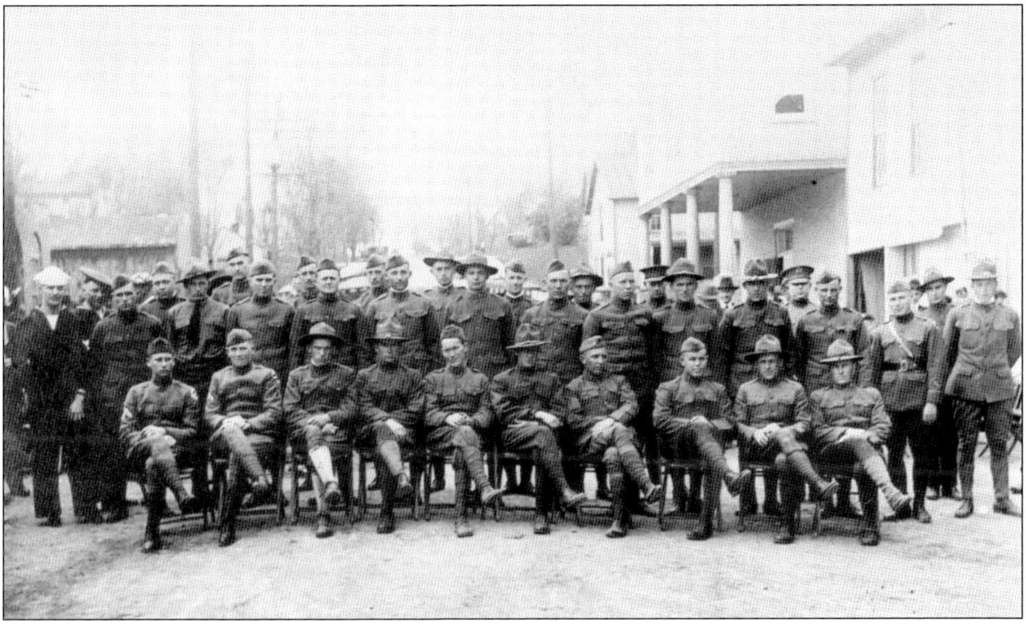

Many Wayne Township men saw service during World War I. This photograph, taken in 1918, shows a group of Waynesville soldiers representing the various branches of military service. The photograph was taken in Miami Street at the intersection of Main Street. Cadwallader Hall, Masonic Lodge No. 163 F&AM, and Waynesville Cracker Factory are visible on the right. (Courtesy of Mary L. Cook Public Library.)

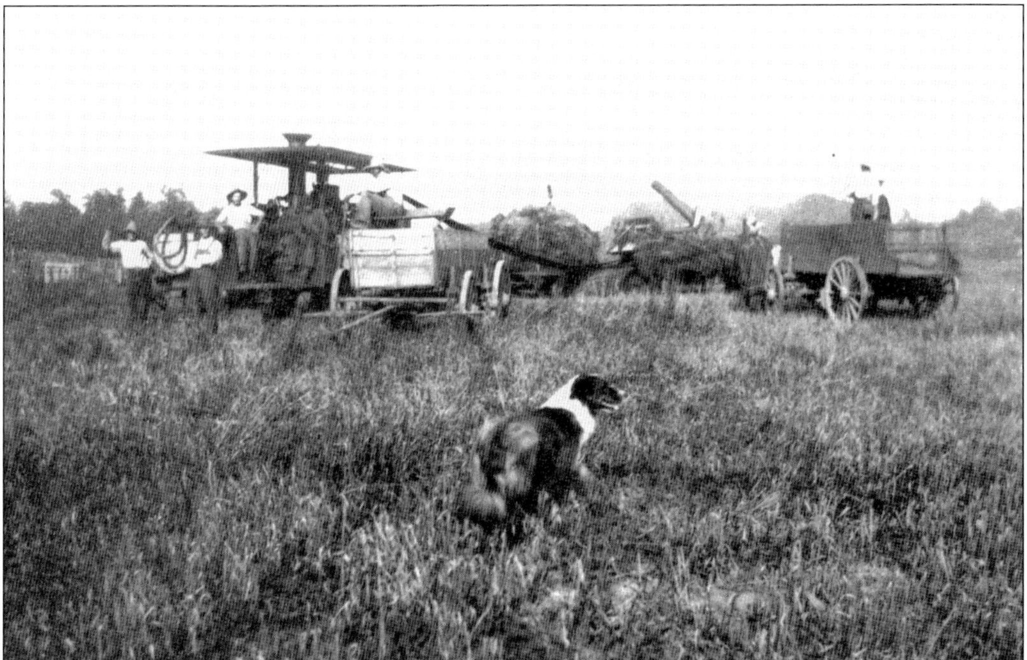

Waynesville farmers are shown in this 1910 photograph harvesting with both steam-powered and horse-powered equipment. In the foreground is someone's faithful collie dog. (Courtesy of Mary L. Cook Public Library.)

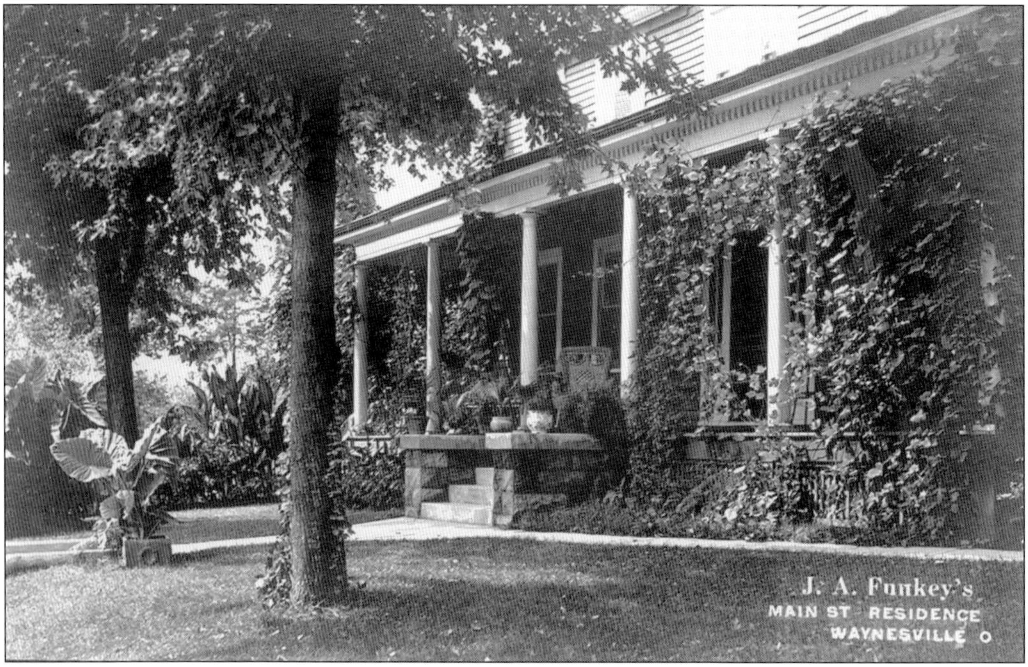

The John A. Funkey residence, on North Main Street, illustrates the gardening style of 1910. The house was built by Joel Evans for his residence in 1874. (Courtesy of Mary L. Cook Public Library.)

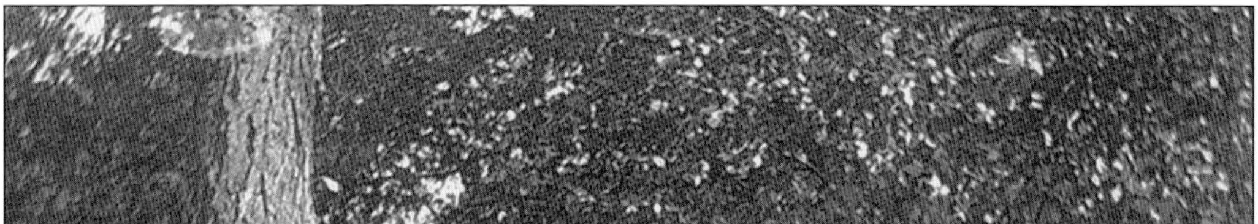

A favorite Edwardian pastime in Waynesville and Corwin was fishing along the Little Miami River. The unidentified young woman in this 1905 photograph is using a bamboo cane pole. (Courtesy of Mary L. Cook Public Library.)

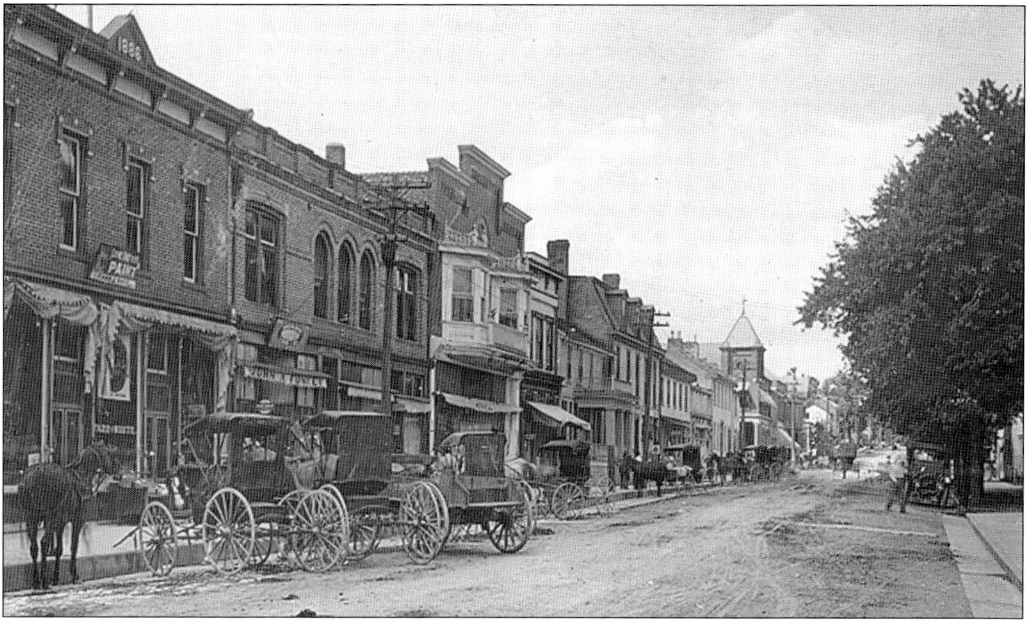

This central view of Waynesville's Main Street business district features horse-and-buggy hitching on the left side of the street and automobile parking on the right side. This photograph, which was taken in 1910, shows the 1886 Farr and White Grocery on the left, with the John A Funkey Trade Palace, built in 1874, and the B.S. Howell Department Store, built in 1905. (Courtesy of Mary L. Cook Public Library.)

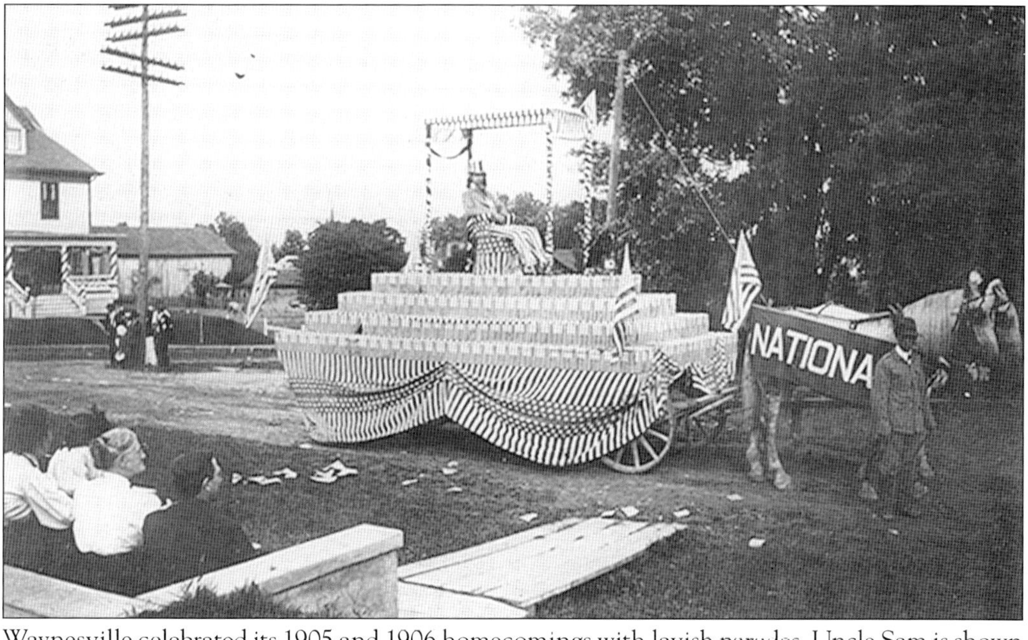

Waynesville celebrated its 1905 and 1906 homecomings with lavish parades. Uncle Sam is shown in this photograph of the 1906 homecoming. At left, spectators are seated on the steps of the Friends Boarding Home, at the corner of Fourth and Miami Streets. St. Mary's Episcopal Church Rectory can be seen at left in the background with the Seth S. Haines barn at its right. (Courtesy of Mary L. Cook Public Library.)

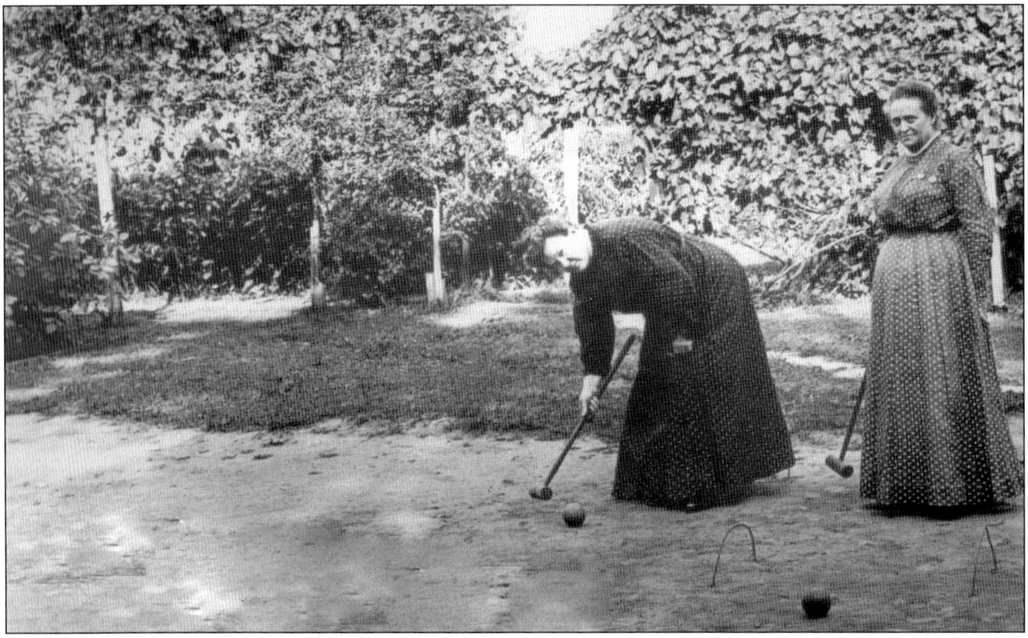

Two Waynesville ladies of the Edwardian era are shown in this 1910 photograph as they play croquet on the lawn of their home. Croquet was a popular pastime in Waynesville, Corwin, and Lytle from the Victorian age onward. (Courtesy of Mary L. Cook Public Library.)

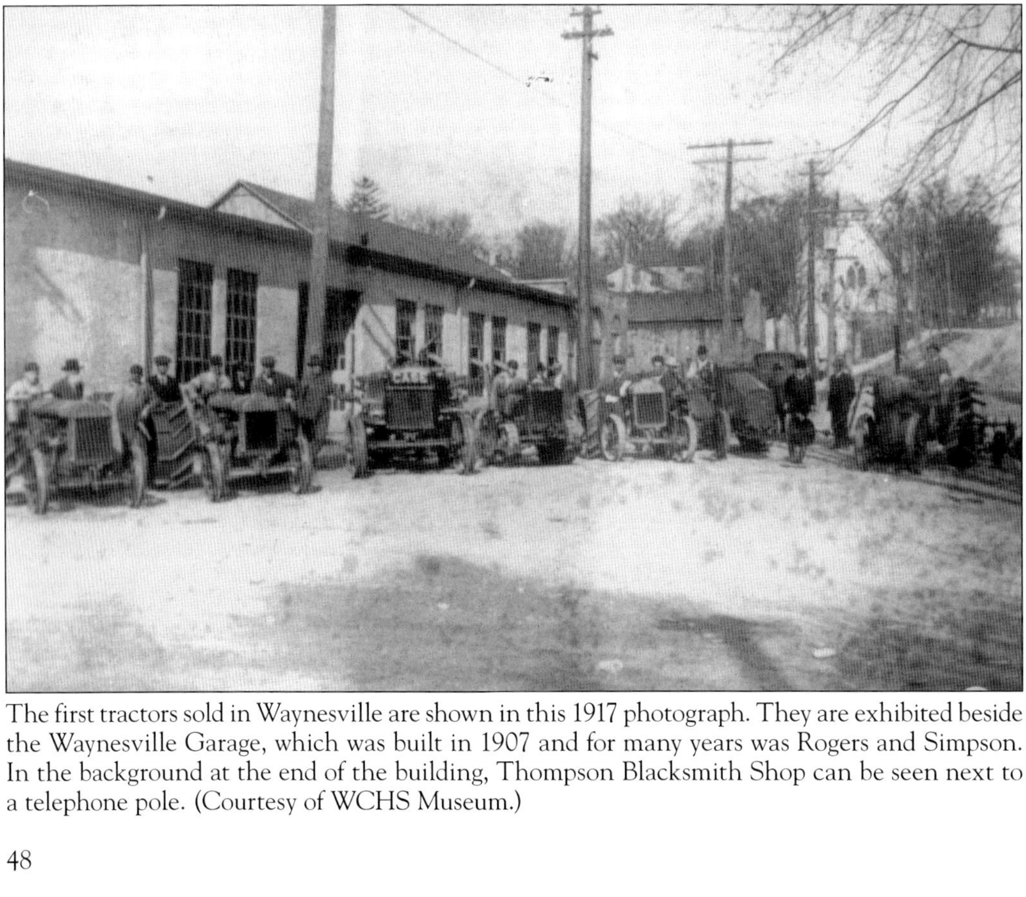

The first tractors sold in Waynesville are shown in this 1917 photograph. They are exhibited beside the Waynesville Garage, which was built in 1907 and for many years was Rogers and Simpson. In the background at the end of the building, Thompson Blacksmith Shop can be seen next to a telephone pole. (Courtesy of WCHS Museum.)

The Hammell House Inn, at 121 South Main Street in Waynesville, was purchased in 1901 by William Gustin and renamed the Gustin House. Gustin catered to travelling businessmen. Gustin had the historic inn's third-floor brick ballroom, originally added in 1843 by Enoch Hammell, removed in 1934. He built a show barn for his Thoroughbred horse sales behind the hotel in 1904. (Author's.)

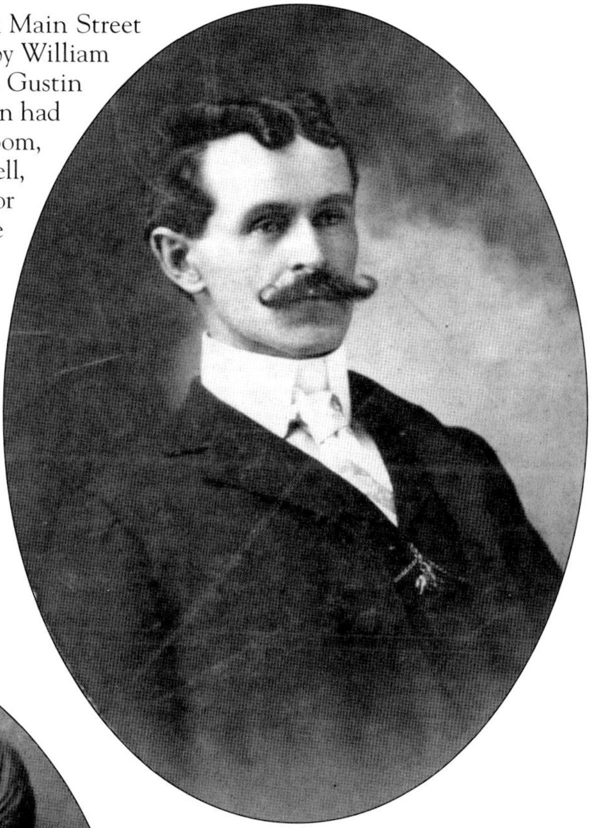

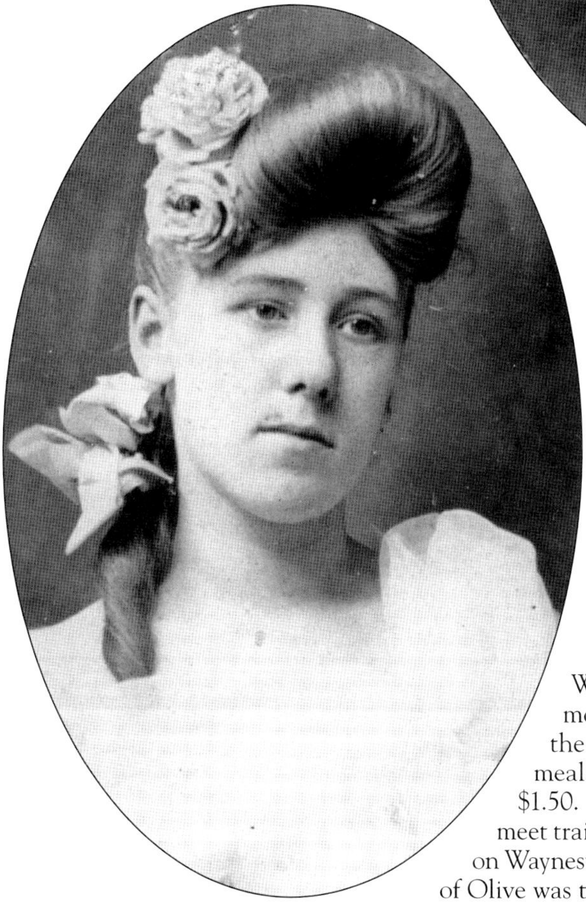

William's wife, Olive Casey Gustin, and her mother-in-law, Mary Combs Gustin, did all the Gustin House cooking and preparing of meals. Meals cost 25¢, and a day's lodging was $1.50. Olive drove a buggy to Corwin daily to meet trains and shuttle guests to the Gustin House on Waynesville's South Main Street. This photograph of Olive was taken in 1905. (Author's.)

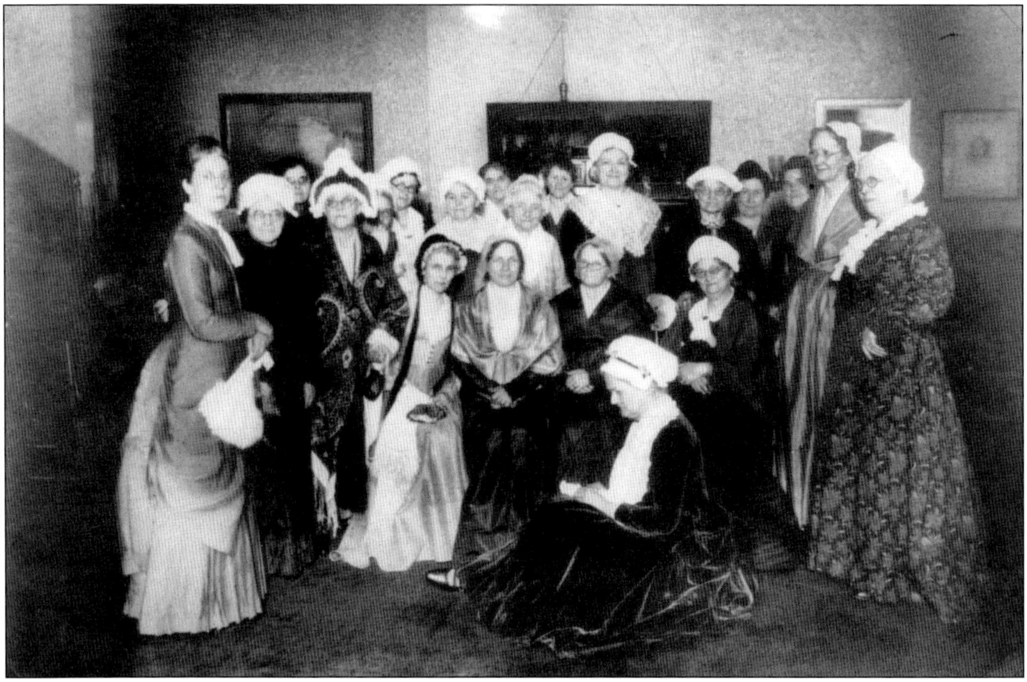

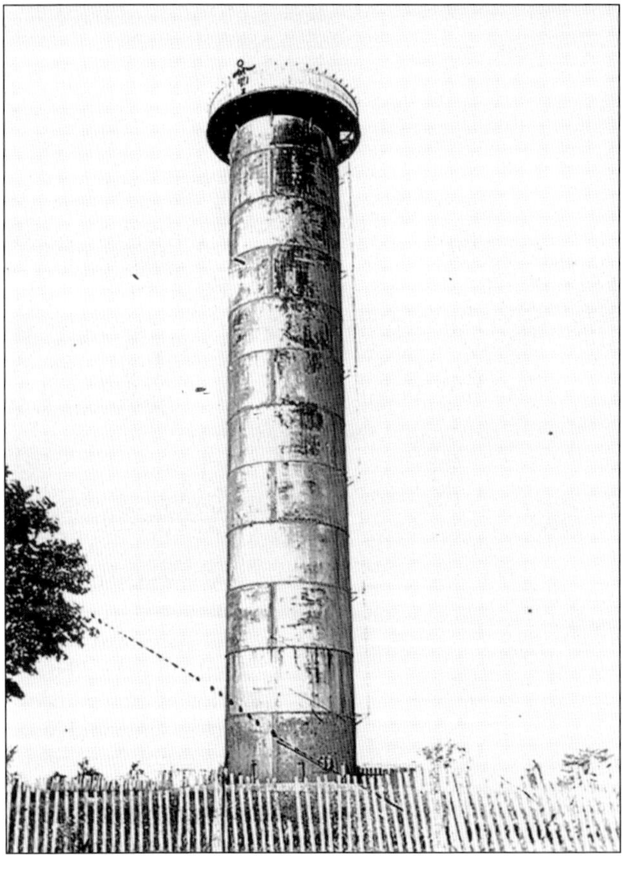

The Current Topic Club organized in Waynesville in 1899. A literary club, it was renamed the New Century Club in 1908, when this photograph was taken. Members are shown in their mothers' and grandmothers' dresses to celebrate the renaming of the club. (Courtesy of Mary L. Cook Public Library.)

Waynesville got both water and electricity in 1901. This photograph of the village's gravity-flow water storage standpipe was taken 1901. The iron storage tank was located on West Chapman Street near the intersection of Fifth Street. The standpipe was demolished in 2006. An unidentified man is perched at the top. (Courtesy of Mary L. Cook Public Library.)

This photograph, taken in 1901, shows the Waynesville Powerhouse just after construction was finished that year. Jesse Burton was the first superintendent who supervised and operated the plant. Electricity would be generated by steam in the early morning hours for village stores and shut down at noon. The electricity would be turned back on in the early evening and then shut down at 8:00 p.m. Burton habitually "winked" the electricity before closing time to signal his family that he was coming home for supper. Burton is standing in the doorway between the two automobiles. (Courtesy of Mary L. Cook Public Library.)

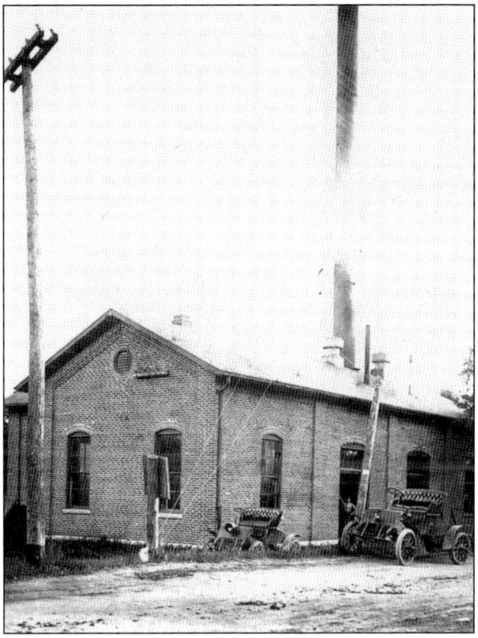

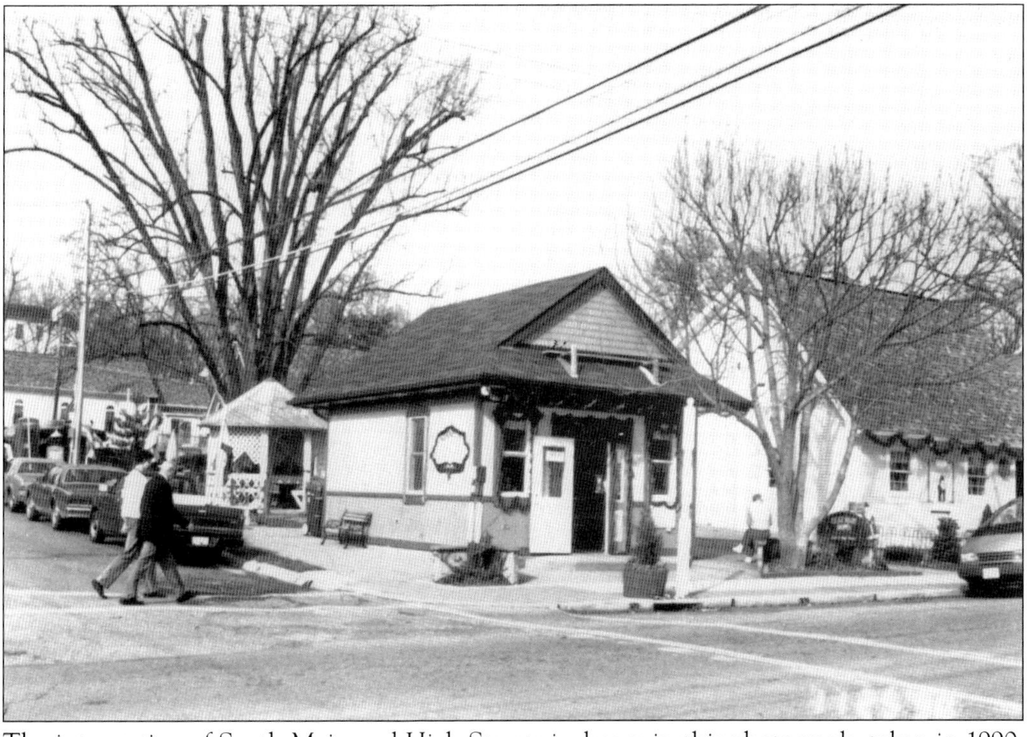

The intersection of South Main and High Streets is shown in this photograph, taken in 1990. This intersection was the site of Waynesville Public Square from 1797 until after the Civil War. St. Augustine's Roman Catholic Church can be seen at left in the background. St. Augustine's was built in 1884 on a part of Lot 5 in Wabash Square. The partial lot purchased by the church from William and Sarah Rogers in 1877 was due to the front corner being tapered to make the public square. (Courtesy of Mary L. Cook Public Library.)

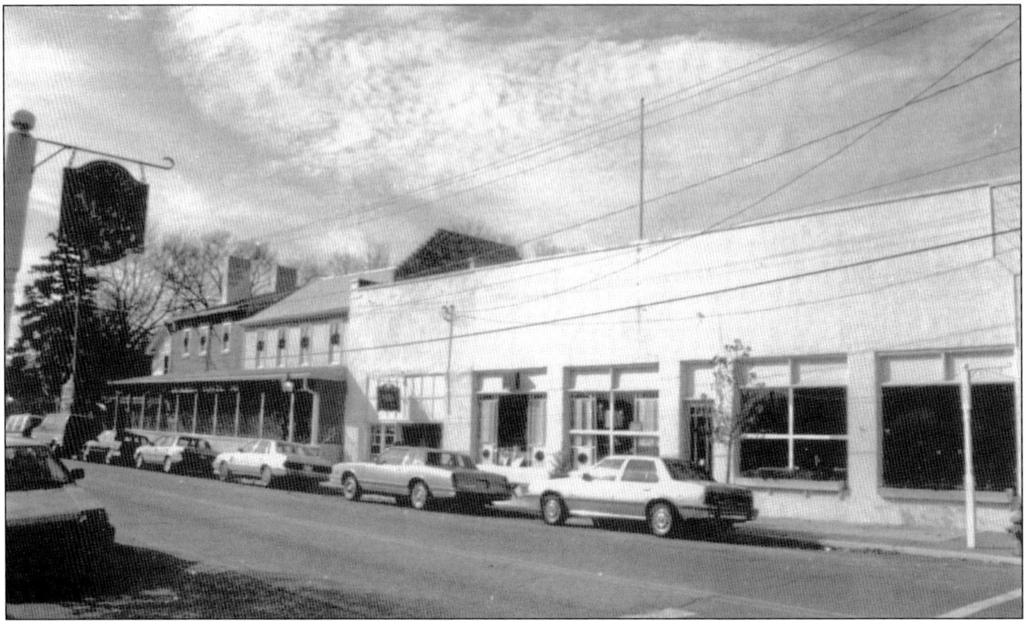

The building that housed the Waynesville Garage and Miami Theater is shown in this 1990 photograph. The building was constructed in 1907 with a theater addition in 1919. The building, which is located at South Main and Miami Streets, occupies the site of the brick J&S Collins Grocery and Bakery, built before 1850. The Hammel House is shown on the left. (Courtesy of Mary L. Cook Public Library.)

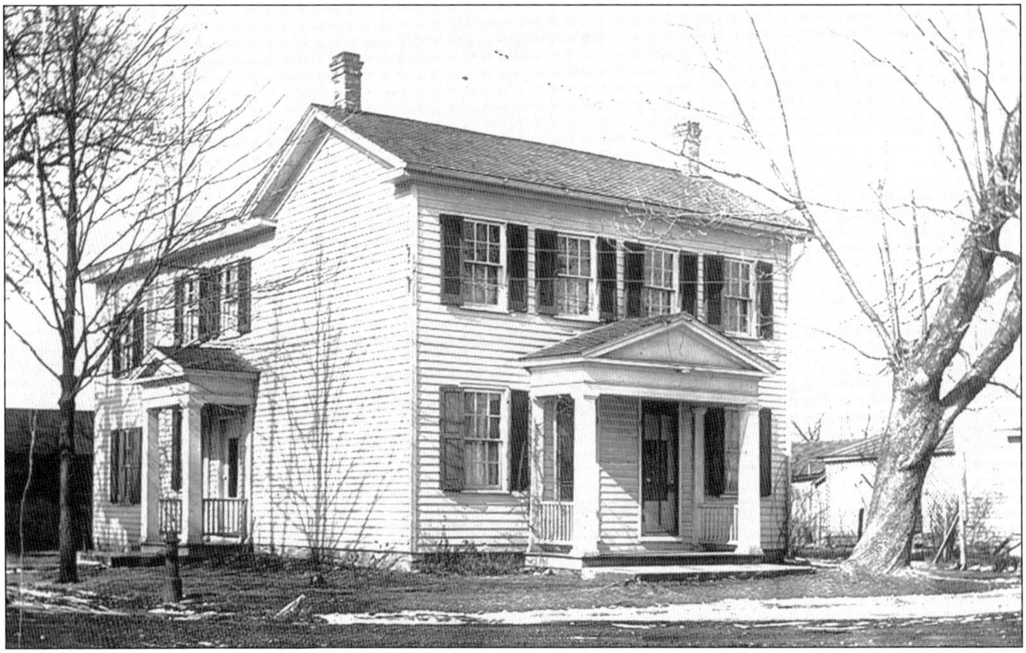

The c. 1850 Dinwiddie-Wardlow residence, on the northwest corner of Fifth and Chapman Streets in Waynesville, is shown in this 1950 photograph. The house for many years was the home of Truman and Olive Wardlow and family. Olive Wardlow's mother, Arabella Dinwiddie, previously owned the house. (Courtesy of Mary L. Cook Public Library.)

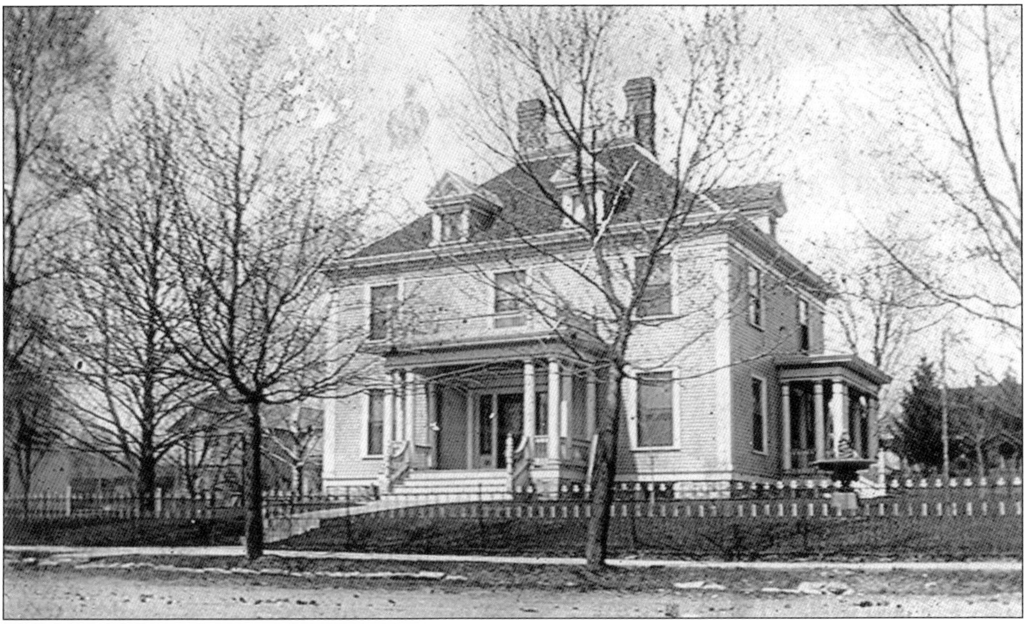

The Phillip Hopkins residence is shown in this photograph, taken in 1900. The house was built by Hopkins around 1900 on the southwest corner of Third and North Streets. The lot was originally part of the grounds of the Seth S. Haines mansion down on Third Street. The ornamental iron fence and the ornate fountain visible on the right were a part of Haines's landscaping. (Courtesy of Mary L. Cook Public Library.)

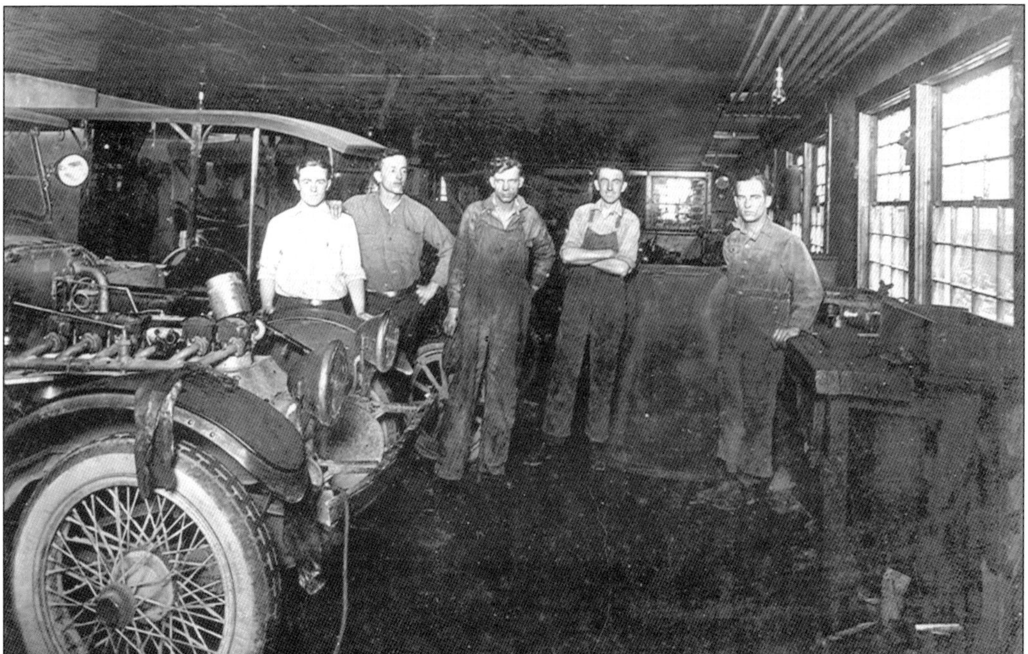

The owners and mechanics of Rogers and Simpson Garage at 109 South Main Street in Waynesville are shown in this photograph, taken in 1932. Mark Rogers is third from the left, and Vern Simpson is at the far right. (Courtesy of Mary L. Cook Public Library.)

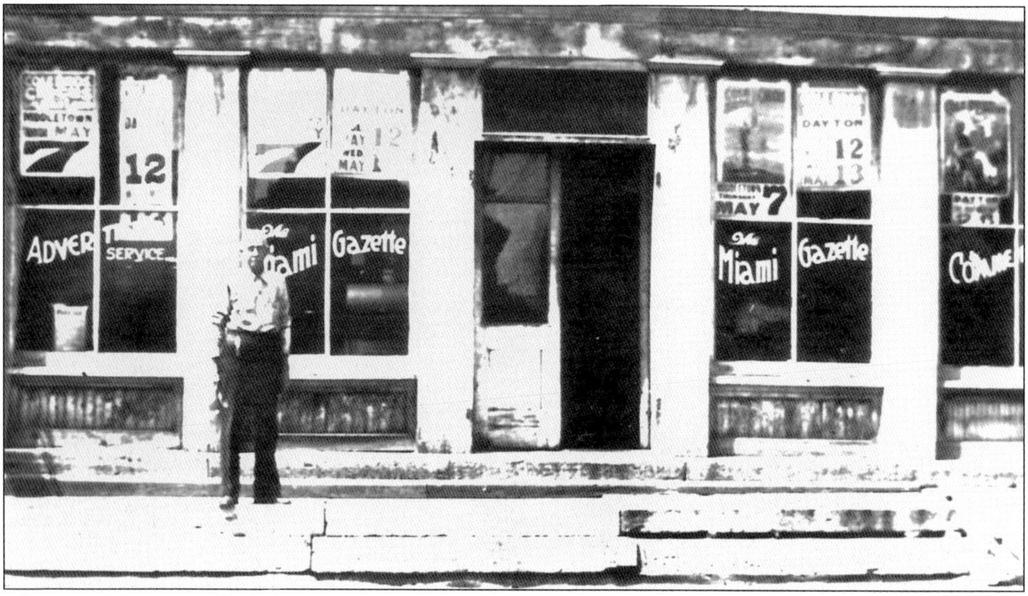

The *Miami Visitor*, which became the *Miami Gazette* in 1865, was founded on the second floor of the building constructed by John Satterthwaite in 1820 at 38 South Main Street in Waynesville. It moved to the first floor of the building when the new owner, James Drew Sweet, changed the name. The *Miami Gazette* was last owned and operated at this location by Paul Shearer Sr. and wife Cecelia in 1955. John C. Hawke is shown in front of the *Gazette* in this 1920 photograph. (Courtesy of Mary L. Cook Public Library.)

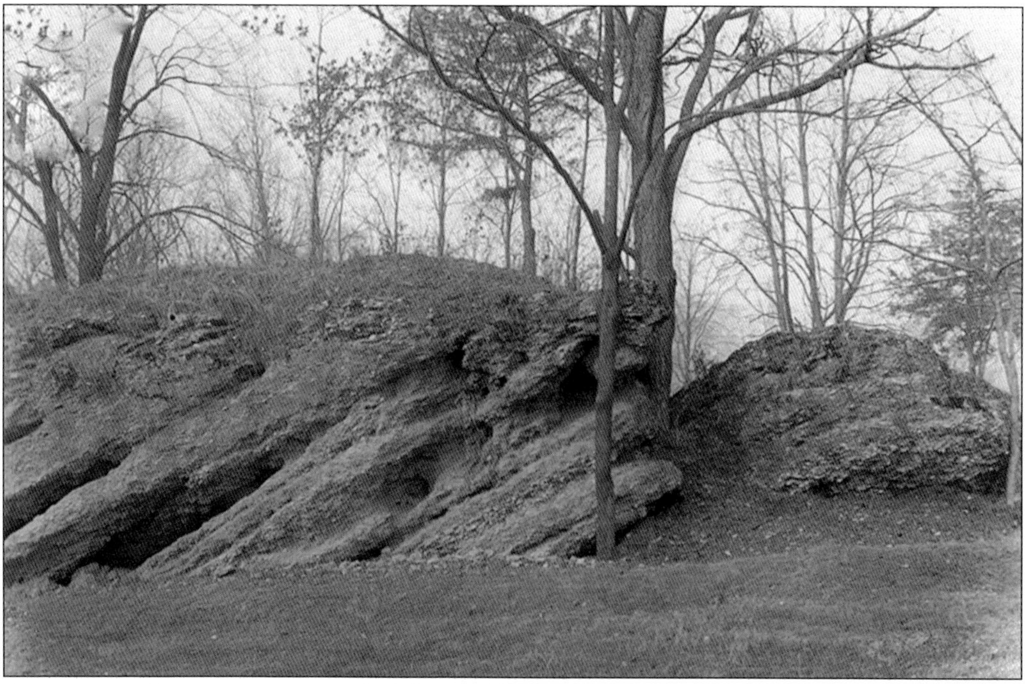

A vast vein of limestone passes under Waynesville, originating at the Ohio River near Cincinnati. The outcropping of limestone in this photograph, taken in 1900, is buried under the hillside near 355 South Main Street. (Courtesy of Mary L. Cook Public Library.)

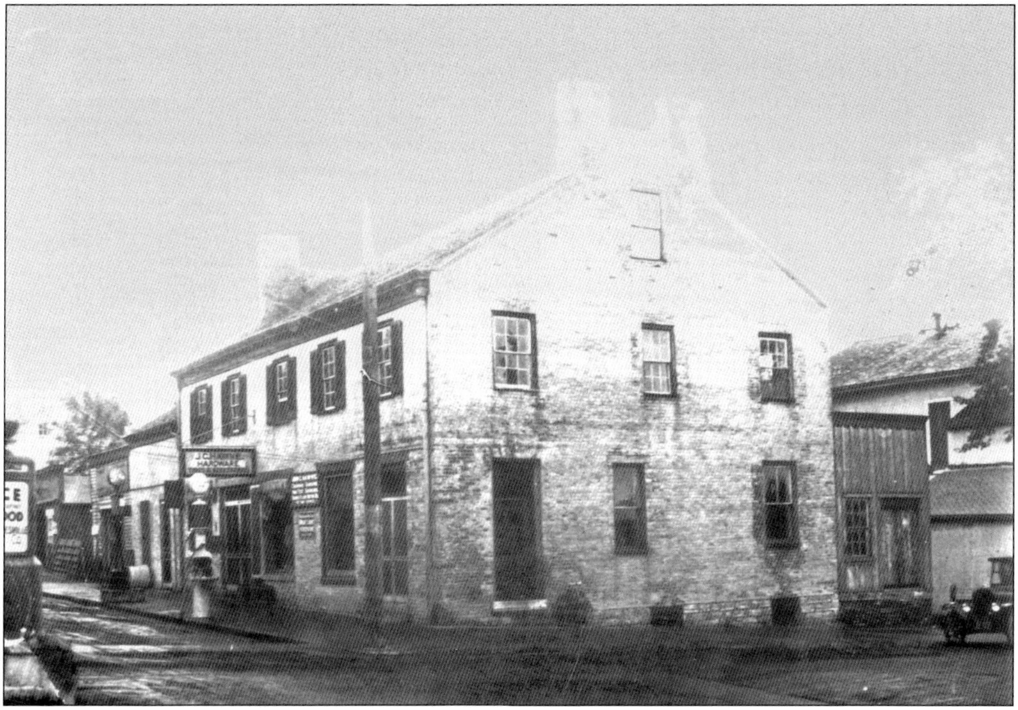

Many historical events happened in the Miami House, shown in this photograph, taken around 1912. The Little Miami Railroad was organized in the dining room in 1835, and the Wayne Township Public Library was founded there in 1917. At the time of this photograph, it was the J.C. Hawke Hardware store. Visible at left is the Odd Fellows Hall. The Miami House, which was located on the northeast corner of Main and North Streets, was demolished in 1955. (Courtesy of Mary L. Cook Public Library.)

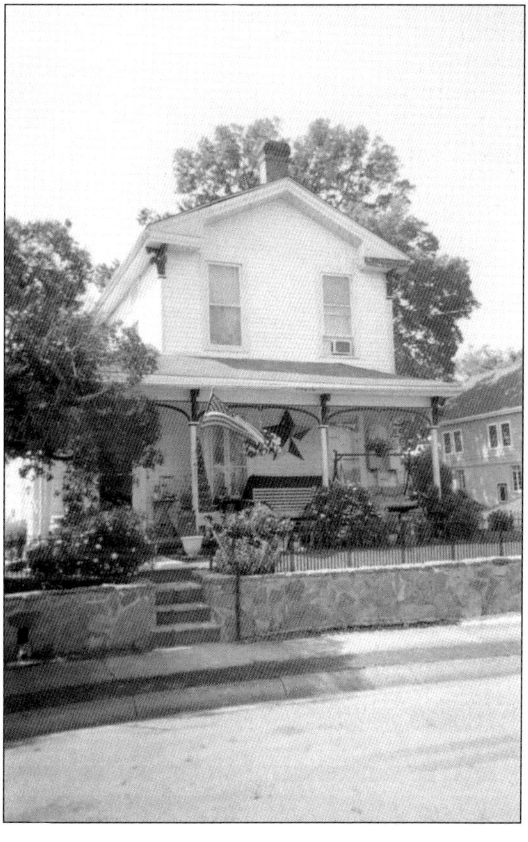

Dr. Edwin F. Dakin, MD, built this home at 143 South Third Street in Waynesville in 1874. Dr. Dakin was the great-grandfather of American playwright Thomas L. "Tennessee" Williams. This photograph was taken in 2012. (Author's.)

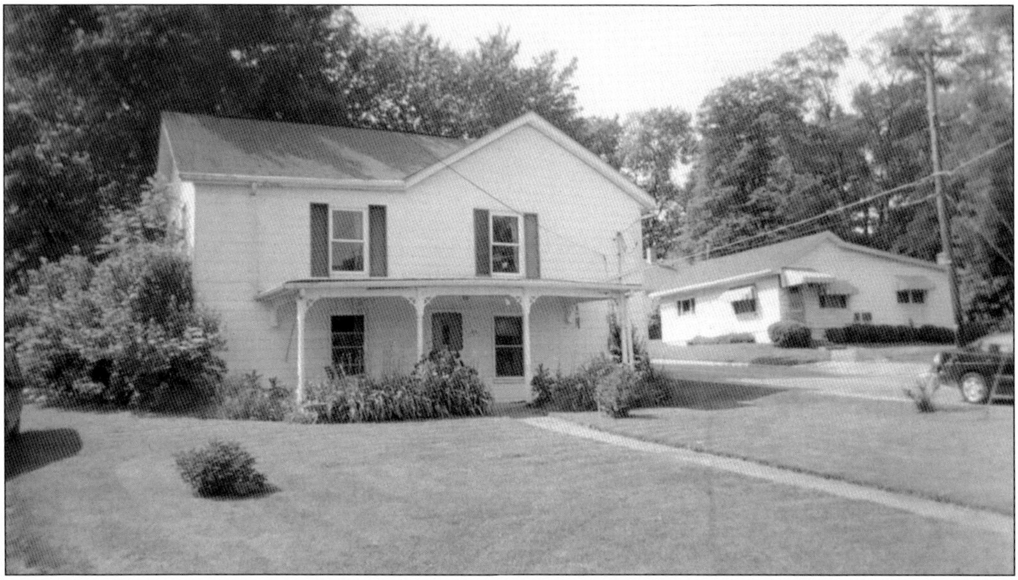

Distilling and brewing were two of Wayne Township's biggest businesses from the early to late 1800s. The kitchen of this building at 221 North Main Street was constructed for a whiskey distillery in 1801 and is of log construction. By 1875, the first two stories were added by the Arbogast Aman Brewery. In the late 1880s, it was a branch of the Sachs Pruden Brewery of Dayton, Ohio. This photograph was taken in 2012. (Author's.)

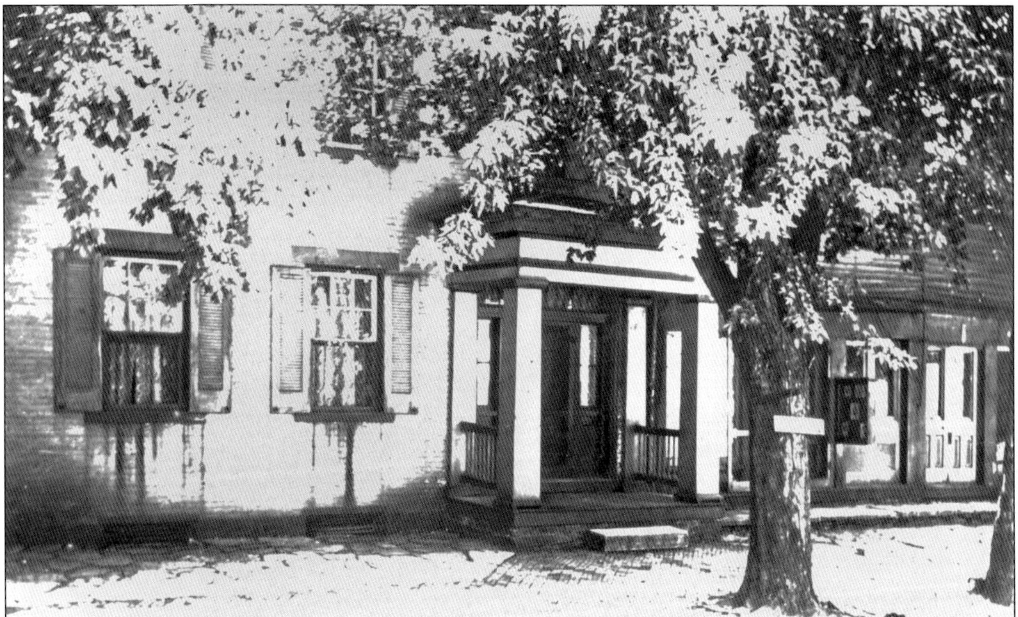

Samuel Linton built the Gideon Leak residence at 38 South Main Street in Waynesville in 1847. This photograph, taken in 1912, shows the Ridge Photography studio next door on the right. Just inside the front door and to the left is a small painting on wood inserted in the door transom. The artwork depicts the Samuel Linton log cabin facing south toward Camp Creek. The Linton cabin, built in 1799, is covered by clapboard and is still a part of the rear of the building. (Courtesy of Mary L. Cook Public Library.)

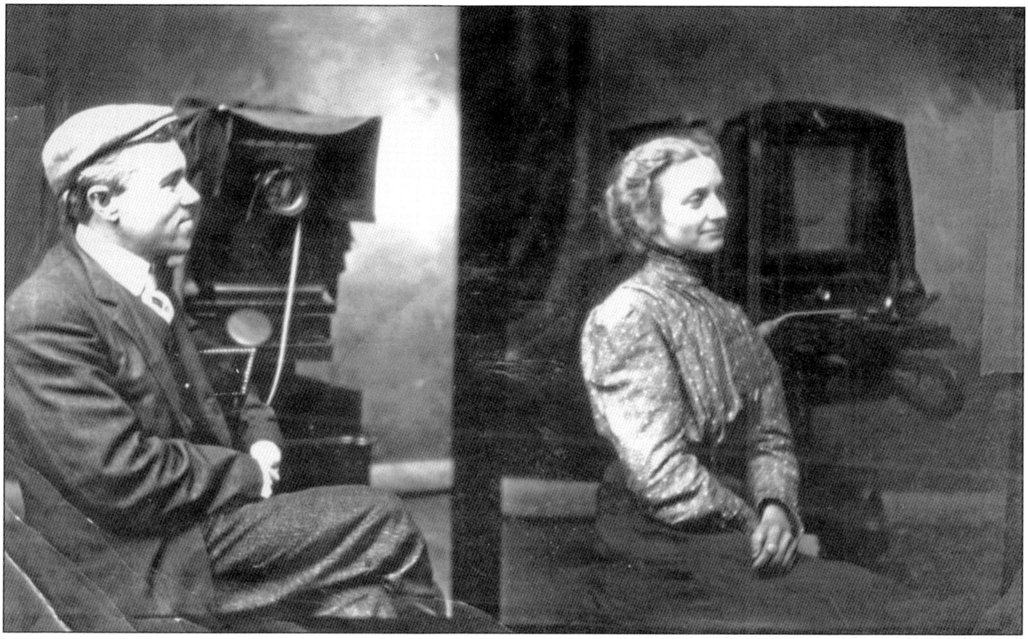

Oakley and Edna Ridge are shown in this 1912 photograph taken in their photography studio on South Main Street. The studio building was built around 1860. (Courtesy of Mary L. Cook Public Library.)

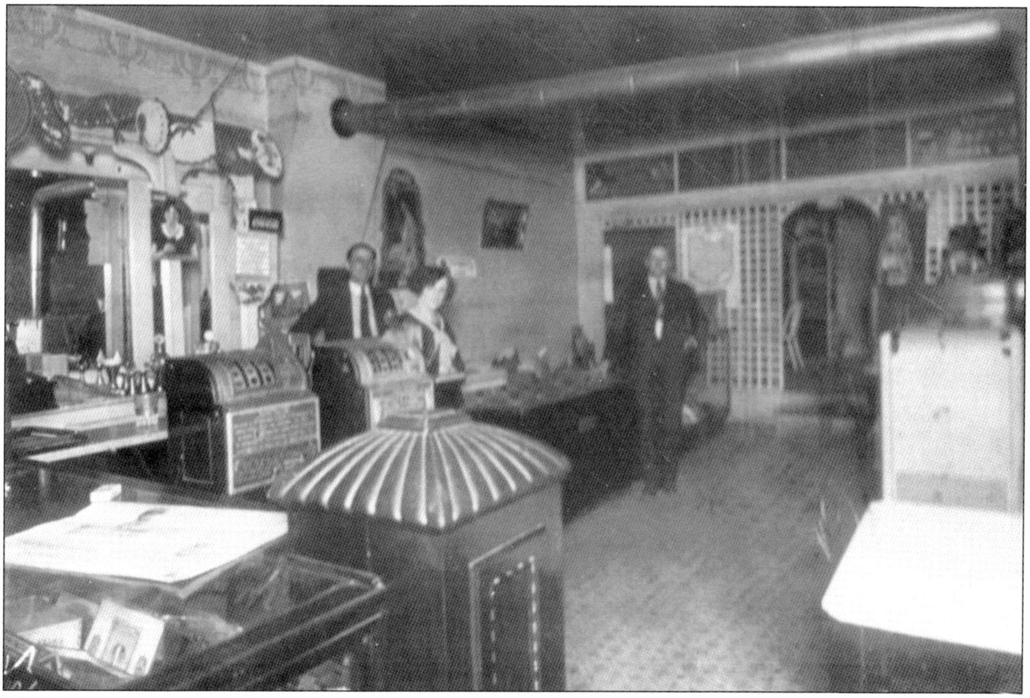

The Burton Restaurant was opened September 15, 1920, in the Susan Scanlon Building on the southwest corner of Main and North Streets. The restaurant was demolished in the 1960s to construct a parking lot. Shown in this 1926 photograph are, from left to right, Robert Burton, Lavonne Burton Waterhouse, and Edward Burton. (Courtesy of the Mary L. Cook Public Library.)

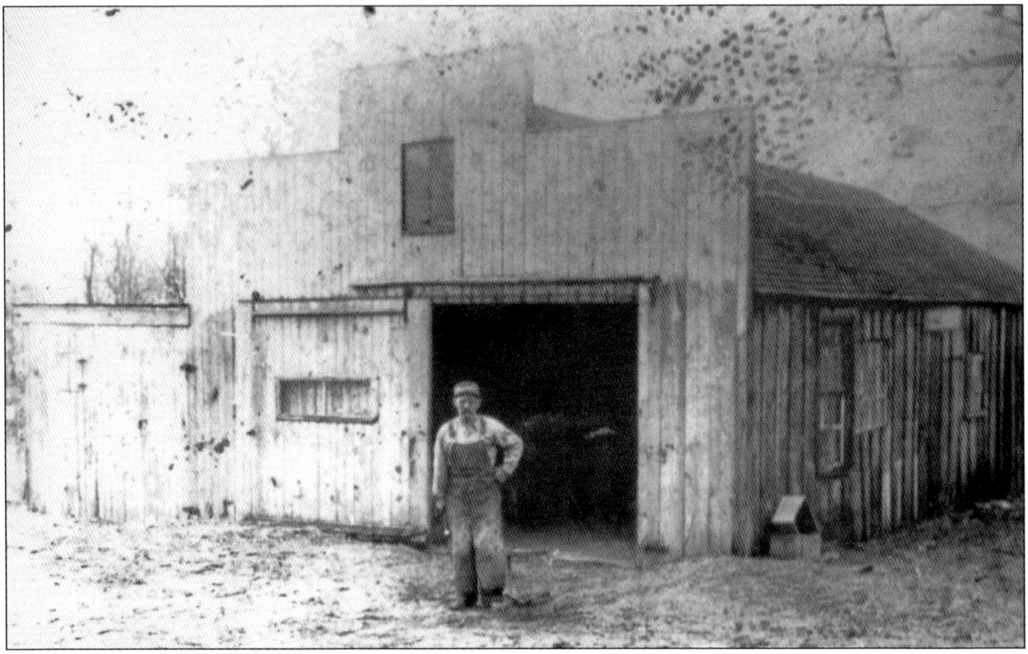

William "Willie" Casperson is shown in front of his blacksmith shop in this 1899 photograph. The shop was located on the northeast corner of North Main Street and Franklin Road. Casperson was also a bricklayer and helped construct the John Funkey mansion. (Courtesy of Mary L. Cook Public Library.)

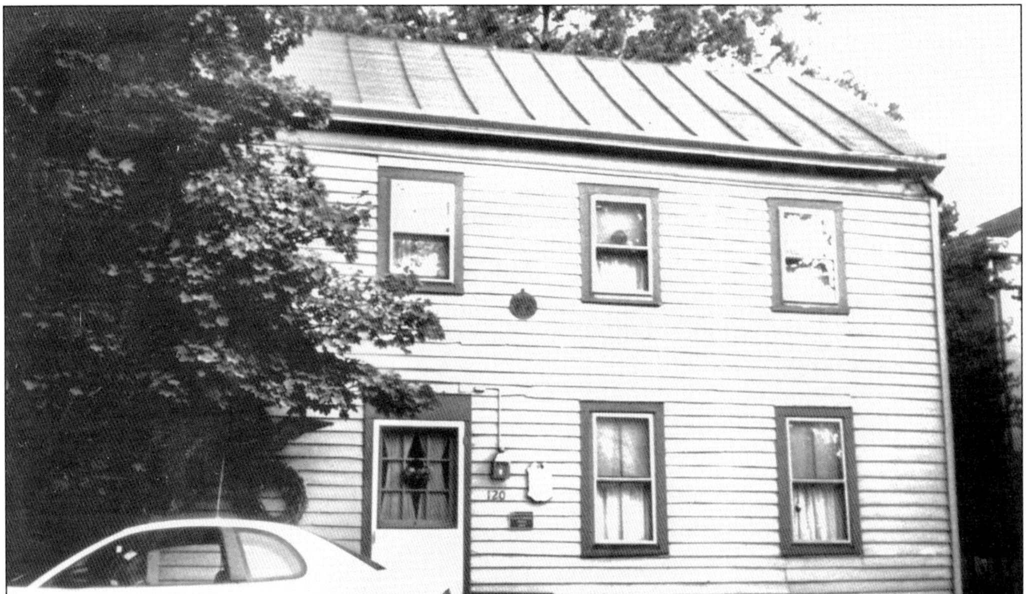

John Haines, a Quaker Virginia miller, built this house in 1803 at 120 North Main Street in Waynesville. Haines's gristmill and sawmill were located at 230 North US Route 42 near the Little Miami River. This photograph was taken in 2000. (Courtesy of Mary L. Cook Public Library.)

Two

Treasure in the River

Freshwater pearl fishing in the Little Miami River caused Israel H. Harris, a Waynesville banker and paleontologist, to open Little Miami Pearl Fisheries, Inc., in 1878. Harris bought only the finest and most exquisite pearls yielded by the mussels of the Little Miami. His "Treasury of Pearls" made Waynesville and its sister village, Corwin, world renowned. Representatives of British and French museums were drawn to the banks of the Little Miami to investigate the river's treasure. Harris sold many of his finest pearls to Tiffany & Co. jewelers in New York. In 1879, Jesse Van Duser of Corwin discovered the rarest pearl ever found in the Little Miami River. Since it was intensely agatized, it brought Van Duser $1,000. The unusual brilliance and colors of the gem earned it the name "Kohinoor" (most beautiful in the world). Harris resold the Kohinoor to Tiffany & Co. for $10,000. In 1889, a selection of Harris freshwater pearls won the gold medal in the American Pavilion at the Paris World Exposition; the collection was split up and bought by American and European jewelers.

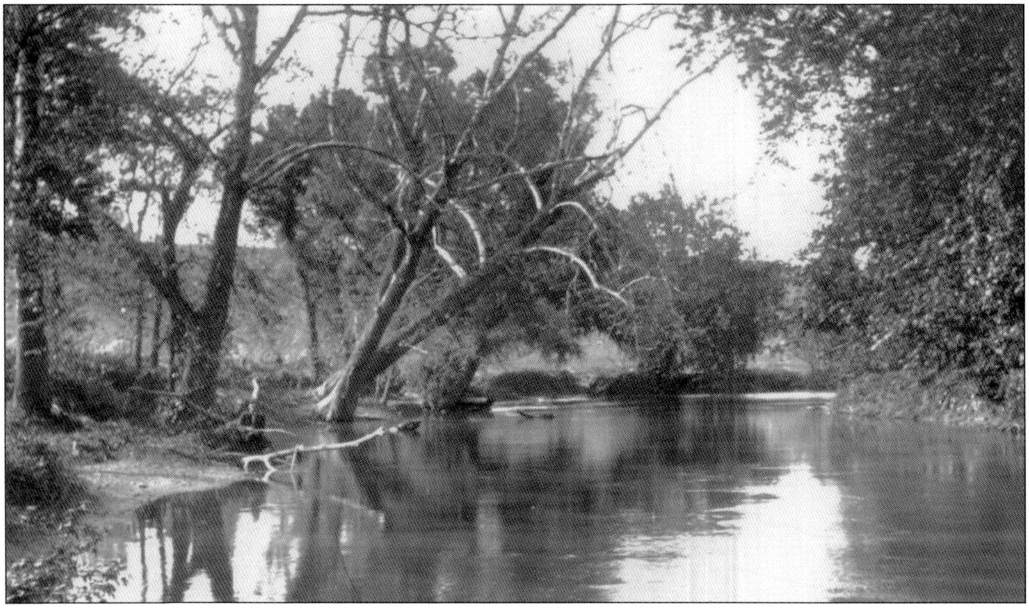

This 1907 photograph of the Little Miami River, which separates Waynesville and Corwin, illustrates good conditions for freshwater pearl fishing. When the water level was low, pearl hunters would wade and locate mussels with the bottoms of their feet. Pearls were sold to Israel H. Harris, a prominent Waynesville banker. As a result, Harris opened the Little Miami Pearl Fisheries, Inc., in 1878. (Courtesy of Mary L. Cook Public Library.)

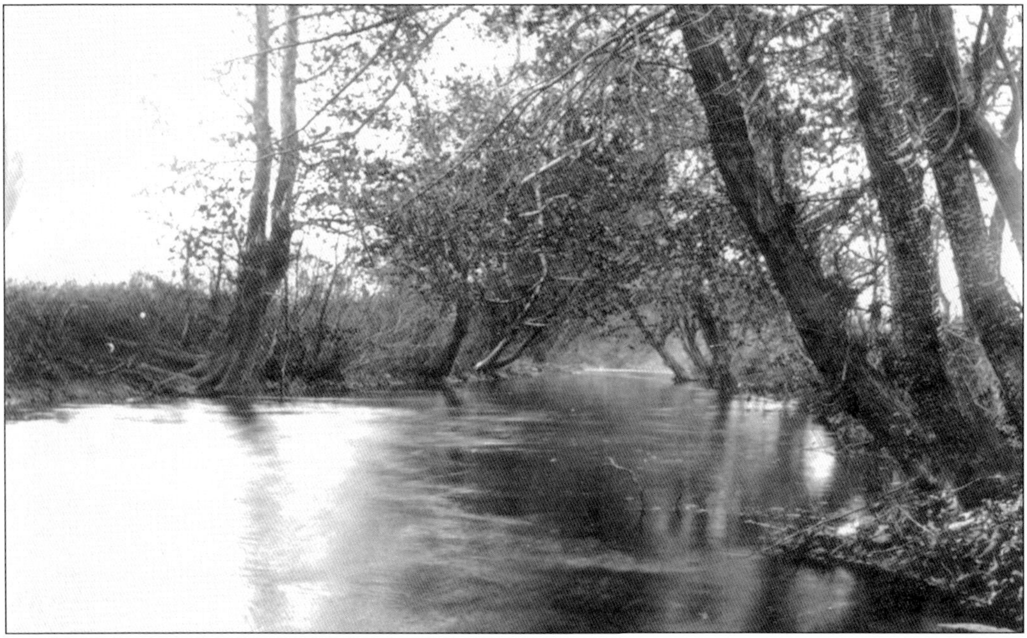

The rarest freshwater pearl ever found in the Little Miami River, shown above in 1907, was a large, brilliant, agatized gem discovered in 1879 by Jesse Van Duser of Corwin. Van Duser sold the pearl to Israel H. Harris for $1,000. Harris named it Kohinoor, which means "most beautiful in the world." He resold the pearl to Tiffany & Co. in New York City for $10,000. (Courtesy of Mary L. Cook Public Library.)

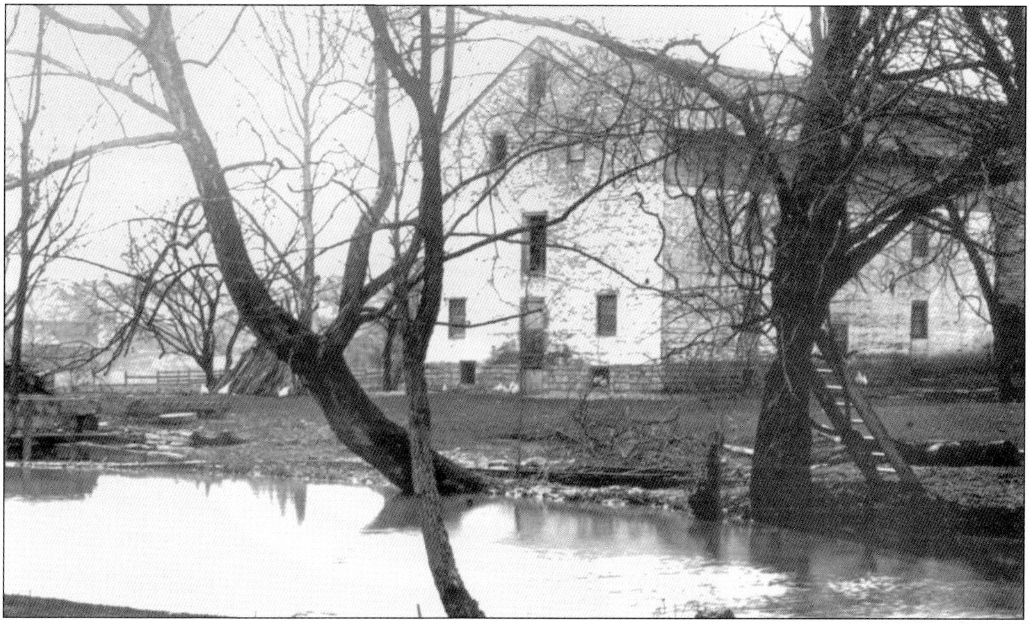

The gristmill was the earliest industry established along the Little Miami River, which at one time was considered the best milling stream in Ohio. John Jennings, a New Jersey Quaker, built the Jennings Mill, pictured above in 1900. It was built in 1825 from handmade bricks fired on the site. A Virginia Quaker, John Haines, operated a gristmill and sawmill at this location in 1801. (Courtesy of Mary L. Cook Public Library.)

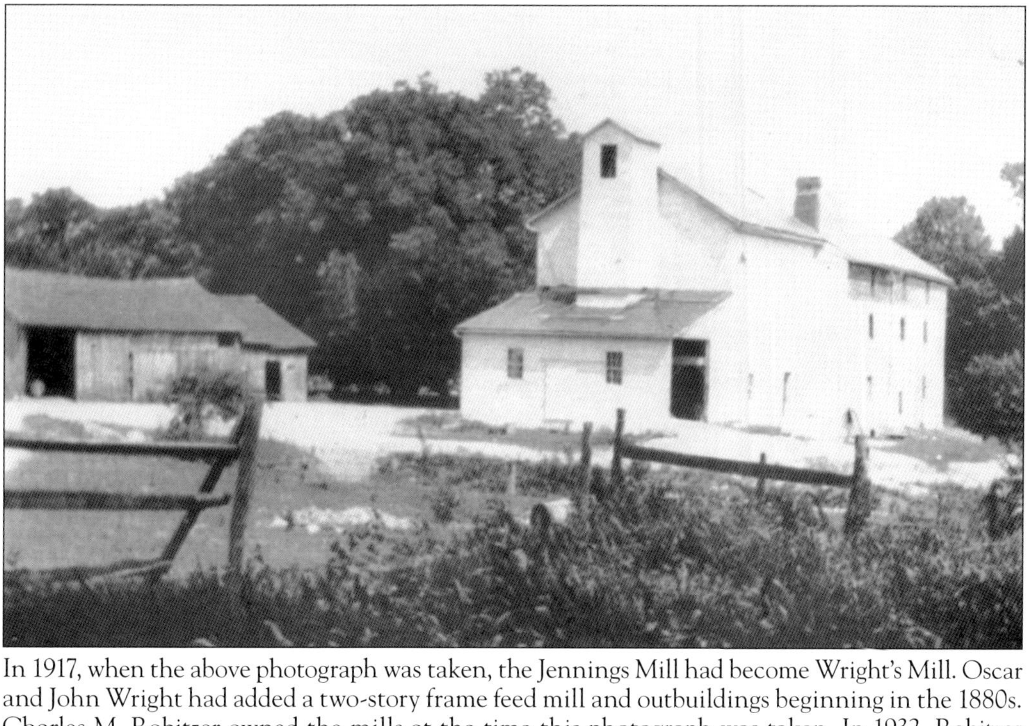

In 1917, when the above photograph was taken, the Jennings Mill had become Wright's Mill. Oscar and John Wright had added a two-story frame feed mill and outbuildings beginning in the 1880s. Charles M. Robitzer owned the mills at the time this photograph was taken. In 1932, Robitzer developed Old Mill Stream Park on the grounds surrounding the buildings. (Author's.)

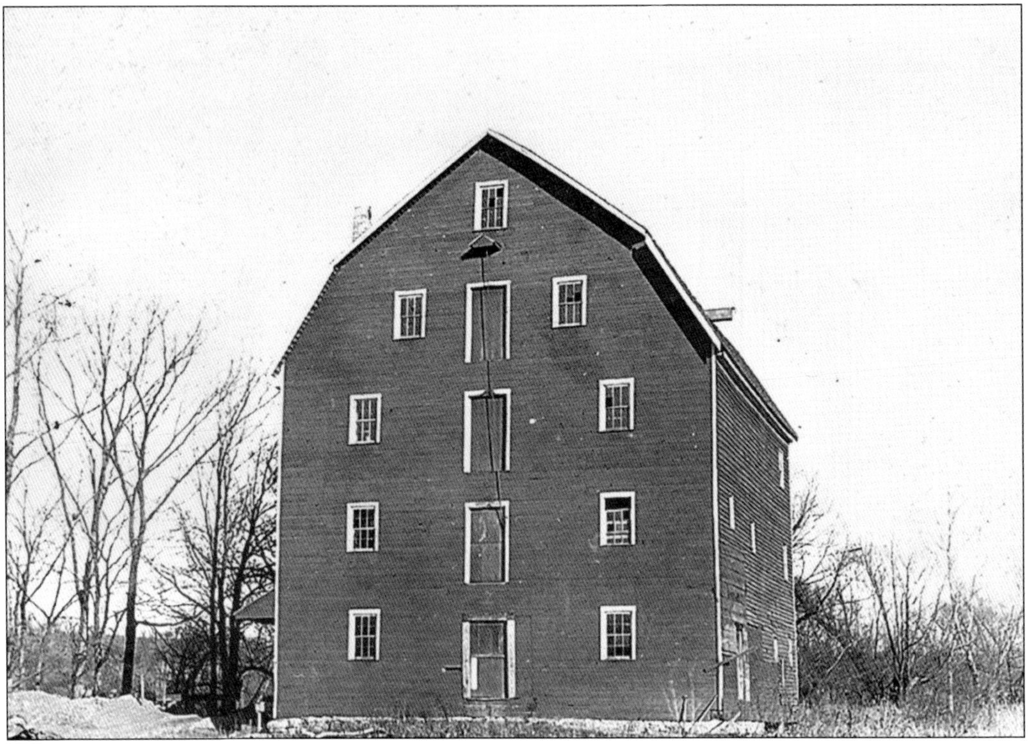

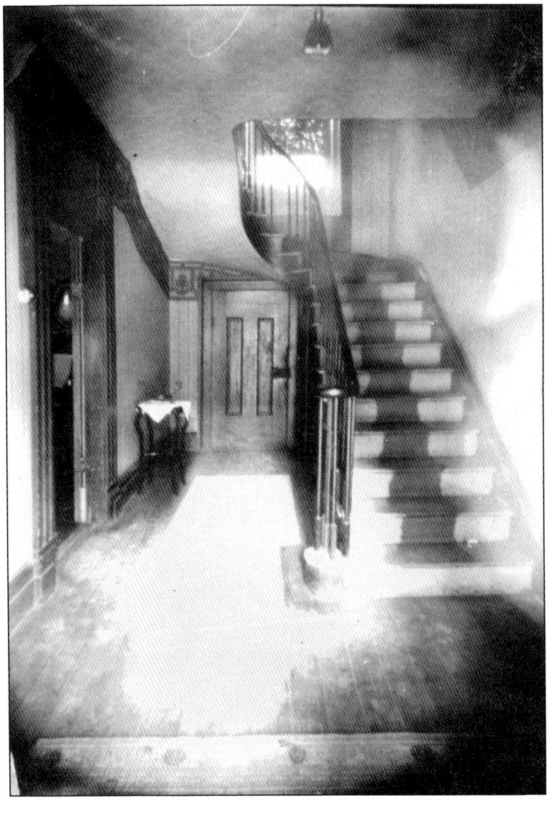

The Taylor Mill, known as "Telegraph Mill," is shown above as it looked in 1900. It received its nickname from the telegraph system centered there. The mill was constructed in 1856 from black walnut timber cut on the site. After the mill was abandoned, souvenir seekers removed siding and pieces of the framework, eventually causing the mill to collapse during a windstorm in the late 1940s. (Courtesy of Mary L. Cook Public Library.)

The main hallway of the I.H. Harris residence is shown in this 1905 photograph. I.H.'s father, James Harris, built the Harris residence in 1844. The residence also housed a general store and the Citizen's Exchange Bank, where I.H. Harris stored his world-renowned collection of 2,000 freshwater pearls from the nearby Little Miami River. Harris's Treasury of Pearls was sold to Tiffany & Co. in New York in 1885. (Courtesy of Mary L. Cook Public Library.)

Israel Hopkins Harris, shown in this 1882 portrait, amassed one of the world's finest collections of lower Silurian fossils. He willed the entire collection in addition to archaeological relics from Wayne Township, Ohio, to the Smithsonian Institution in 1897. The collection is still preserved at the Smithsonian in Washington, DC. (Courtesy of Mary L. Cook Public Library.)

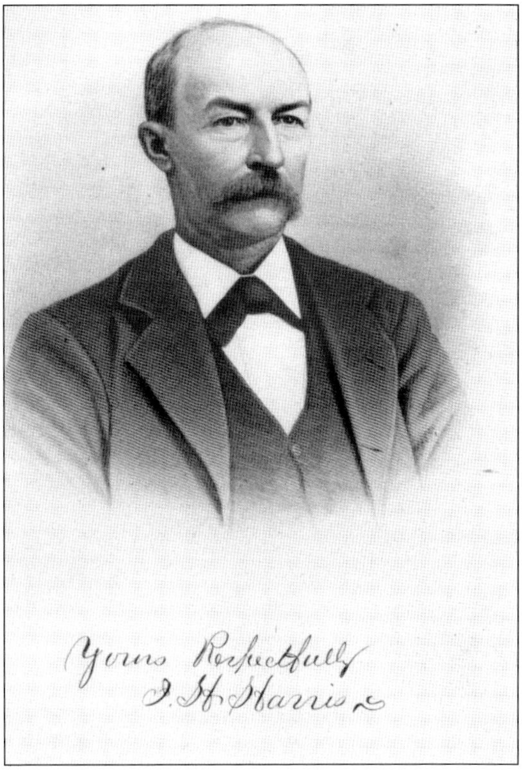

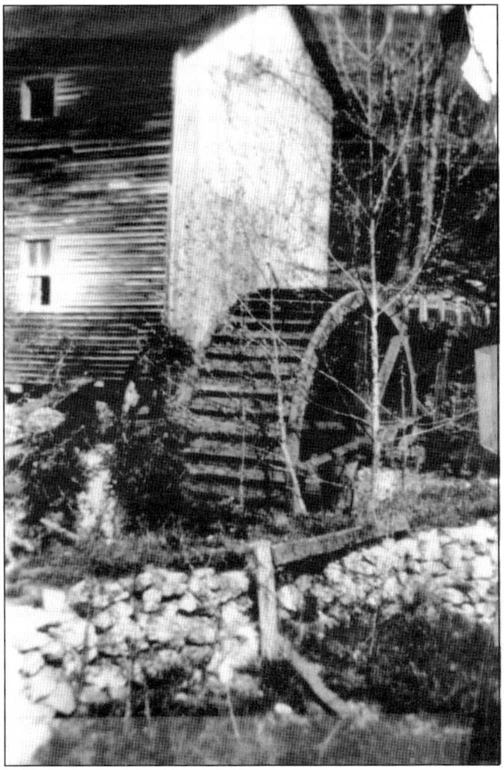

The Elliott gristmill was built in 1831 on the Little Miami River at the south end of Waynesville and also served Corwin. This 1920 photograph shows the mill, abandoned at the time. The mill was owned and operated by Sidwell Taylor in 1860. Taylor also owned a feed and flour store on North Main Street in Waynesville. Note the overshot waterwheel. (Courtesy of Mary L. Cook Public Library.)

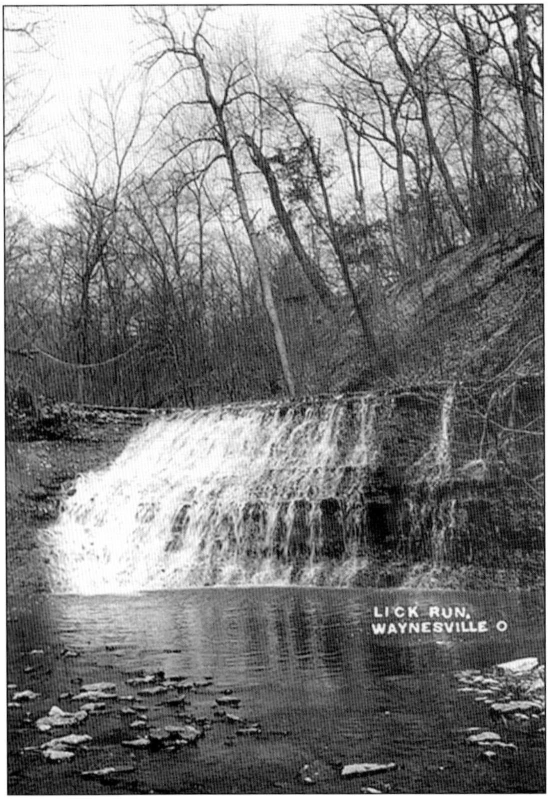

The Little Miami River had some of the most scenic tributaries of any stream in Ohio a century ago. This 1910 photograph shows a picturesque waterfall along Lick Run, one of the Little Miami's branches in Wayne Township, Ohio. (Courtesy of Mary L. Cook Public Library.)

The spring thaw is shown in this 1905 photograph of the Waynesville-Corwin Avenue covered bridge. The Little Miami River is choked with the ice flow and flooding. The photograph was taken from the Corwin side. (Courtesy of Mary L. Cook Public Library.)

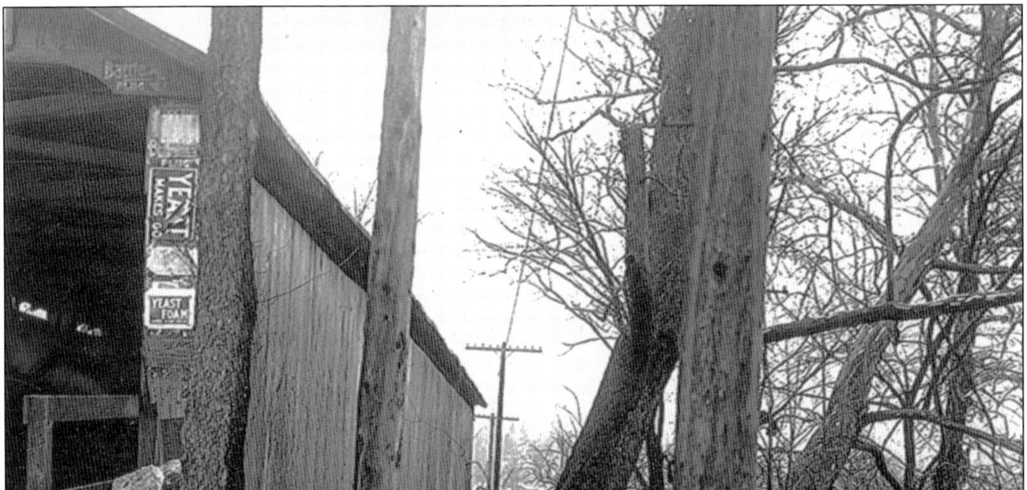

Three

MR. DICKENS, I PRESUME

Waynesville, Ohio, has hosted the curious and famous throughout its history. Among its influential visitors have been authors, politicians, US presidents, actors, and oddities. Charles Dickens refreshed himself with plain cold water at the Holloway House Inn on April 21, 1842. Travelling by stagecoach, he was on his first American tour. Dickens had anticipated brandy, but temperate Quakers owned the inn. Dickens's great-great-grandson and actor Gerald Charles Dickens visited from his home in England in late April 1999. He gave riveting performances at the Angel of the Garden Tearoom and Waynesville High School. Prince Henry of Germany stopped at the Pennsylvania Railroad depot in Corwin, Waynesville's sister village, in March 1902. Corwin station was his only stop between Columbus and Cincinnati. The royal party dined during its 17-minute stop while its train took on water.

The most notable visit made by a dignitary at Corwin station was that of Pres. Abraham Lincoln. Hundreds of local citizens crowded the depot platform for a glimpse of Lincoln, who made a speech from the back of his car. Seldom did dignitaries ignore Corwin and Waynesville as they passed through via the railroad. However, former president Ulysses S. Grant did not stop on October 12, 1879. Grant was insulted when Waynesville's mayor neglected to greet him and rode directly to Cincinnati without stopping anywhere.

US president Theodore Roosevelt spoke to a group at Corwin station in 1905. The president was eating breakfast at the time. He was moved to greet the crowd when one little Corwin boy and his mother peered through a window and watched him eat.

A stagecoach brought Pres. Martin Van Buren to the Hammell House Inn on Main Street in 1842. American playwright Thomas Lanier "Tennessee" Williams repeatedly visited Waynesville throughout his life. His maternal great-grandfather, Dr. Edwin F. Dakin, his wife, and their family moved next door to St. Mary's Episcopal Church in 1874. Walter E. Dakin, the doctor's son, was in St. Mary's first confirmation class in 1881. Walter eventually became a church deacon and was ordained to the Episcopal priesthood in 1892. Tennessee Williams frequently visited his beloved grandfather Dakin as a child and young adult. The congregation of St. Mary's knew him as Tom Williams.

Colorado governor John Evans did not just visit Waynesville but was born here. John, the son of David and Rachel Burnet Evans, early members of Miami Friends Meeting at Waynesville, brought more national fame to his hometown than anyone else. After a log cabin youth and formal medical education, Dr. John Evans founded Northwestern University at Evanston, Illinois, and the University of Denver, Colorado. In 1862, Pres. Abraham Lincoln appointed him the second territorial governor of Colorado. The oddest visitors Waynesville ever hosted were Cheng and Eng Bunker, the original Siamese Twins. The curious-looking brothers were exhibited at McKay's Hall on the public square in 1833. Other unusual characters who visited the village were the world's smallest man, Tom Thumb, and Captain Foote, another miniature man who awed audiences.

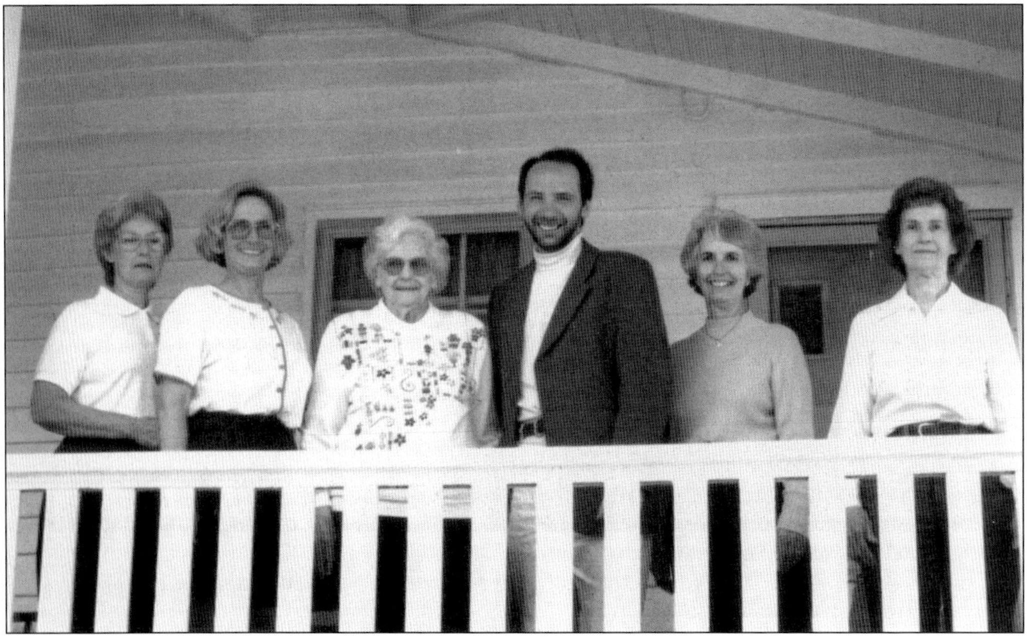

Gerald Charles Dickens followed in the footsteps of his noted great-great-grandfather in Waynesville in April 1999. Gerald, a professional actor, was brought to Waynesville from England to perform excerpts from *A Christmas Carol*. He is shown in this 1999 photograph on the porch of the Holloway House, then the home of Laura Brown. From left to right are Joanne Brown Dakin, Charlotte Brown Lucas, Laura Brown, Gerald Charles Dickens, Janice Brown Powell, and Virginia Brown Hill. (Author's.)

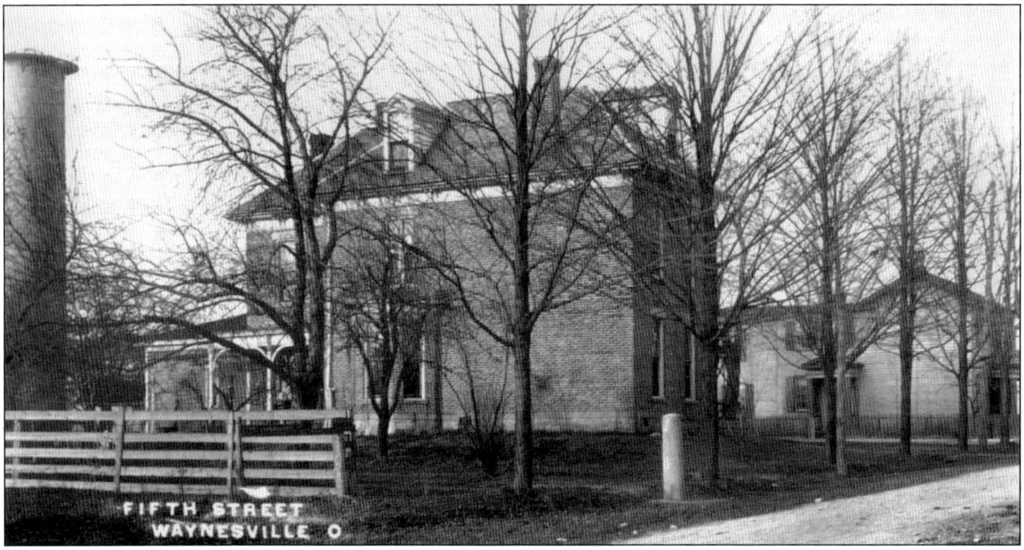

Thomas and Mary Brown, publishers of the *Miami Gazette*, built the home shown in this 1910 photograph in 1882. Mary Brown was an avid Dickens reader and named the residence Bleak House from a Dickens novel. The Oglesbee sisters, Bette, Nettie, and Lida, bought the home, which is on the southwest corner of Fifth and Chapman Streets, in 1917. The village water tower is shown at left, and the Dinwiddie Wardlow home is on the right. The original concrete hitching post is shown near the center. (Courtesy of Mary L. Cook Public Library.)

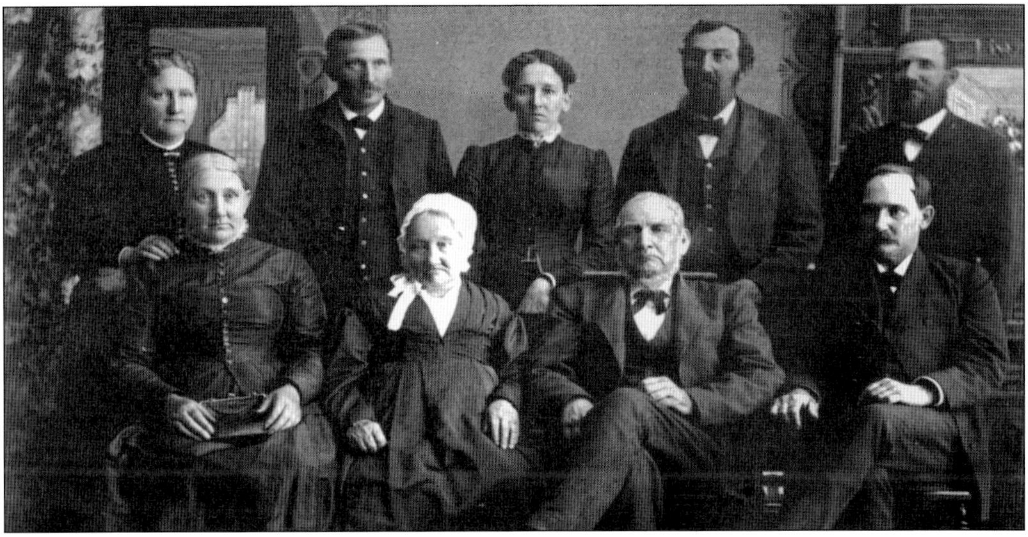

Charles Dickens's sister Frances married Henry Burnet in England. Their son Henry Burnet Jr. was the model for Tiny Tim in *A Christmas Carol*. Henry Burnet Jr.'s relatives settled in Waynesville in 1804. Stephen and Hannah Jones Burnet and children are shown in this 1883 photograph during the celebration of their 50th wedding anniversary. Pictured are, from left to right, (first row) Lydia Ann Burnet Gordon, Hannah Jones Burnet, Stephen Burnet, and Joseph Burnet; (second row) Emma Burnet Keys, Franklin Burnet, Sarah Burnet Butterworth, John Burnet, and Owen Jones Burnet. (Courtesy of Wilma Surface Coyan.)

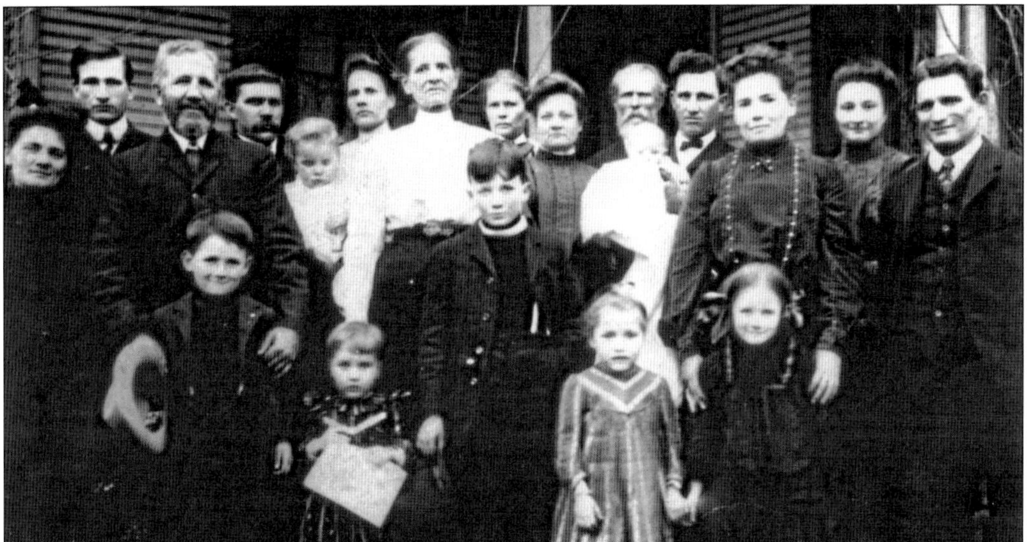

The Owen Jones Burnet family is shown in front of their home at 38 North Main Street in Waynesville on Christmas Day, 1904. The children are, from left to right, (first row) Russell Burnet, Antha Dinwiddie, Harry Burnet, Helen Dinwiddie, and Mildred Burnet; the adults are, from left to right, (second row) Bertha Worthington Burnet, Whittier Burnet, Owen Jones Burnet, John Dinwiddie with baby Rue Dinwiddie, Mabel Burnet Dinwiddie, Catherine Munger Gregg, Roweena Muger Gregg, Adelaide Thackera Burnet, Allen Gregg, Harvey Burnet and baby Catherine Burnet, Edna Burnet, Sarah Burnet, and Stephen H. Burnet. (Courtesy of Wilma Surface Coyan.)

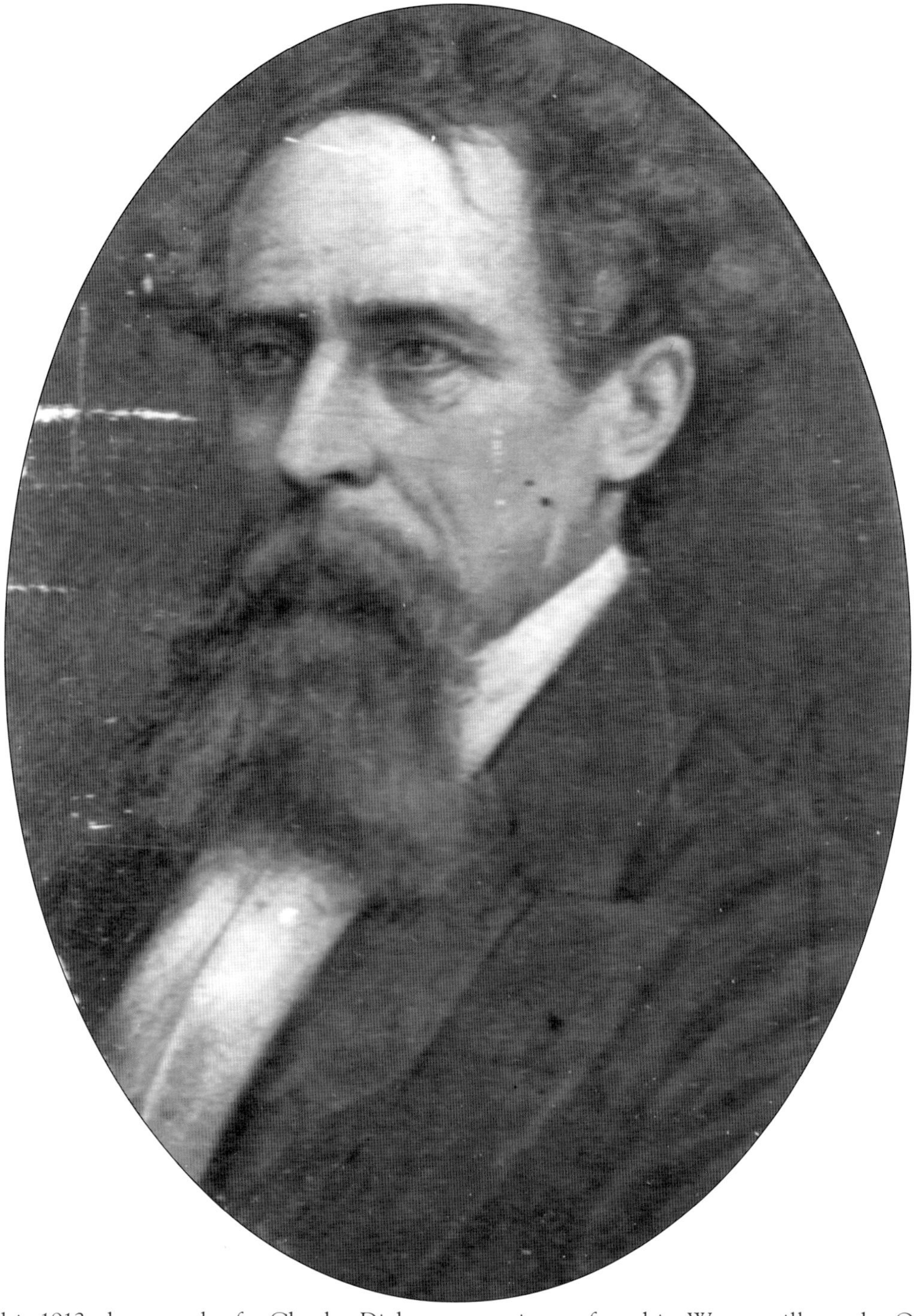

This 1912 photograph of a Charles Dickens portrait was found in Waynesville at the Old Curiosity Antiques Shop. A likeness of Dickens in his later years, it is a reminder of the 200th anniversary of Dickens's birth. Dickens's relatives, the Burnet family, were Wayne Township pioneers and settled near Lytle, Ohio, in 1804. The Burnets were early members of Miami Friends Meeting. (Author's.)

Four

Hickory Stick Education

The first schools in Wayne Township were opened in log cabins in 1801 by the Religious Society of Friends (Quakers). The Friends School, built on High Street in 1814, and Gravel Hill School, constructed in 1829, served Waynesville until 1857, when the two-story brick Union School was constructed at Fourth and Miami Streets. After Waynesville and Wayne Township were divided into districts in 1846, brick schools began to replace log ones. One-room country schools were often identified with names such as Buckeye, Spring Branch, Sugar Grove, College Hill, Harmony Grove, and Greenbrier.

Waynesville Academy, which still stands at 185 North Main Street, was a forerunner of high school. Students were taught the arts, languages, and sciences. Waynesville Academy, which was built in 1844, consolidated with the Union School in 1857. Miss Taylor's School for Young Ladies was opened in 1852 in a house that still exists on the northeast corner of North and Fourth Streets. Young girls received instruction in decorative arts and music. After Miss Taylor's death in 1881, it became a school for African American students. Embroidery was added to the curriculum of Waynesville School when it was located in the 1805 Miami Friends log meetinghouse. The instructors were Elizabeth and Susan B. Wright, who had been educated at the Friends School in Westtown, Pennsylvania. The schoolgirl samplers, produced in the school from 1807 until after 1814, are now rare and much sought-out museum pieces.

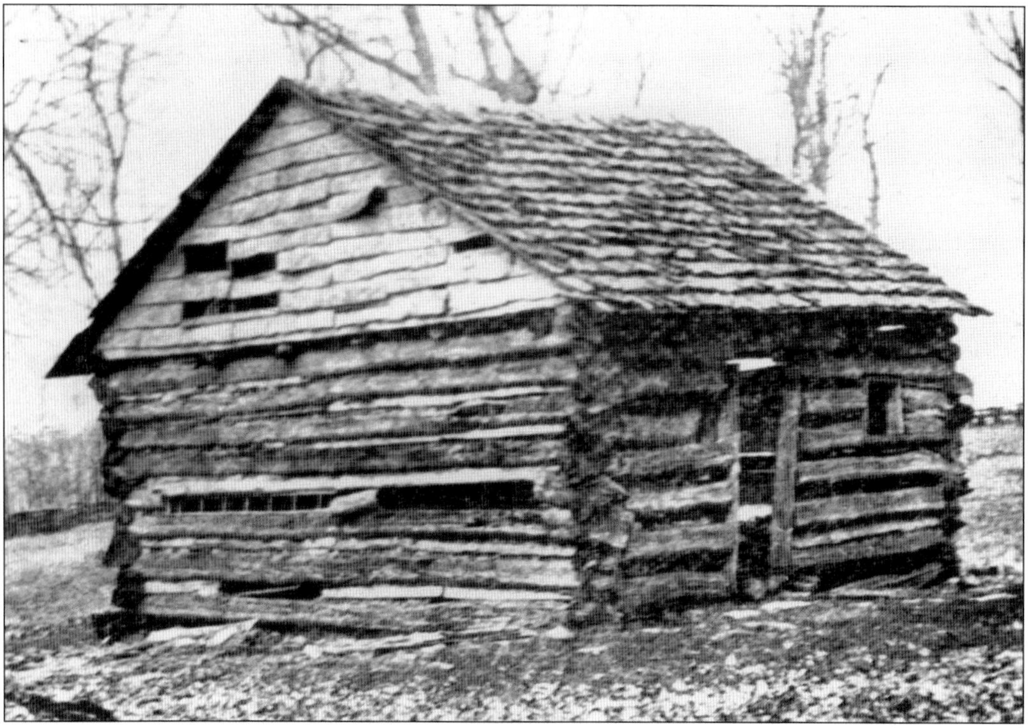

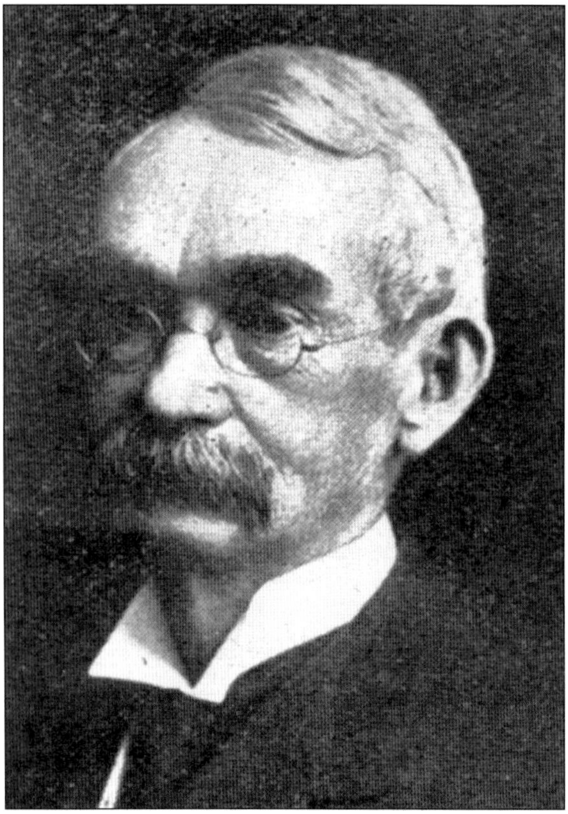

Wayne Township's first schools in 1801 were one-room primitive log structures like the one in this 1903 photograph. This early log school was originally located on the Cook farm on Lower Springboro Road. Students reciting their lessons in this country school could be heard a half-mile away. (Courtesy of Mary L. Cook Public Library.)

William Henry Venable, one of Ohio's most venerated educators, is shown in this 1905 photograph. Venable, a graduate of the National Normal University in Lebanon, Ohio, also wrote poetry and an American history book used nationally in schools. He was born in 1836 in a log cabin south of Waynesville on the Little Miami River. During his career, he was presented an honorary degree for law and literature from Ohio University at Athens. (Courtesy of Mary L. Cook Public Library.)

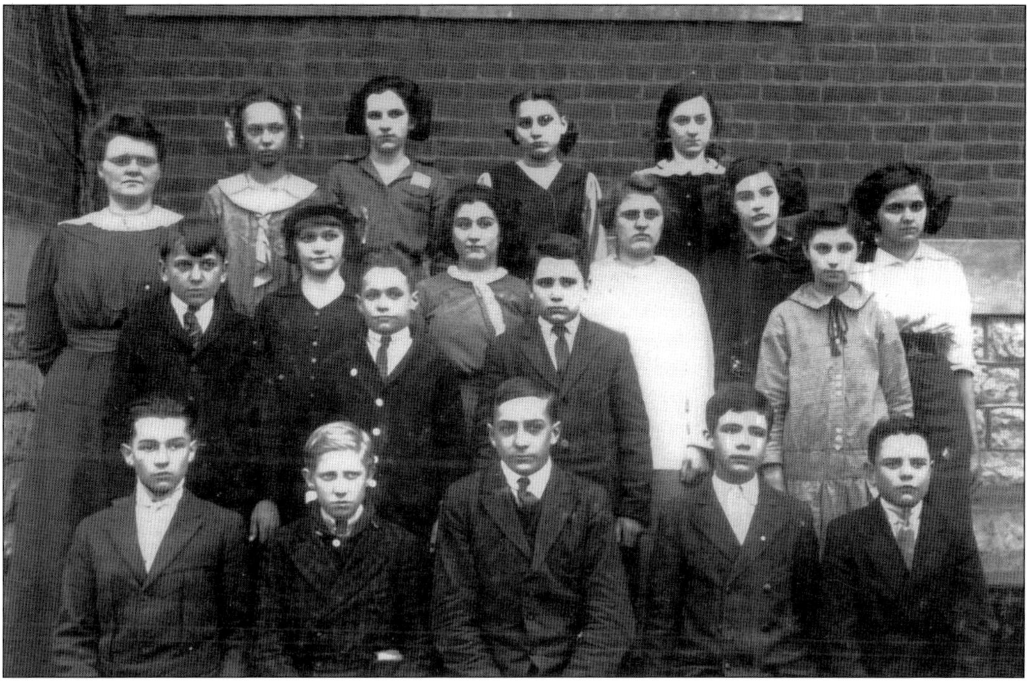

The seventh and eighth grades of Waynesville School are shown with their teacher in this 1911 photograph. Pictured are, from left to right, (first row) Elmer Wills, Warren Miller, Ernest Earnhart, Jim ?, and Ethan Crane; (second row) Harold Earnhart, Lavonne Burton, Ed Burton, Marie Burnside, Rue Dinwiddie, Mabel Cast, Adria Braddock, Clara Berryhill, and Cora McKeever; (third row) teacher Anna Vandervoort, Glenna Cook, Hazel Salisbury, Antha Dinwiddie, and Frances Janney. (Courtesy of Mary L. Cook Public Library.)

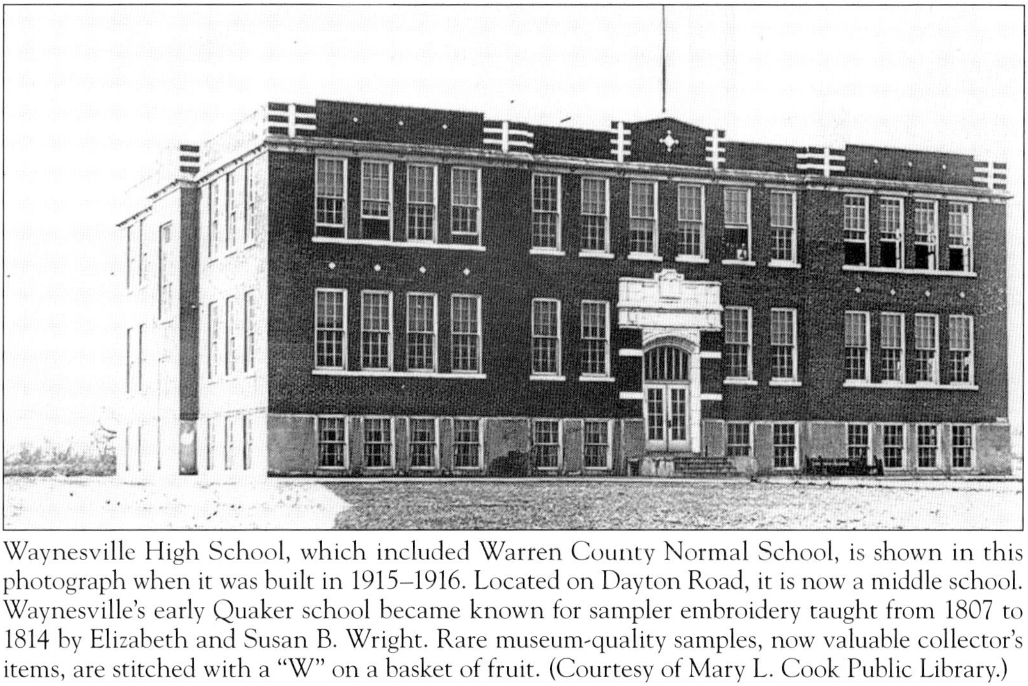

Waynesville High School, which included Warren County Normal School, is shown in this photograph when it was built in 1915–1916. Located on Dayton Road, it is now a middle school. Waynesville's early Quaker school became known for sampler embroidery taught from 1807 to 1814 by Elizabeth and Susan B. Wright. Rare museum-quality samples, now valuable collector's items, are stitched with a "W" on a basket of fruit. (Courtesy of Mary L. Cook Public Library.)

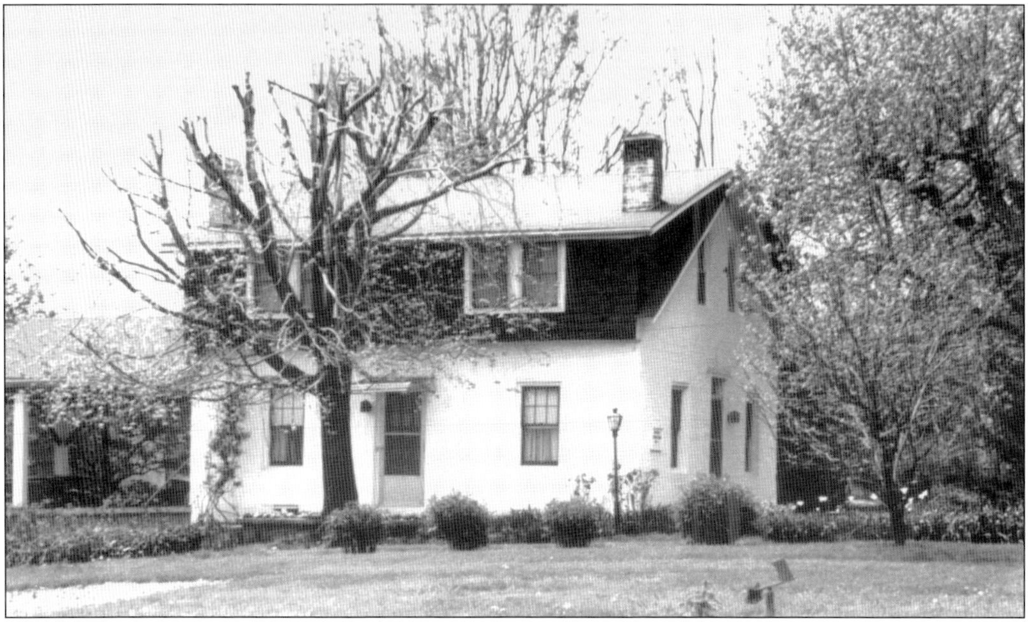

The Waynesville Friends School was built on West High Street in Waynesville in 1814. It replaced the log school, accommodated by the 1805 meetinghouse, just east of it. The Hopkins family added the second-floor dormer when the brick structure was converted to a residence. This 1972 photograph shows the building in preservation by Harold and Josephine Harlan Earnhart. (Courtesy of Mary L. Cook Public Library.)

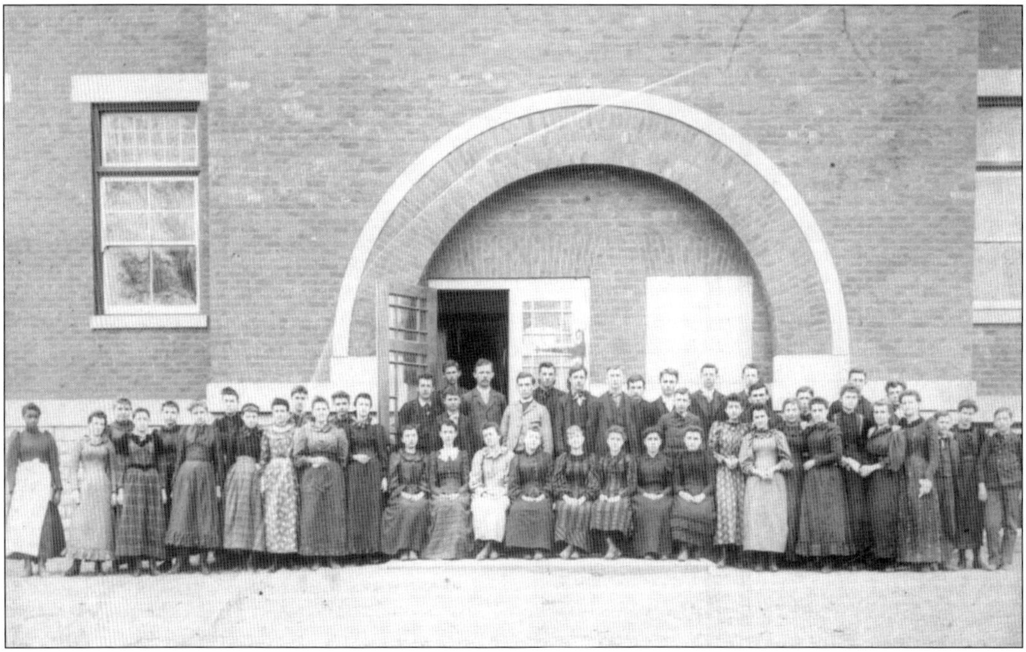

Waynesville High School students are shown in this 1895 photograph taken in front of the south entrance to the building at Fourth and Miami Streets. The high school was located on the second floor. Elementary school was taught on the first floor, with two grades to a classroom. (Courtesy of Mary L. Cook Public Library.)

Five

We Shall Come Rejoicing

The hymn "Bringing in the Sheaves" was written in Waynesville by Rev. Knowels Shaw in 1874. Shaw, who was nicknamed "the Singing Preacher," founded the Church of Christ in the village in 1869. Miami Friends Meeting was established in 1803 by a delegation of Quaker settlers from Red Stone, Pennsylvania. The initial group of Quakers, who settled as early as 1801, increased so rapidly that, by 1805, Waynesville had the largest Quaker settlement in the nation. A log meetinghouse built in 1805 on West High Street was replaced with a larger brick structure in 1811 on the northwest corner of Fourth and High Streets. The 1811 meetinghouse, which is still in use, is the oldest Quaker meetinghouse in continuous service west of the Allegheny Mountains.

St. Mary's Episcopal Church, at 103 South Third Street, was completed in 1881. Its cornerstone was laid on August 4, 1870. It was designed by Cincinnati architect Edwin Proctor. The primary organizers of the church were Mary Brown and James Drew Sweet. Organizational meetings were held as early as 1867 in the Third Street home of Isabella Brown. The Reverend W.T. Helms, who helped found the church in 1869, conducted worship services at Cadwallader Hall. In 1871, the church moved to Pugh's Chapel, a former stable that was remodeled by ecumenical Quaker Achilles Pugh and given to the parish rent-free. Michael Shea, a wealthy Irish stock dealer, headed the founding of St. Augustine's Roman Catholic Church. The group organized a church at the Shea farmhouse in 1867. Mass was held next in Cadwallader Hall, where on July 30, 1876, Archbishop John B. Purcell conducted the new church's first Confirmation service. In late 1876, the parish moved to Pugh's Chapel, also given the members rent-free by Achilles Pugh. Roman Catholics constructed their first church at the foot of High Street Hill in 1884. At first, supply priests served the parish from Cincinnati. The church was named in honor of its first regular priest, the Reverend Fr. Augustine Anderson. Wayne Township had a large enough African American population after the Civil War to support a small church located on Wilkerson Lane, a mile south of Waynesville. The small frame building was near the bank of Newman's Run and was still thriving in 1904. The church, possibly African Methodist Episcopal or Baptist, was founded by former slaves. The African American farmhands were brought to Union Place Farm from Kentucky by Alvin Sellers, the farm manager. Waynesville's A.M.E. church first met in the village's African American School in 1885. The church was headed by Rev. A.M. Palmer, a theological graduate of Wilberforce University. The building still exists on the northeast corner of North and Fourth Streets in Waynesville. The two-story brick building at 232 Miami Street in Waynesville was built in 1874 by Miami Valley Baptist Church. The church was organized and headed by the Wright family, which separated from Middle Run Predestinarian Primitive Baptists, located northwest of Waynesville. The Gen. William Buckles family from Virginia settled the Middle Run Predestinarian Primitive Baptist Church in 1799. Henry Buckles was the first justice of the peace of Wayne Township in 1804.

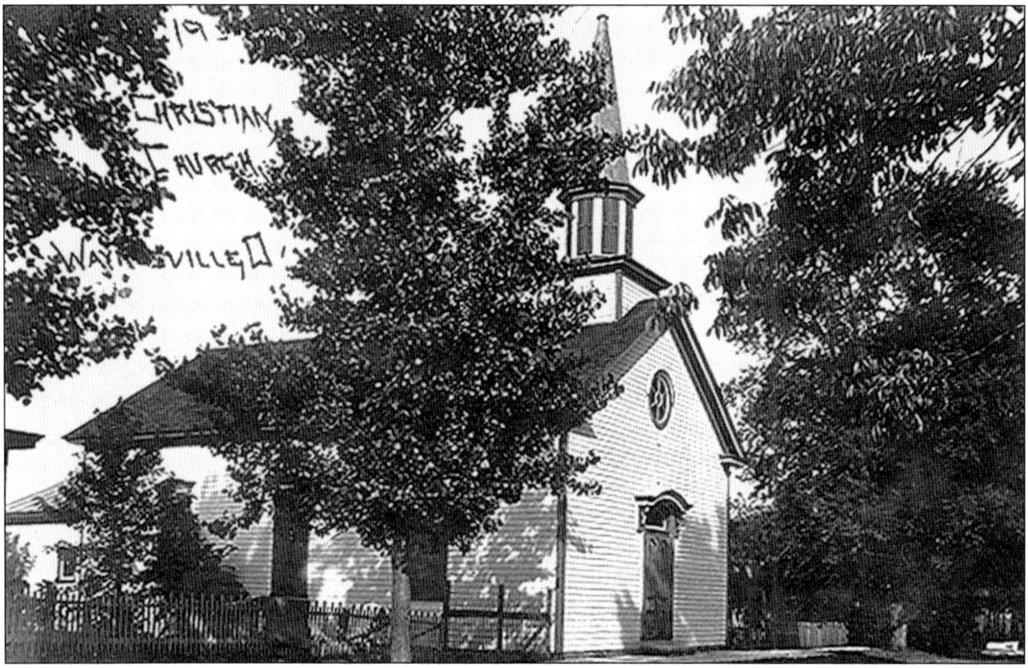

The hymn "Bringing in the Sheaves" was written in Waynesville by Rev. Knowels Shaw in 1874. Shaw, nicknamed "the singing preacher," founded the Church of Christ in the village in 1869. The church, shown in this 1910 photograph, was constructed in 1877 on High Street. (Courtesy of Mary L. Cook Public Library.)

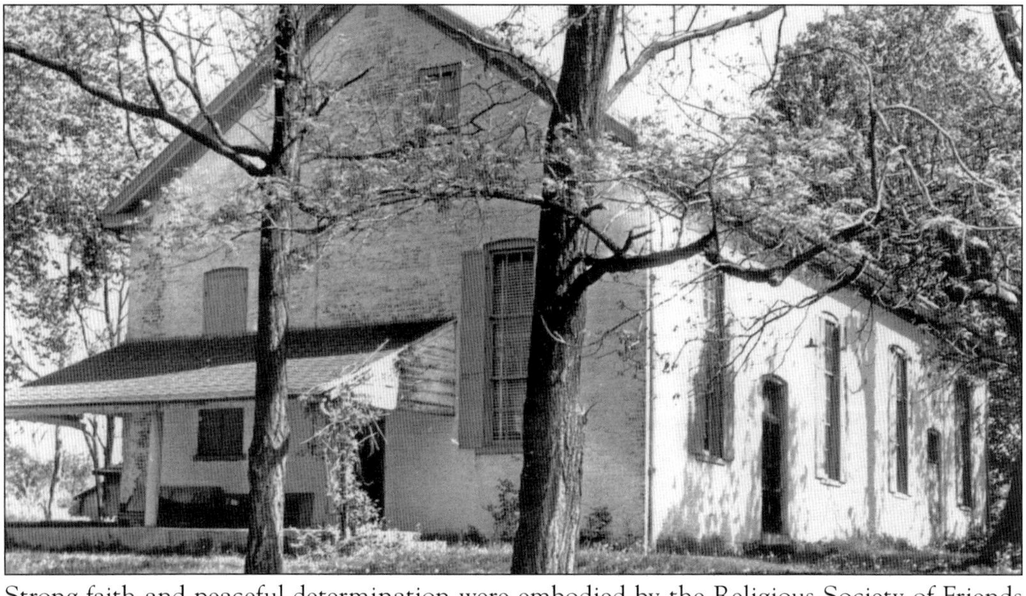

Strong faith and peaceful determination were embodied by the Religious Society of Friends (Quakers). George Harlan was Waynesville's first Quaker settler in 1796. Harlan's descendant Mary Eunice Harlan married Robert Todd Lincoln. The Miami Friends Meetinghouse, on the northwest corner of Fourth and High Streets, is shown in this photograph in 1972. The meetinghouse was constructed in 1811. It is the oldest Quaker meetinghouse in continuous use west of the Allegheny Mountains. (Courtesy of Mary L. Cook Public Library.)

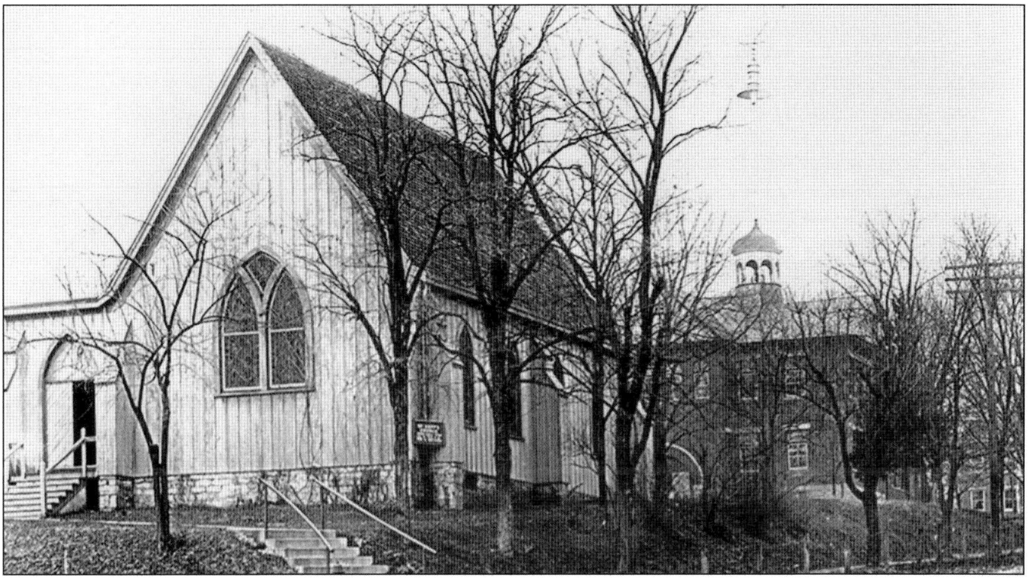

St. Mary's Episcopal Church, at 107 South Third Street in Waynesville, is shown in this 1910 photograph. Established in 1869 at Cadwallader Hall, the parish finished building this church in 1881. Among the church's early members and clergy was Rev. Walter Edwin Dakin, the maternal grandfather of American playwright Thomas "Tennessee" Williams, who attended services here while visiting during his youth. American actor Ethan Hawke's grandparents were also members. (Courtesy of Mary L. Cook Public Library.)

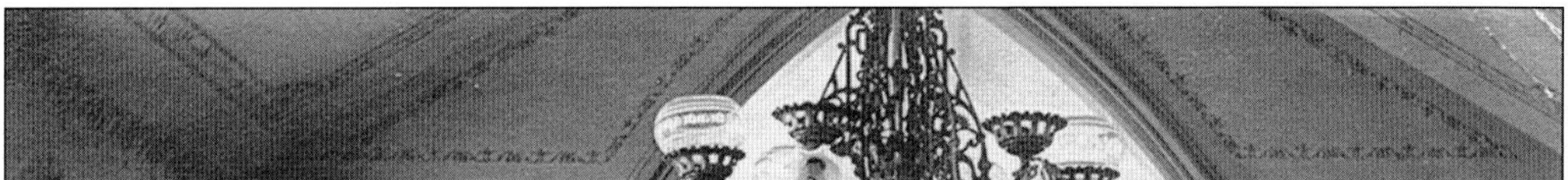

The interior of St. Mary's Episcopal Church is shown in this 1910 photograph. Emma Heighway and her grandparents William H. and Julia Heighway, descendants of Waynesville's founder, were the last of the Heighway family to worship here. Edwin Proctor, the church's Cincinnati architect, had St. Mary's remarkable stained-glass windows made in Cincinnati. (Courtesy of Mary L. Cook Public Library.)

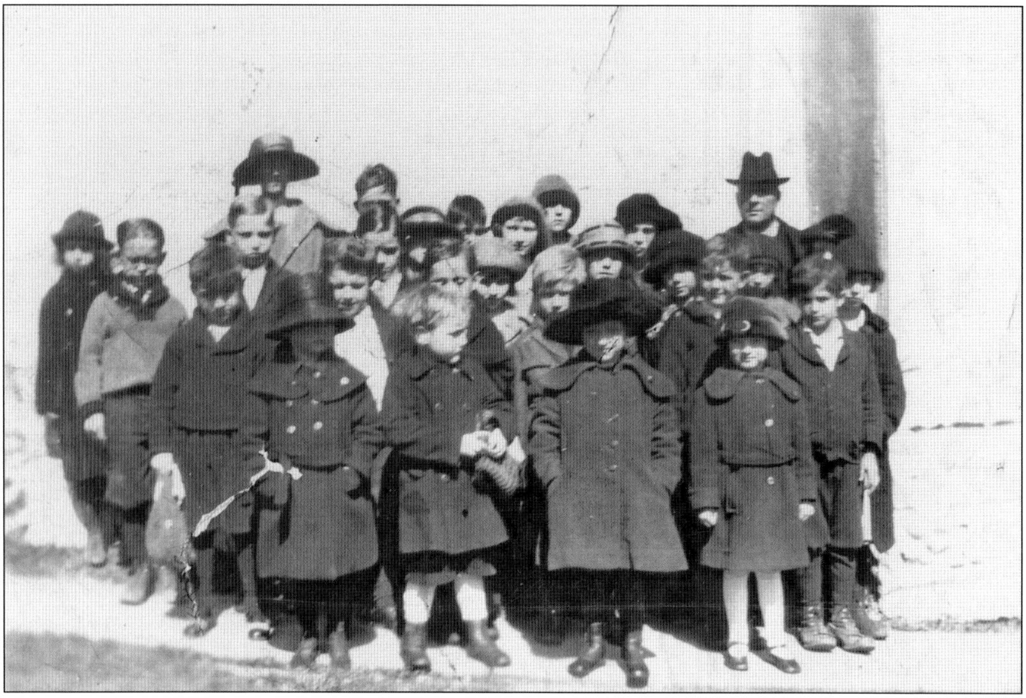

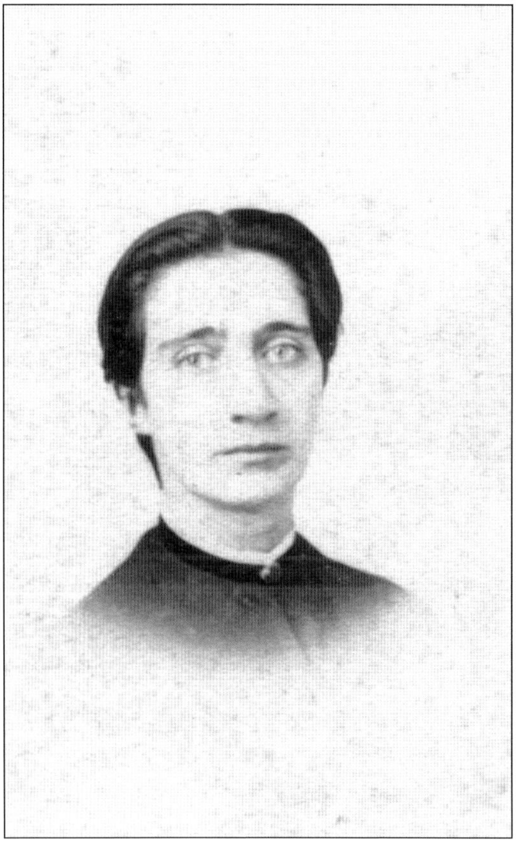

St. Mary's Episcopal Church's Sunday school is shown in this 1921 photograph in front of the church. The woman at left in the back row is Mrs. John Fallis Cadwallader (Anna). The Reverend John Fallis Cadwallader is shown at right in the back row. The Reverend Cadwallader did more to build St. Mary's than any other of its clergy. He built the church rectory in 1901 on the northeast corner of Miami and Fourth Streets. He also provided funds in his estate to build St. Mary's Parish House in 1950. Among the children are Gladys Adams of Corwin (third row, center) and Margaret Pence (first row, third from left). (Author's.)

Isabella Brown is shown in this photograph, taken in 1875. St. Mary's Episcopal Church was organized at her home on Third Street in 1869. Prior to officially organizing, meetings for the church were held in her home as early as 1867. Isabella kept Waynesville women busy at her home sewing bandages and packing food boxes for soldiers during the Civil War. (Courtesy of Mary L. Cook Public Library.)

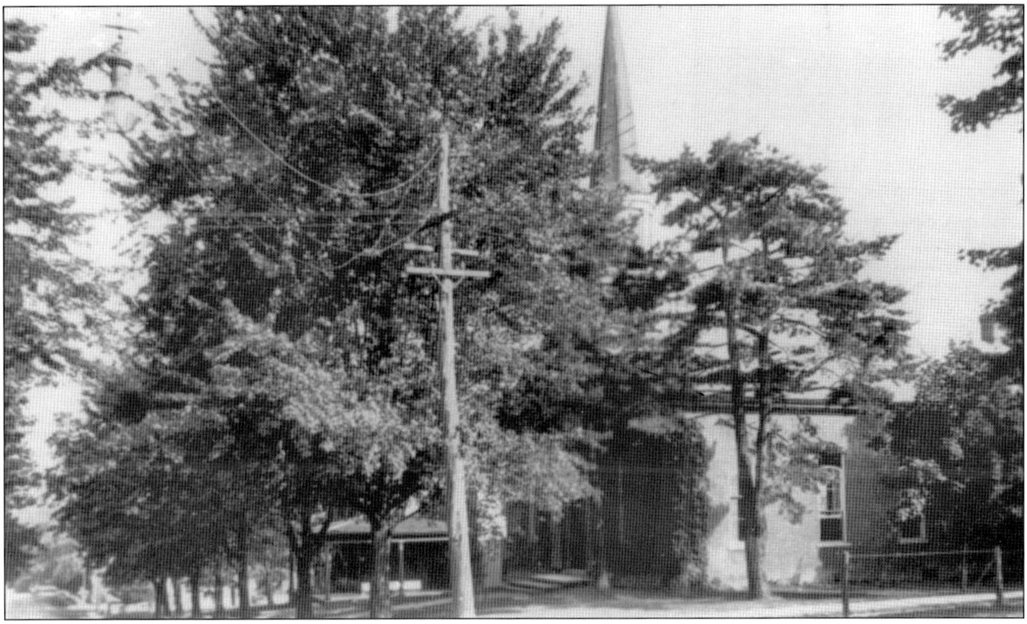

The Waynesville United Methodist Church first worshiped in a log building in 1807 near the mouth of Caesar's Creek southeast of the village. Methodists held services in the Burwell Goode home on East State Route 73 before building a small brick church in 1826 on the village common. This photograph, taken in 1910, shows the Methodist church that was built in 1840 on the southeast corner of North and Third Streets. (Courtesy of Mary L. Cook Public Library.)

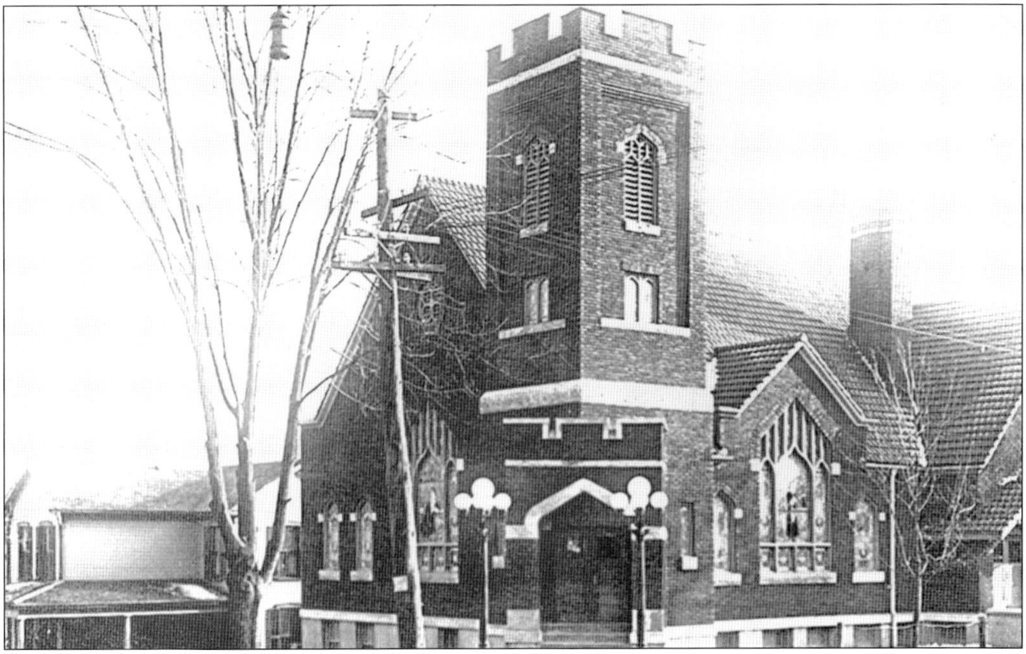

The Waynesville United Methodist Church shown here in 1915 replaced the 1840 edifice. Bricks from the old church were cleaned by the churchwomen and used in the construction of the new building. The church parsonage is also shown at the left. It was built in the 1870s. (Courtesy of Mary L. Cook Public Library.)

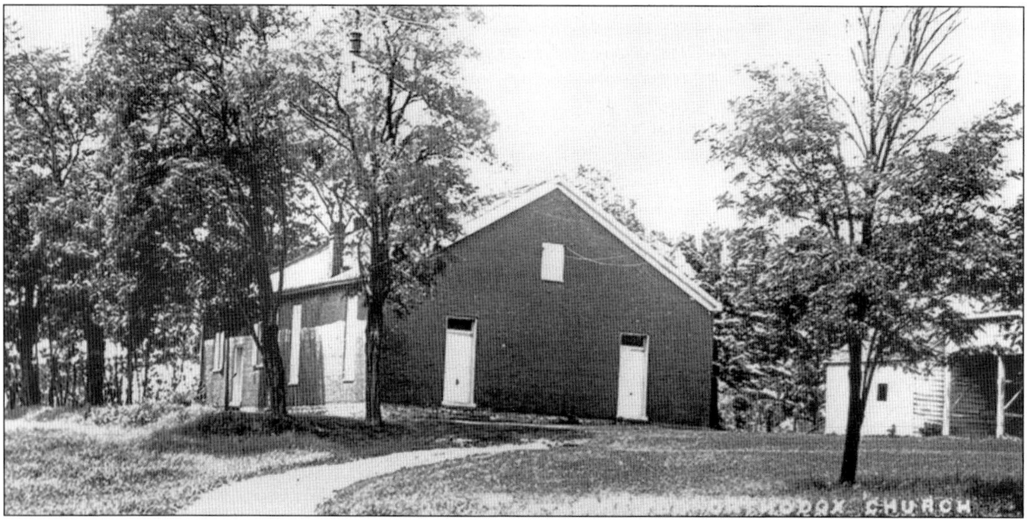

The Orthodox Friends Meetinghouse of Miami Friends Meeting is shown in this photograph in 1915. The meetinghouse was constructed in 1834 on the site of the original Friends log meetinghouse built in 1805. The original buggy sheds are shown on the right at the edge of the Friends Cemetery, which was established in 1808. Miami Friends Meeting split in 1828 over differences of opinion on their religious beliefs. The Orthodox branch moved to the old log meetinghouse until the "Red Brick" could be built. It is now a social room and apartments. (Courtesy of Mary L. Cook Public Library.)

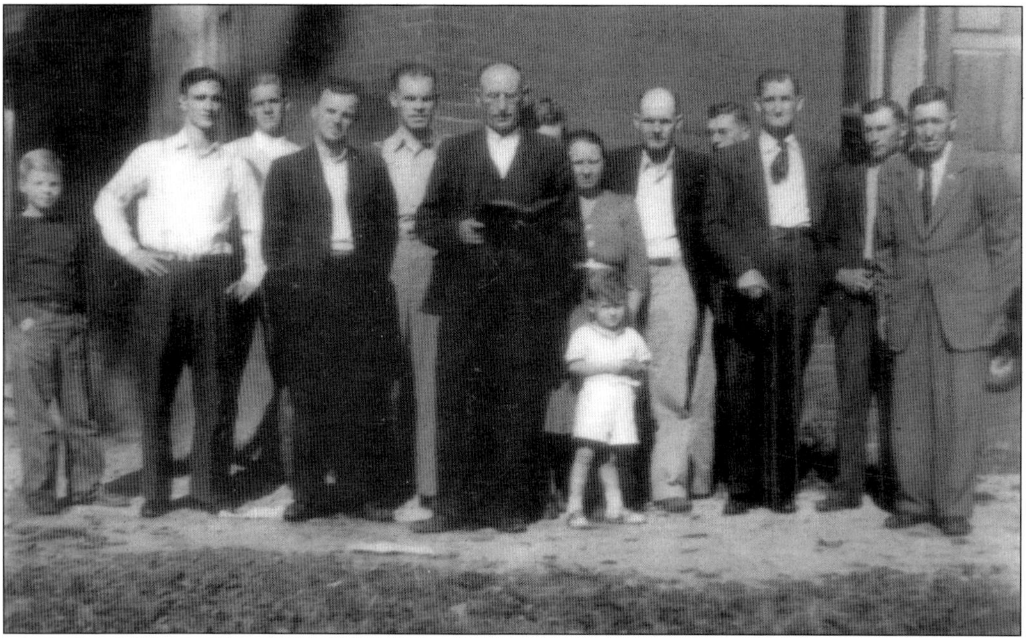

Members of the Greenbrier Pentecostal Church are shown in this pre-1945 photograph in front of the church on Elbon Road southeast of Corwin. From left to right are an unidentified boy and young man, Emery Lamb, Sanford Lainhart, Elmer Lamb, Mike Lamb holding Bible, Virgie Lamb, Gilbert Lamb, Eli Reynolds, two unidentified, and Henry Werkahn. The group formed the nucleus of the Pentecostal church built in Corwin, Ohio, in 1945. The Corwin church was established and built through the efforts of Rev. James P. Lamb. (Courtesy of Lucille Lamb Henry.)

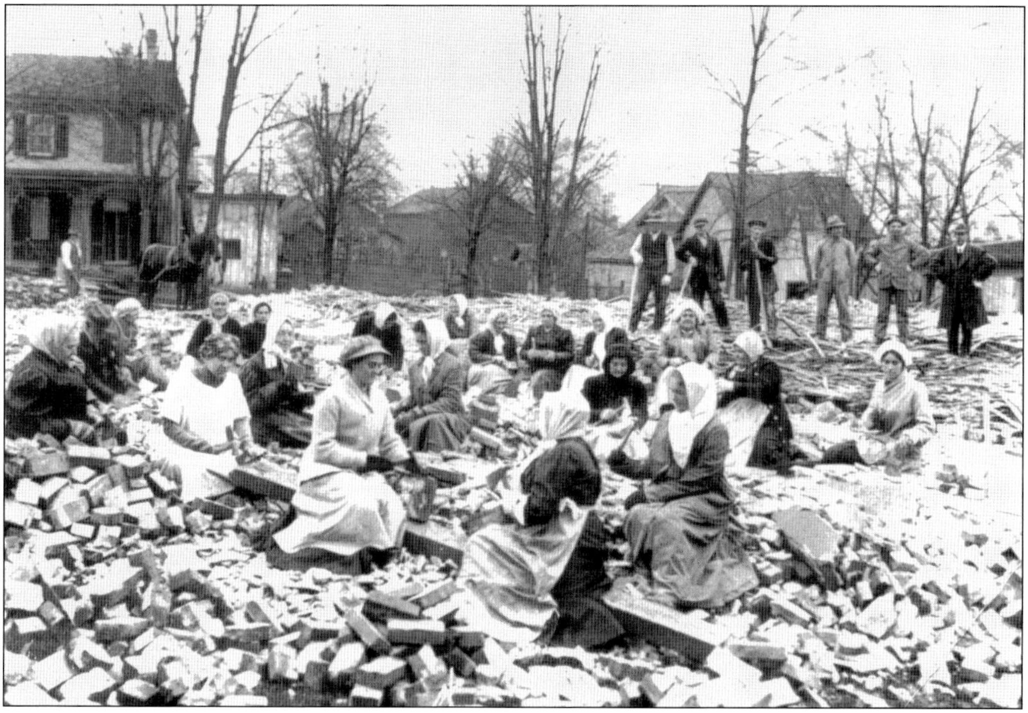

Waynesville Methodist Church women are shown in this 1915 photograph as they clean bricks from the 1840 church demolition. The bricks were used in the new church at North and Third Streets. In the background at left can be seen Old Dex, the horse that helped pull down the 1840 structure. A crew of workmen can be seen at the right. The Joseph Keys home, which in 1859 was the home of Coates Kinney, author of the poem "Rain on the Roof," can be seen in the background at the left. (Courtesy of Mary L. Cook Public Library.)

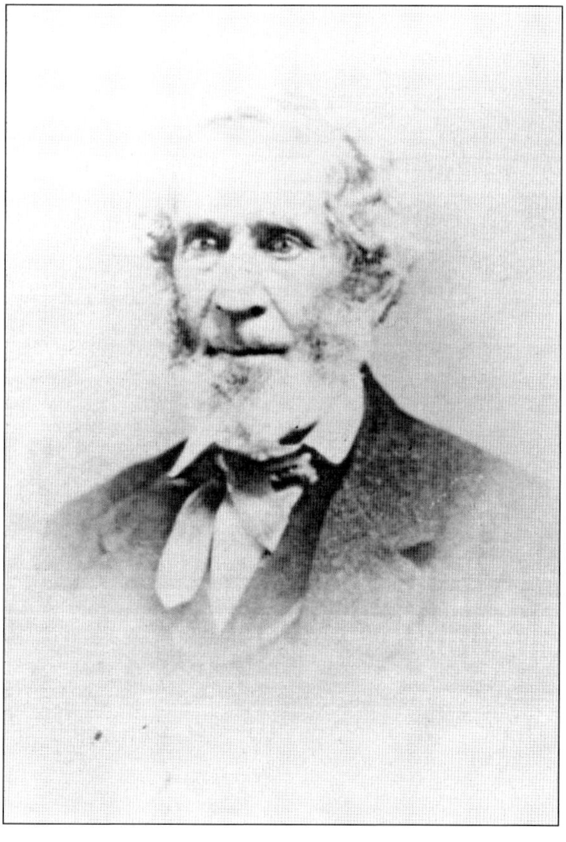

Patrick and Sophia Apjohn Kearney came to Cincinnati from Ireland in 1830. They moved in 1865 to the house that would become the home of Dr. Mary Cook at 5323 Wilkerson Lane in Waynesville. The Kearneys and their children were early members of St. Mary's Episcopal and St. Augustine's Roman Catholic Churches. Patrick had been a civil engineer in Ireland. This photograph was taken in 1875. (Author's.)

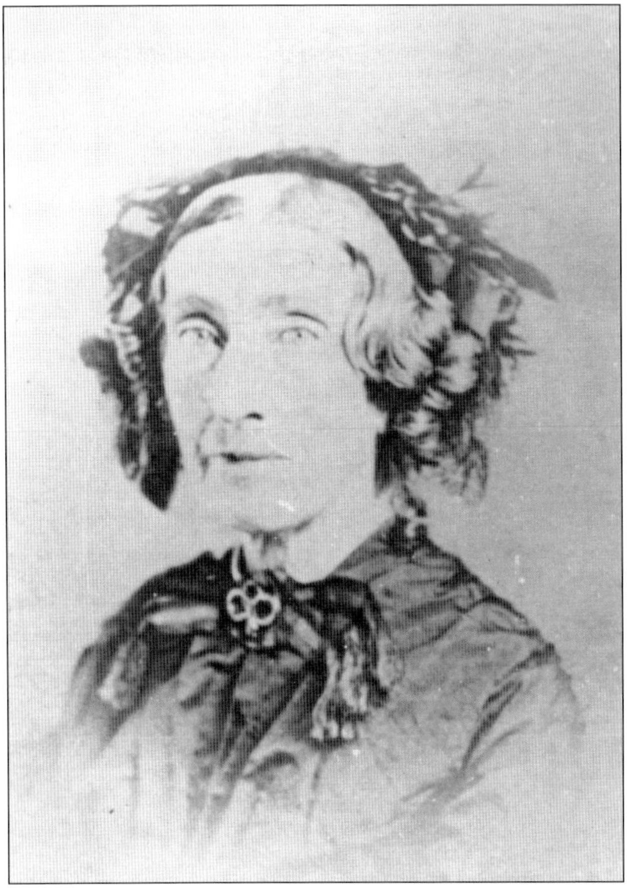

Sophia Apjohn Kearney of Waynesville was a descendant of Irish nobility. Her son-in-law was James Drew Sweet, a founder of St. Mary's Episcopal Church and owner-publisher of the *Miami Gazette* and the *Waynesville News*. This photograph was taken in 1875. (Author's.)

The Third Street Church of Christ was built in 1955 at 95 South Third Street on the northwest corner of Third and Miami Streets in Waynesville. Its membership has always been involved in community interests. This photograph was taken in 2006. (Courtesy of Mary L. Cook Public Library.)

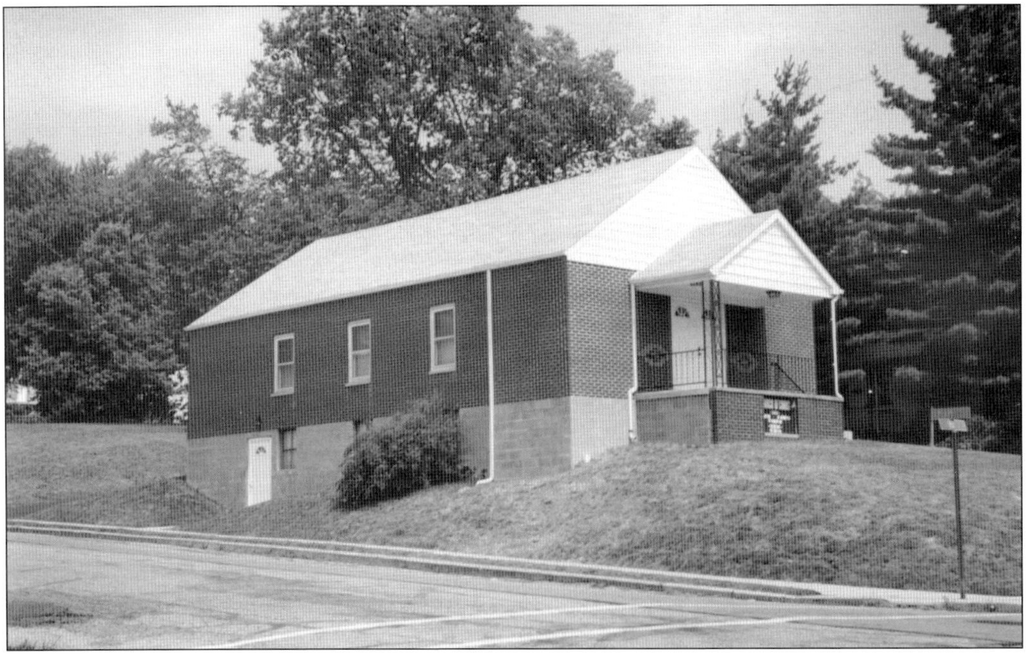

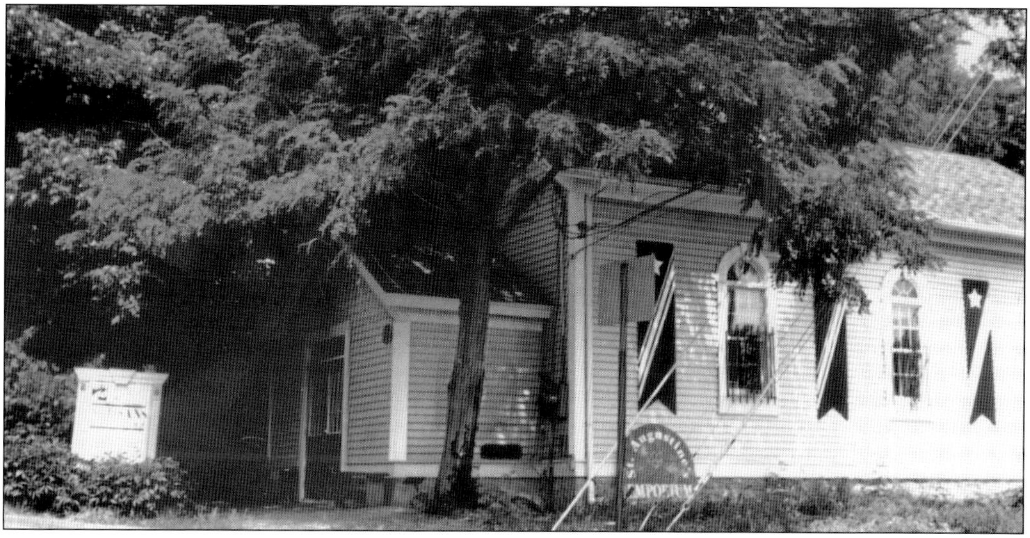

St. Augustine's Roman Catholic Parish members and their priest, Father Augustine, built their first church at the foot of High Street Hill on High Street in 1884. The church was organized as early as 1867 and met in members' homes. Mass was also conducted in Cadwallader Hall and Pugh's Chapel from 1871 until the new church could be constructed on High Street. (Courtesy of Mary L. Cook Public Library.)

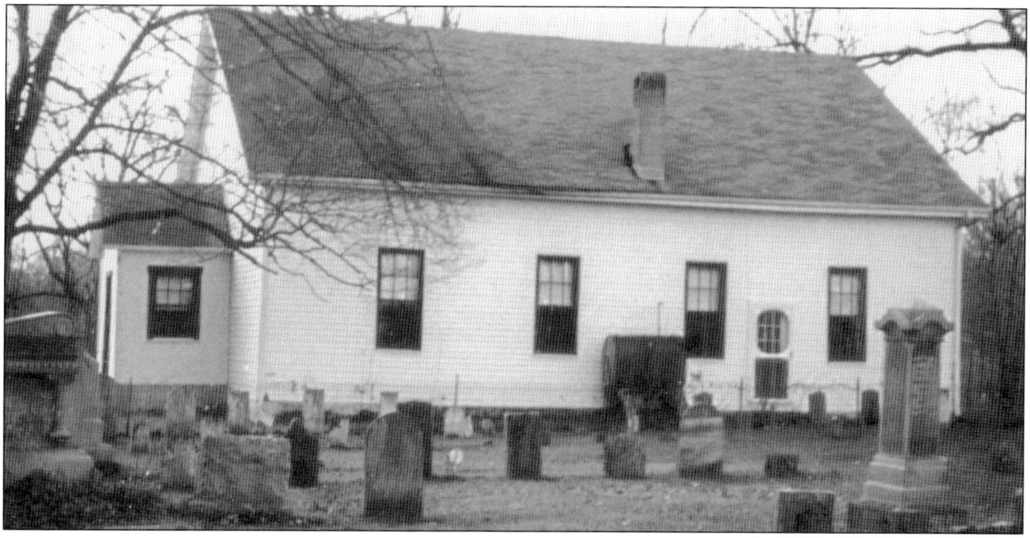

The Middle Run Predestinarian Primitive Baptist Church was founded primarily by William Buckles in 1799. Three churches have occupied the Baptist church site established by the Buckles family from Virginia. The present 1850s building is shown in this 2006 photograph. The first church was built of logs, followed by a brick church, which was destroyed by fire. The church's cemetery is shown in the foreground. The earliest standing headstone is that of Goodone Bright, who died in 1806. Church member John Wilson was also a member of Ohio's Constitutional Committee in 1802. William James, a judge and member of the first Ohio House of Representatives, and his wife, Jane, are buried in the church cemetery. The historic church, which is located at the intersection of Middle Run and Waynesville Bellbrook Roads near the north edge of Wayne Township, is currently preserved by the Middle Run Primitive Baptist Church Preservation Association, Inc. (Courtesy of Mary L. Cook Public Library.)

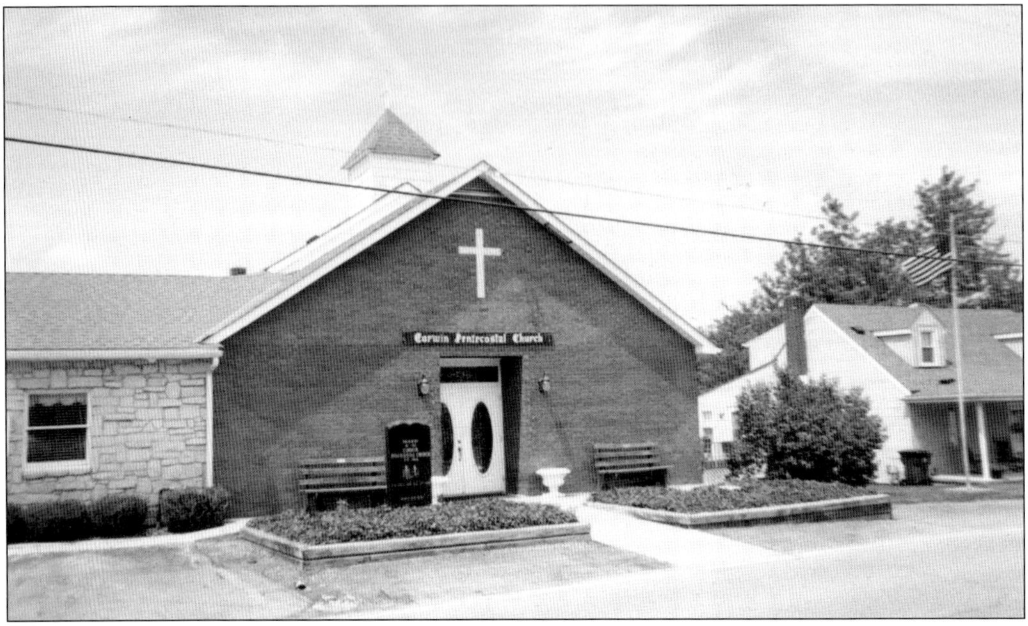

The Corwin Pentecostal Church is shown in this photograph, taken in 2012. The church has been the religious and civic heart of Corwin since Rev. James P. Lamb, who headed a group of church organizers, established it in 1944. (Author's.)

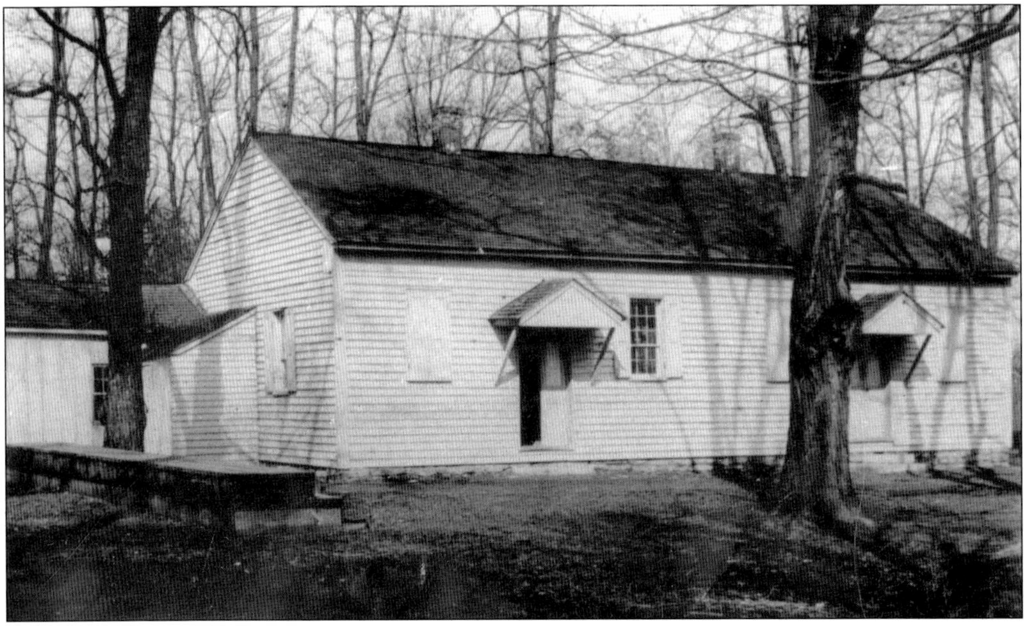

The Caesar's Creek Friends Meetinghouse is shown in this 1905 photograph. The meetinghouse was built in 1849, replacing a log building constructed when the meeting was founded in 1805. The meetinghouse, which originally was located off New Burlington Road north of Corwin, is now preserved at Caesar's Creek Pioneer Village southeast of Waynesville. Henry Milhouse, who is buried in the cemetery beside this meetinghouse, was the Caesar's Creek Meeting's first clerk and a seventh cousin of US president Richard Milhous Nixon. (Courtesy of Mary L. Cook Public Library.)

Six

Corwin

Corwin, Ohio, has always maintained its own individual identity. It grew up as a result of the Little Miami Railroad on July 22, 1844. Corwin was honchoed by John and Joel E. Johnson and called Farmersville at first, when the founders declined the honor of Johnsonville. The name was changed with the opening of the post office in 1898 to avoid confusion with another Farmersville in Montgomery County. Ohio governor Thomas Corwin had attended the Little Miami Railroad dedication banquet in the village, and so the name was changed. A water-and-wood station was the nucleus of Corwin when it was settled at the head of the construction of the Little Miami Railroad. An 1840 pork-packing house was converted into a depot. In 1866, the depot, then called the "Old Rickety," was demolished, and a new railroad station was built on the spot. The new depot served until 1938, when the Pennsylvania Railroad, which had leased the line in 1869, discontinued passenger service.

William Golden, a local carpenter, constructed the frame hotel on the northeast corner of Main Street and Clarksville Road in 1845 for Jonathan Linton. It became the Franey House. Israel Woodruff built another hotel, the brick Woodruff House, in 1845 on the opposite corner. In 1845, a Little Miami Railroad Warehouse completed the heart of the village. The tiny village boomed as a railroad shipping point for livestock and farm produce. In 1876, the Shakers of Union Village near Lebanon, Ohio, shipped a $2,000 calf to a Cincinnati farmer. In 1853, Corwin had an antislavery society. Basically Quaker, the village became a haven for fugitive runaway slaves who were channeled through the village hidden in trains or concealed in their undercarriages.

Corwin's first school was held in an 1802 log cabin built by Abijah O'Neall, a South Carolina Quaker who had settled on the hilltop overlooking the village in 1798. A stone schoolhouse was constructed off North Main Street in the 1840s. The brick two-room school at the top of the old State Route 73 hill was built in 1876. In 1869, Corwin had an African American school.

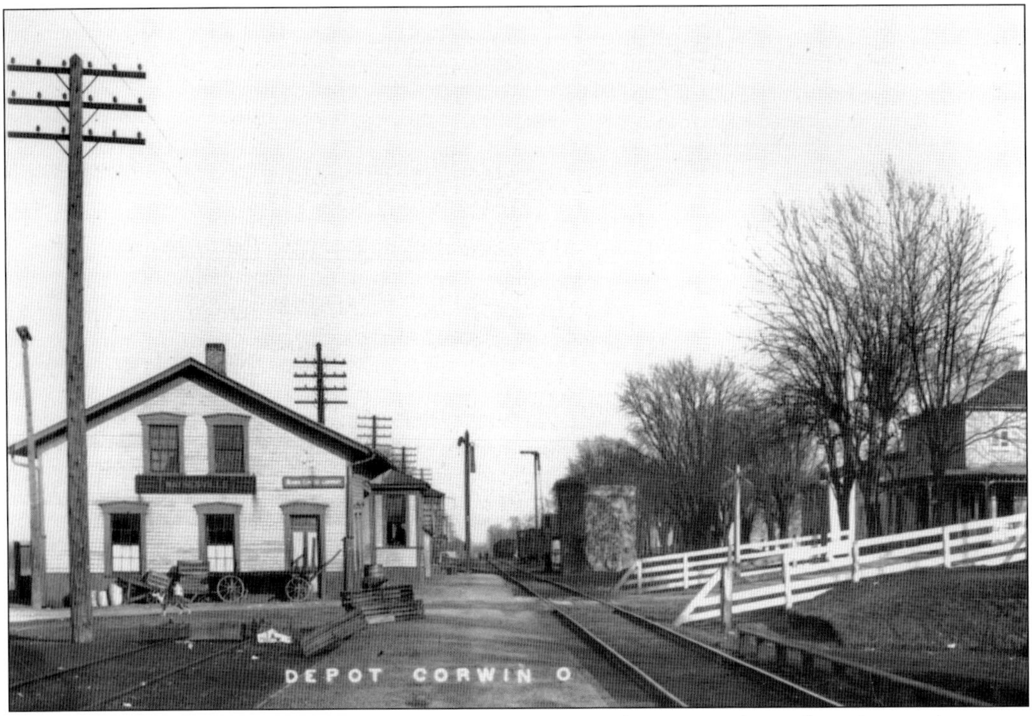

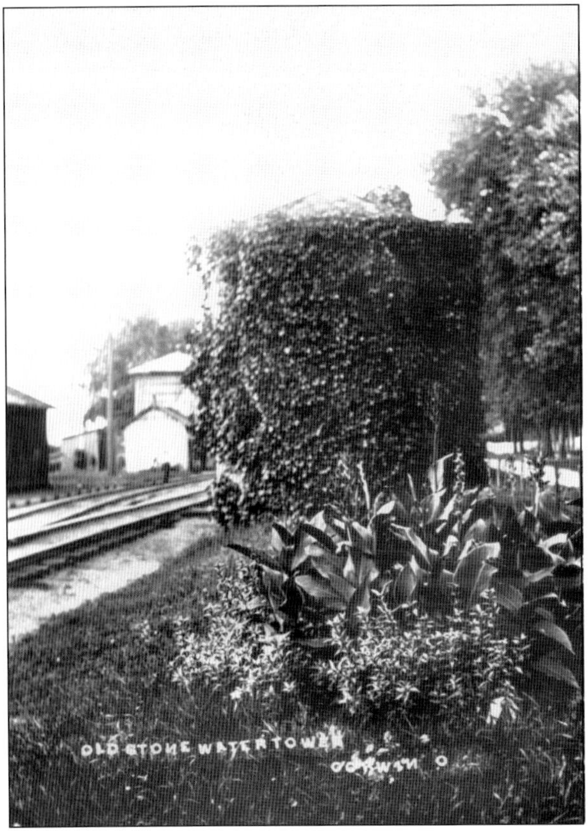

A water-and-wood station at the head of the Little Miami Railroad was the nucleus of Corwin, Ohio, when it was settled on July 22, 1844. This photograph, taken in 1910, shows the beginnings of Corwin at the intersection of Corwin Avenue and the Little Miami Railroad. The 1866 Corwin depot on the left occupies the first train station, an 1840 pork-packing building converted in 1844. The original stone water tower, built in 1844, can be seen at the center. The train transporting the Liberty Bell from Philadelphia to New Orleans passed here on January 31, 1885. (Courtesy of Lucille Lamb Henry.)

The 1844 ivy-covered stone water tower across from the Corwin depot is shown in this 1904 photograph. The flowerbed in the foreground was planted by the Pennsylvania Railroad, which bought the Little Miami in 1869. The railroad company landscaped and maintained the area along the tracks. (Courtesy of Mary L. Cook Public Library.)

A new wooden water tower was built near the north side of the Corwin depot in 1905, as shown in this photograph when it was new. Corwin children in the 1920s cooled off in the summer by boosting someone to pull the chain to release the water flow. (Courtesy of Mary L. Cook Public Library.)

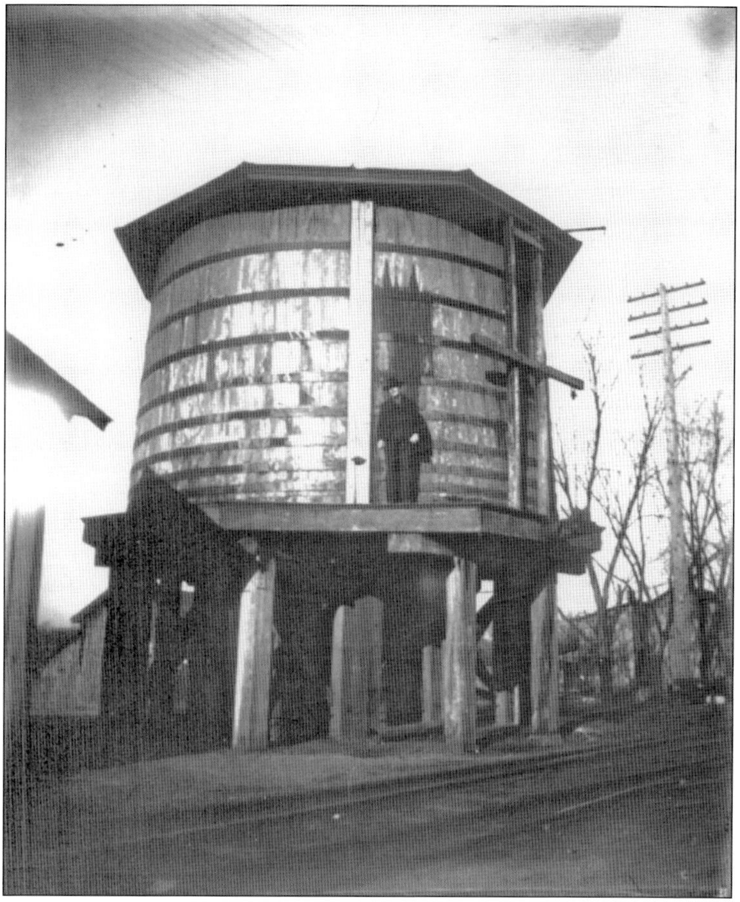

This photograph, taken in 1900, shows a train arriving at the Corwin depot. Daily trains transported passengers and freight south to Cincinnati and north to Springfield. Passenger service was discontinued in 1938. (Courtesy of Mary L. Cook Public Library.)

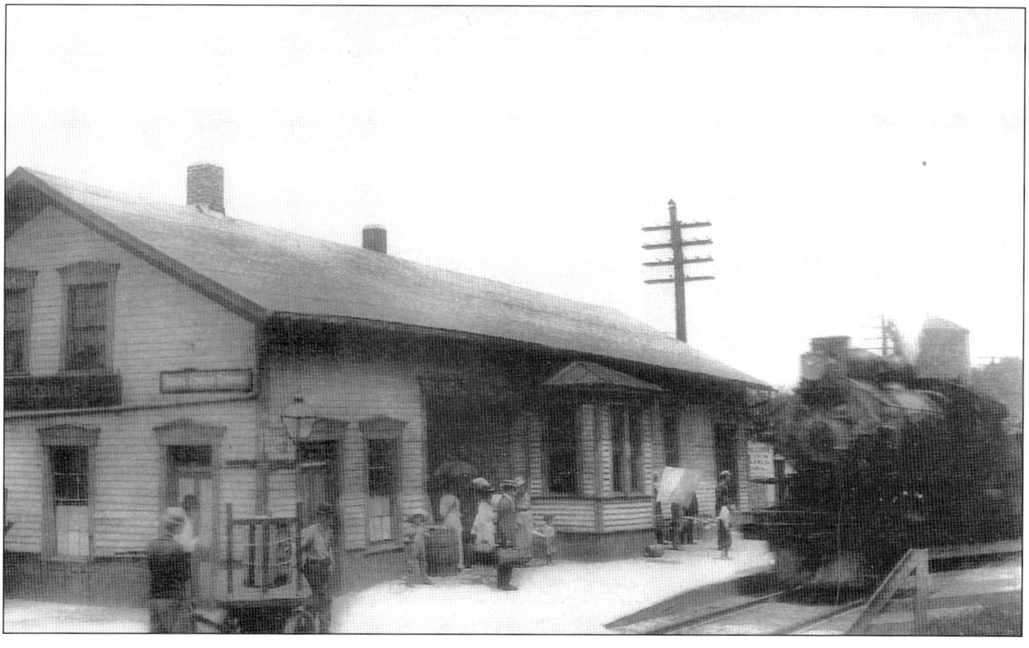

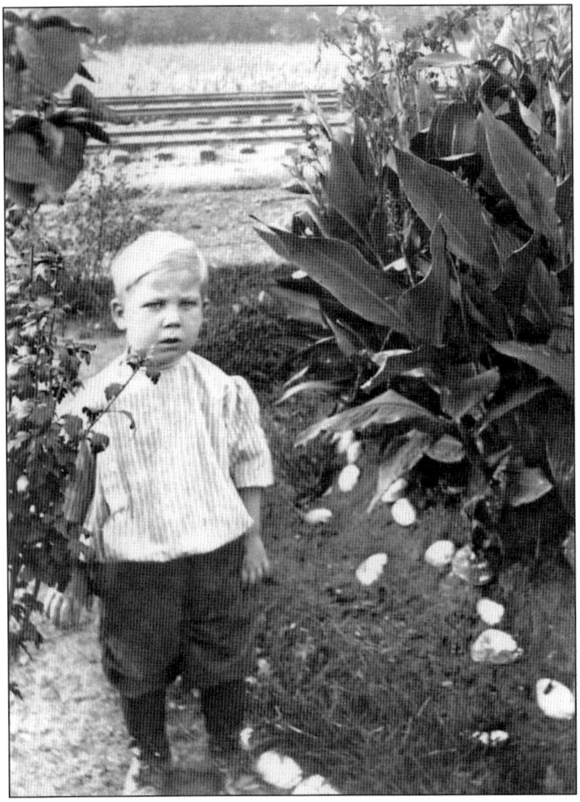

Marion Adams is shown in this 1911 photograph beside a Pennsylvania Railroad flowerbed trimmed at the base with freshwater pearl mussel shells. Corwin citizens often edged their lawns and flowerbeds with the discarded shells. Harold Earnhart fished the last pearls from the Little Miami River in 1930. (Author's.)

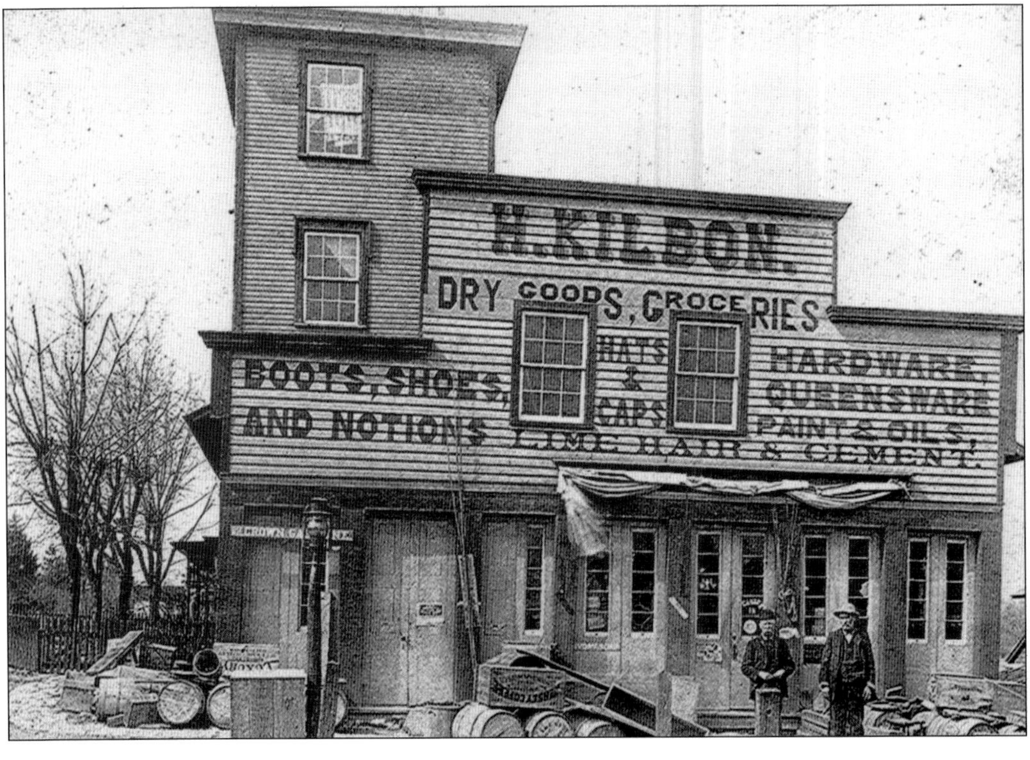

The Kilbon General Store in Corwin is shown in this 1904 photograph. Hiram Kilbon built it in 1866. Legendarily, its inventory included everything from a paper of pins to a threshing machine. The tower was added to hold a gravity-flow water storage tank. (Courtesy of Mary L. Cook Public Library.)

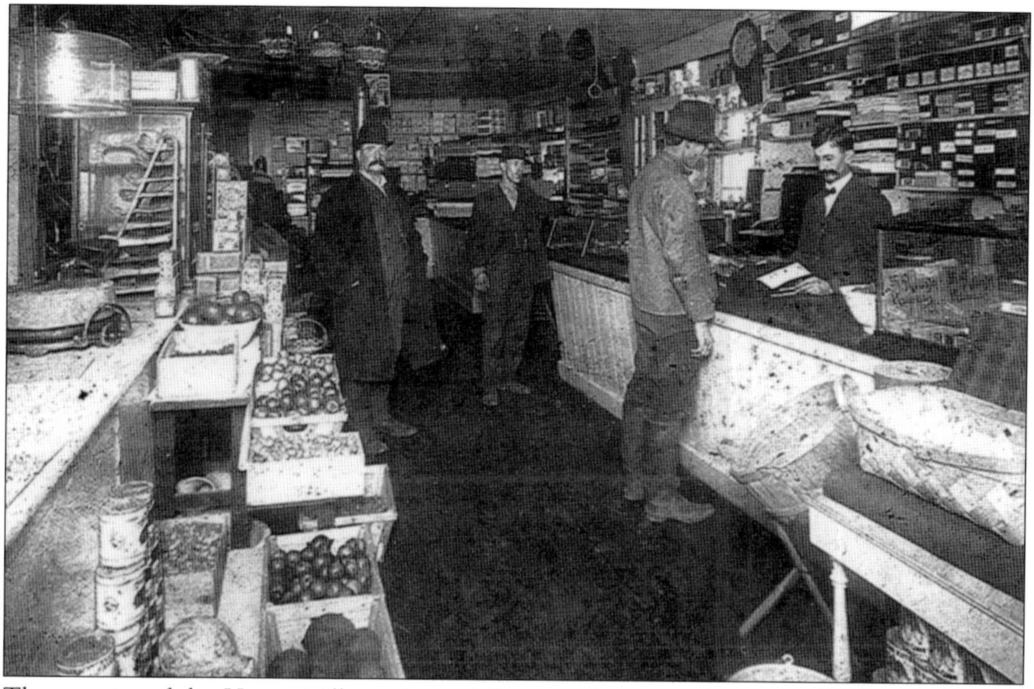

The interior of the Hiram Kilbon General Store is shown in this 1904 photograph. Walter Kilbon, Hiram's son, waits on an unidentified customer at the counter. (Courtesy of Mary L. Cook Public Library.)

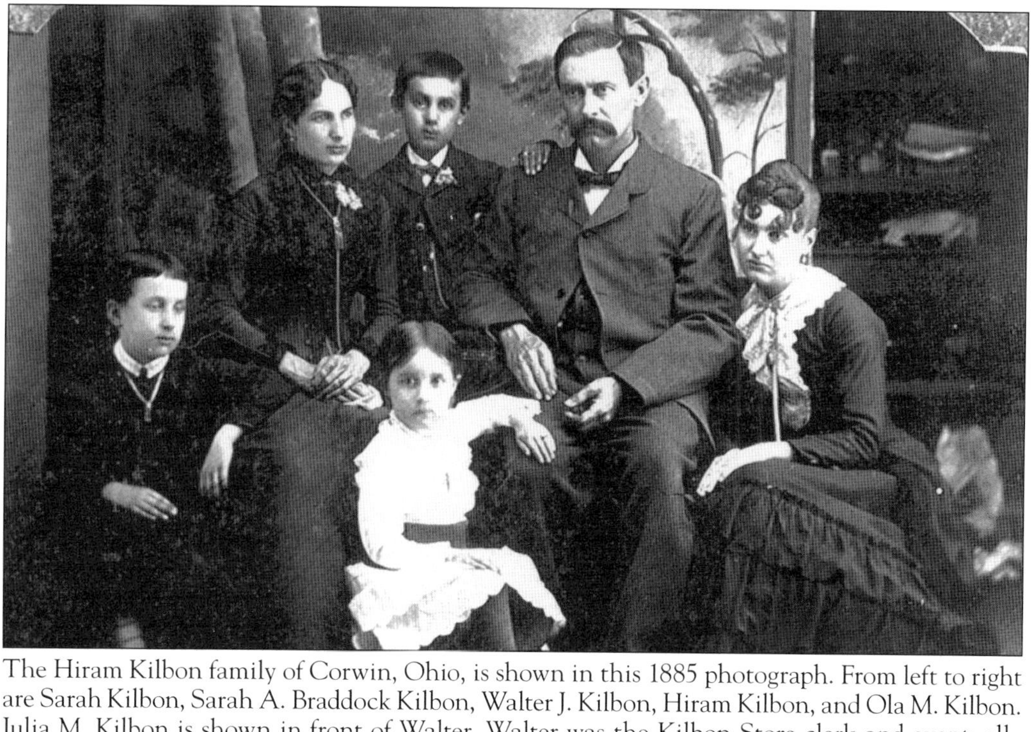

The Hiram Kilbon family of Corwin, Ohio, is shown in this 1885 photograph. From left to right are Sarah Kilbon, Sarah A. Braddock Kilbon, Walter J. Kilbon, Hiram Kilbon, and Ola M. Kilbon. Julia M. Kilbon is shown in front of Walter. Walter was the Kilbon Store clerk and eventually succeeded his father as owner. (Courtesy of Mary L. Cook Public Library.)

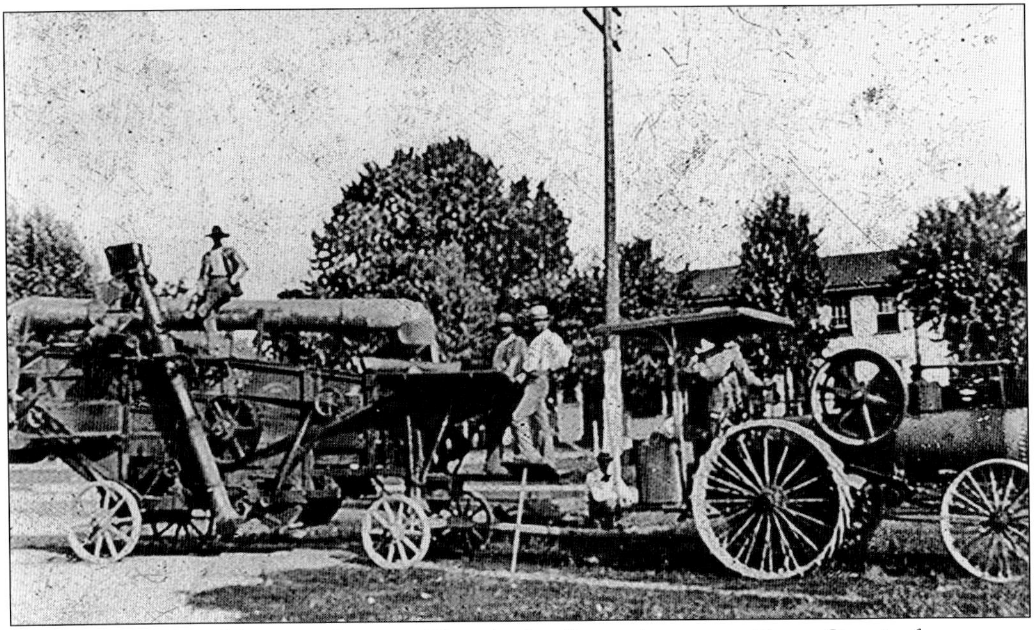

The Kilbon General Store in Corwin, Ohio, had a diverse inventory. Some Corwin farmers are shown in this 1900 photograph with a steam threshing machine outside the Kilbon store. The thresher had apparently just been delivered by train on the Pennsylvania Railroad, which is visible just under the machine. (Courtesy of Mary L. Cook Public Library.)

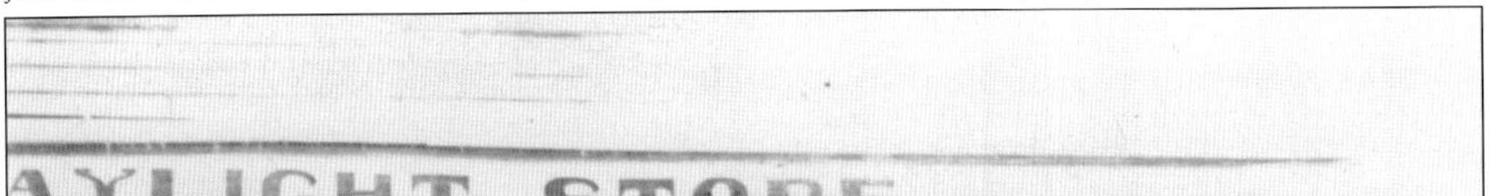

Hiram Kilbon's son Walter became the owner of the Kilbon Grocery in Corwin in 1904. Walter changed the name of the business to the Daylight Store. An unidentified Corwin boy is shown in front of the store in this 1912 photograph. A sign at the left advertises "Fresh Oysters Today." At that time, the oysters sold for 10¢ a pint. The reflection of the Grange Market Building across the street can be seen in the window on the left. (Courtesy of Mary L. Cook Public Library.)

Corwin's postmaster, Jacob R. Hisey, is shown in this 1900 photograph of the interior of the post office. The post office, being established in 1898, caused Corwin to change its name. The village had been named Farmersville from 1844 until that time. There was another Farmersville in Montgomery County. To avoid confusion, the village was renamed Corwin after Ohio governor Thomas Corwin, who attended the banquet celebrating the arrival of the Little Miami Railroad in 1844. (Courtesy of Mary L. Cook Public Library.)

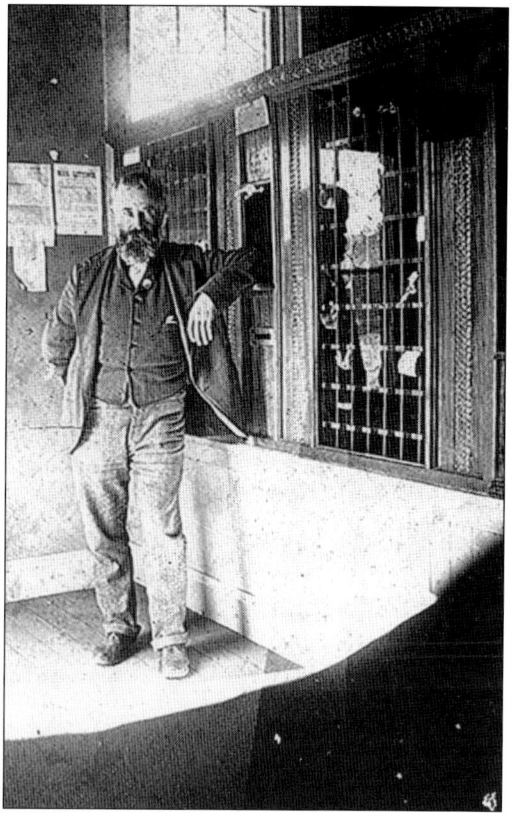

Waynesville Farmer's Grange No. 13, Ohio, Patrons of Husbandry built this market house in Corwin in 1876. It was constructed for shipping farm produce and local manufactured items on the railroad. Nathan Harlan and Morrison Van Duser made brooms in the building in 1879. This photograph was taken around 1876. The Corwin Post Office was in the right-side rooms. An undertaker was in the left-side rooms in 1898. The building still stands on the corner of Corwin Avenue and New Burlington Road. (Courtesy of Mary L. Cook Public Library.)

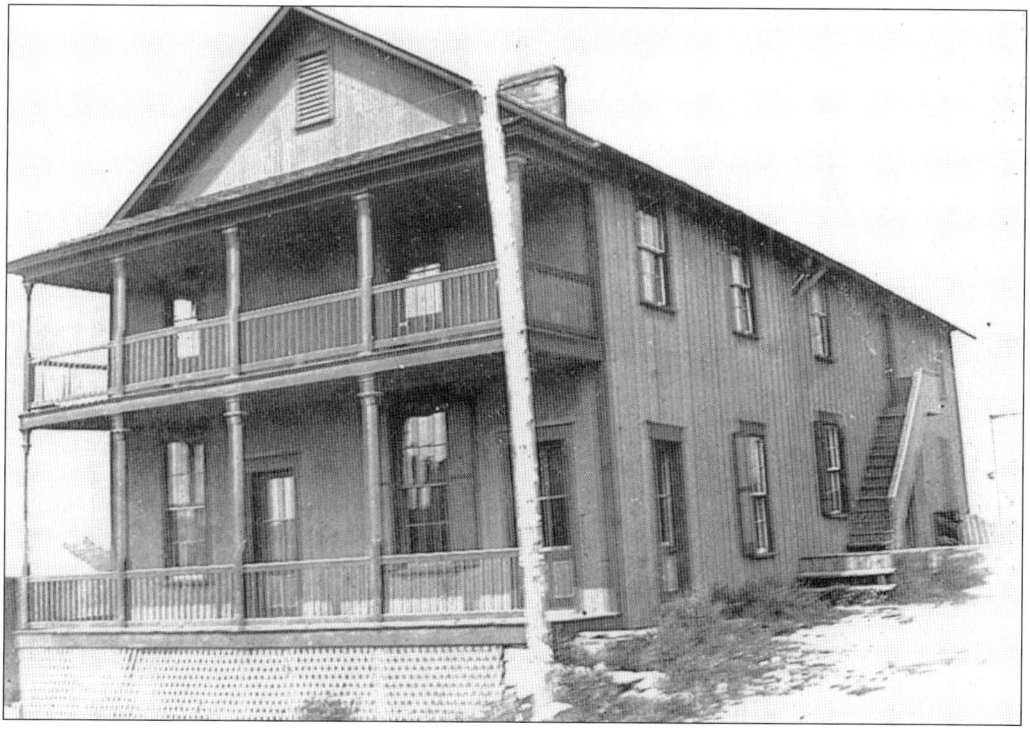

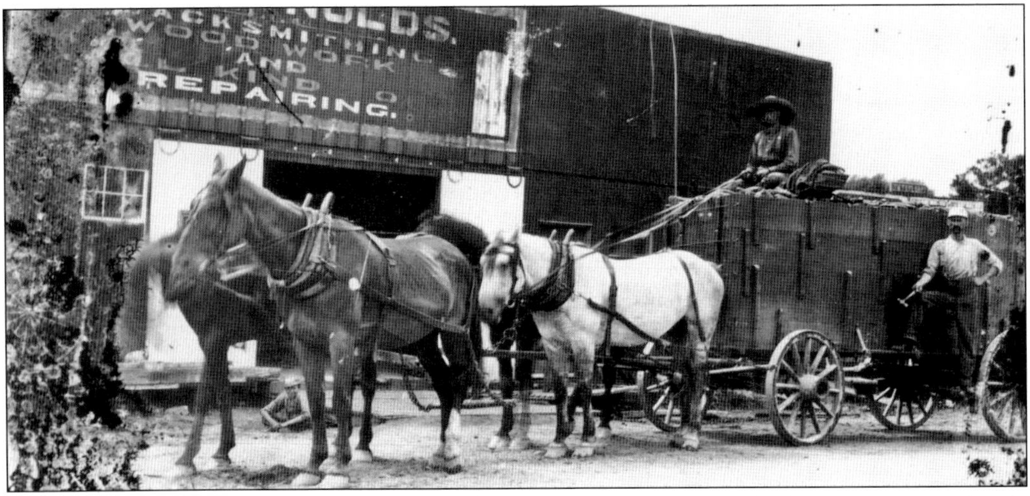

This photograph was taken in 1904 of the Charles Reynolds Blacksmith Shop, on the north side of Corwin Avenue next to the Grange Market Building. Reynolds is shown with a hammer in his hand while standing on the wagon. An unidentified farmer is in the driver's seat of the wagon. (Courtesy of Mary L. Cook Public Library.)

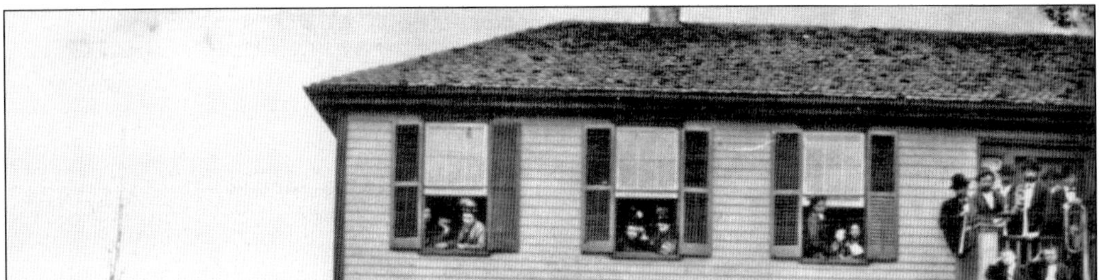

The Franey House Hotel, in Corwin, is shown during a Crusaders Temperance Union visit in 1874. The building was constructed on the northeast corner of Corwin Avenue and Clarksville Road in 1846. In 1853, owners Thomas and Mary Franey hid fleeing slaves snuck in on trains. A tunnel on the east side of the hotel concealed the slaves' entry. (Courtesy of Mary L. Cook Public Library.)

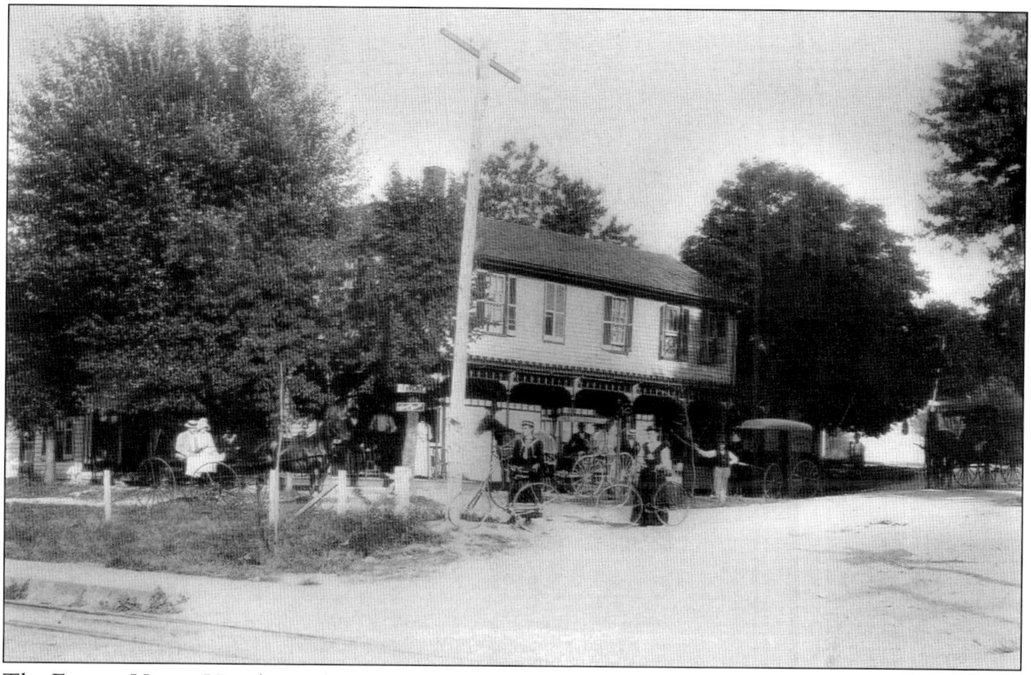

The Franey House Hotel was the Panhandle Hotel owned by William Arnold in 1900, when this photograph was taken. Corwin citizens are shown out for an afternoon buggy and bicycle ride. (Courtesy of Lucille Lamb Henry.)

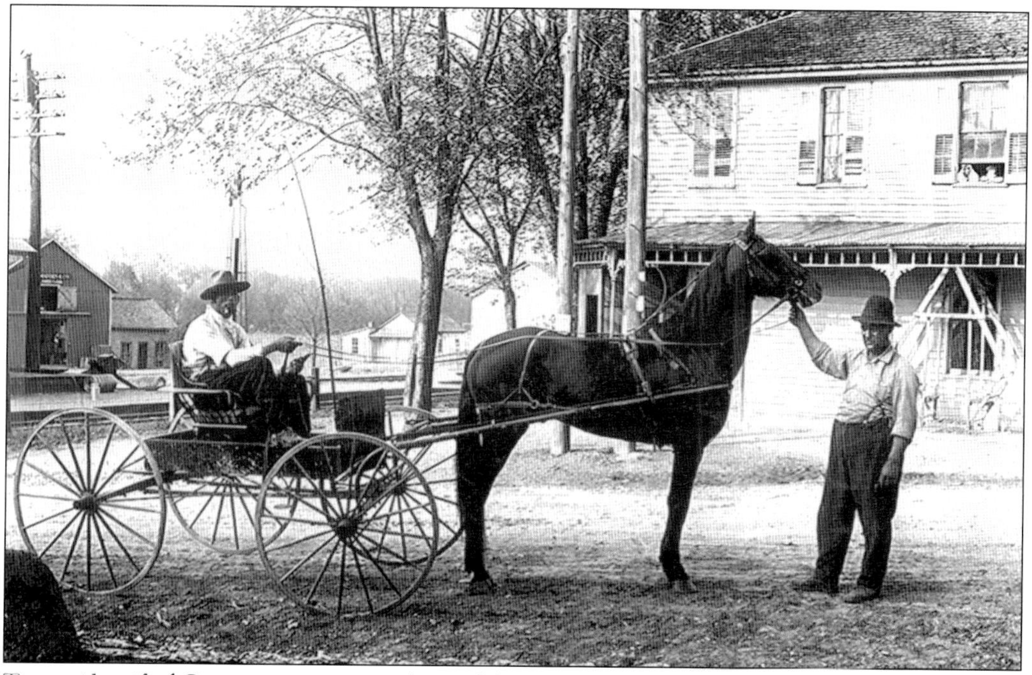

Two unidentified Corwin men pause in front of the former Panhandle Hotel in this 1912 photograph. The hotel had been converted into a residence. Seth Cook's coal yard barn can be seen at the far left. The hotel, last owned by William Arnold, became the home of the Rev. James P. Lamb family. It was destroyed by fire in 1932. (Courtesy of Mary L. Cook Public Library.)

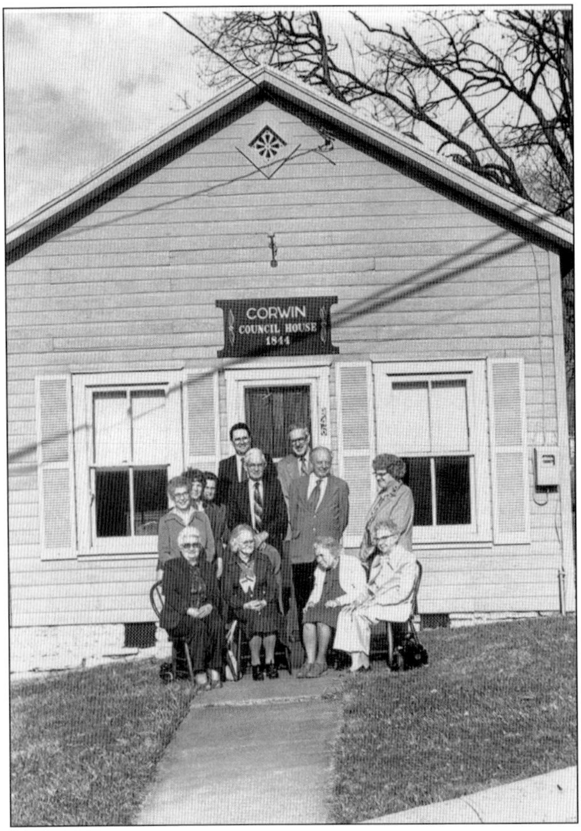

The Corwin Council House, shown in this 1970 photograph, was built in 1895 and still exists. A reunion of Corwin natives is gathered in front for a commemorative program. Pictured are, from left to right, (first row) Gladys Adams Dalton, Grace Hockett Prendergast, Minerva Harlan Hough, and Josephine Harlan Earnhart; (second row) Leeada Werntz Yenger, George Henderson, Raymond Braddock, and Virginia Hardin; (third row) Mrs. William Purkey (Diane), Lucille Lamb Henry, Mayor William Purkey, and Tressler Hardin. (Courtesy of Mary L. Cook Public Library.)

A single jail cell was added to the interior of the Corwin Council House in a separate room. The cell, patented in 1888, usually held prisoners just overnight. An occasional brawl would break out in one of the village saloons, and the ringleader would sober up here. (Courtesy of Mary L. Cook Public Library.)

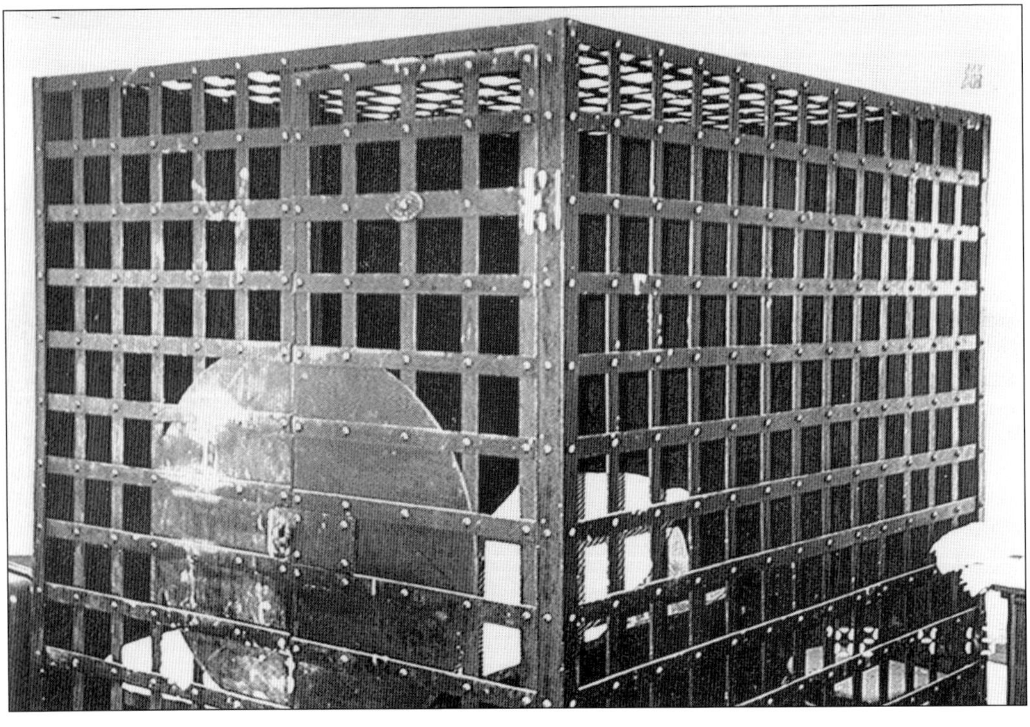

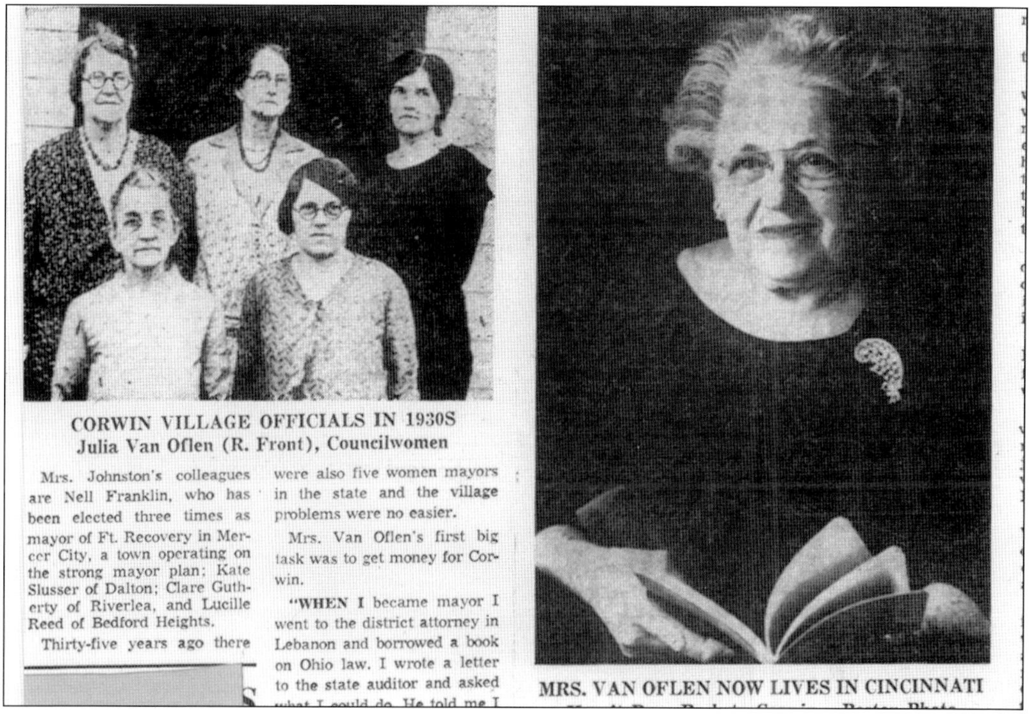

CORWIN VILLAGE OFFICIALS IN 1930S
Julia Van Oflen (R. Front), Councilwomen

Mrs. Johnston's colleagues are Nell Franklin, who has been elected three times as mayor of Ft. Recovery in Mercer City, a town operating on the strong mayor plan; Kate Slusser of Dalton; Clare Guth-erty of Riverlea, and Lucille Reed of Bedford Heights.

Thirty-five years ago there were also five women mayors in the state and the village problems were no easier.

Mrs. Van Oflen's first big task was to get money for Corwin.

"WHEN I became mayor I went to the district attorney in Lebanon and borrowed a book on Ohio law. I wrote a letter to the state auditor and asked

MRS. VAN OFLEN NOW LIVES IN CINCINNATI

Corwin, Ohio, made national history in 1930 when it had an all-woman government. The men of the village of 236 refused to tackle the administration, so the women ran for the offices. In the 1930 photograph are, from left to right, (first row) Councilwoman Amanda Norton and Mayor Julia Van Oflen; (second row) Councilwoman Ethel Beckett, Treasurer Dora Stiles, and Councilwoman Laura Werntz. (Courtesy of Mary L. Cook Public Library.)

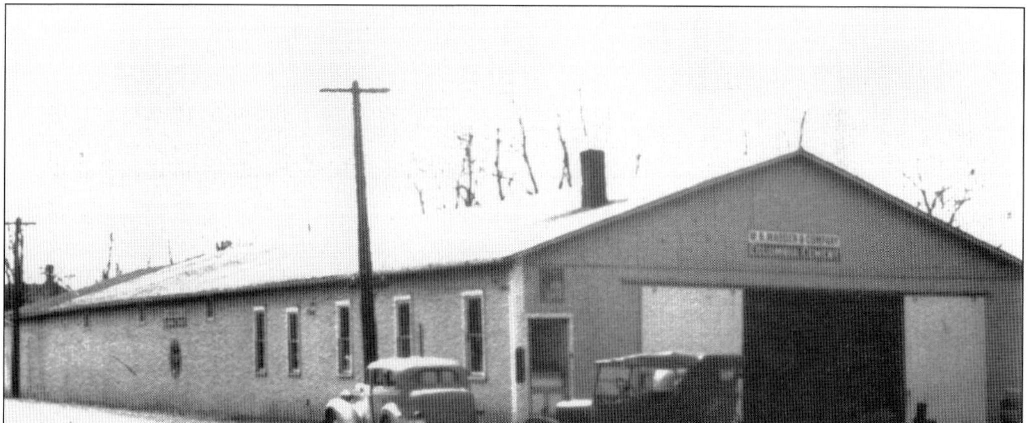

The W.H. Madden Lumber Company is shown in this 1930s photograph. The business was opened in 1905. The building and a lumber and supply business still exist at 39 Maple Street in Corwin. (Courtesy of Mary L. Cook Public Library.)

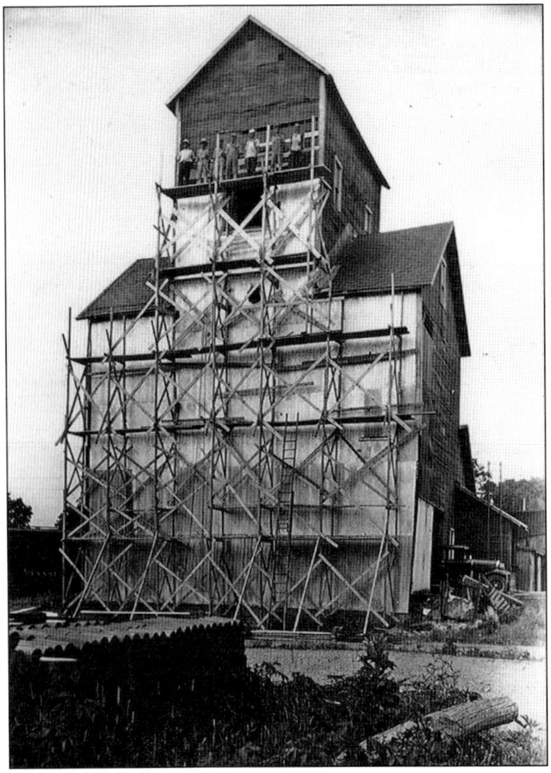

This 1903 photograph of the Henry Jay Feed Mill shows it being constructed. It was for many years located on the Pennsylvania Railroad on the south side of Corwin, Ohio. Later used as the Waynesville Farmer's Exchange Building, the mill was demolished in April 2012. (Courtesy of Mary L. Cook Public Library.)

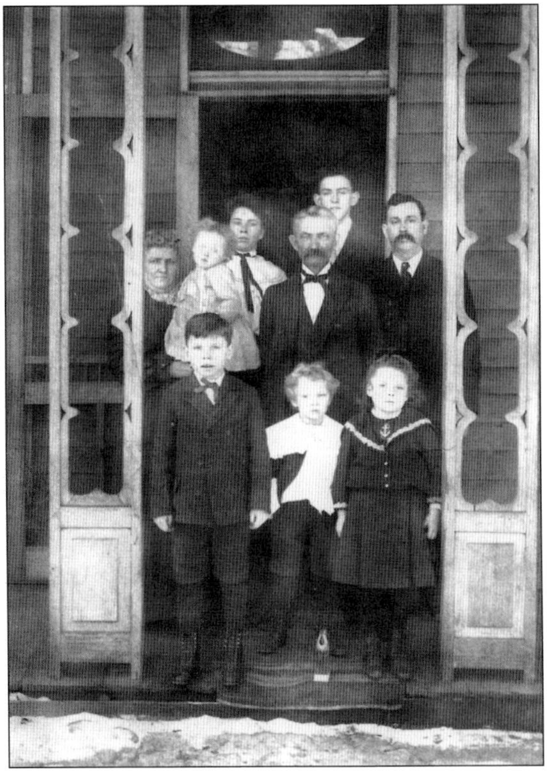

George Harlan settled in Wayne Township in 1796. A group of his descendants is shown on the porch of the home in Corwin at 40-B South Main Street. Pictured are, from left to right, (first row) Ernest Lawrence Harlan, Everett Paul Harlan, and Francis Minerva Harlan; (second row) Naomi Van Duser Harlan, Mary Josephine Harlan, and Morrison Van Duser; (third row) Viola Harlan, Raymond Harlan, and Otto Harlan. (Courtesy of Suzanne Harlan Andrews.)

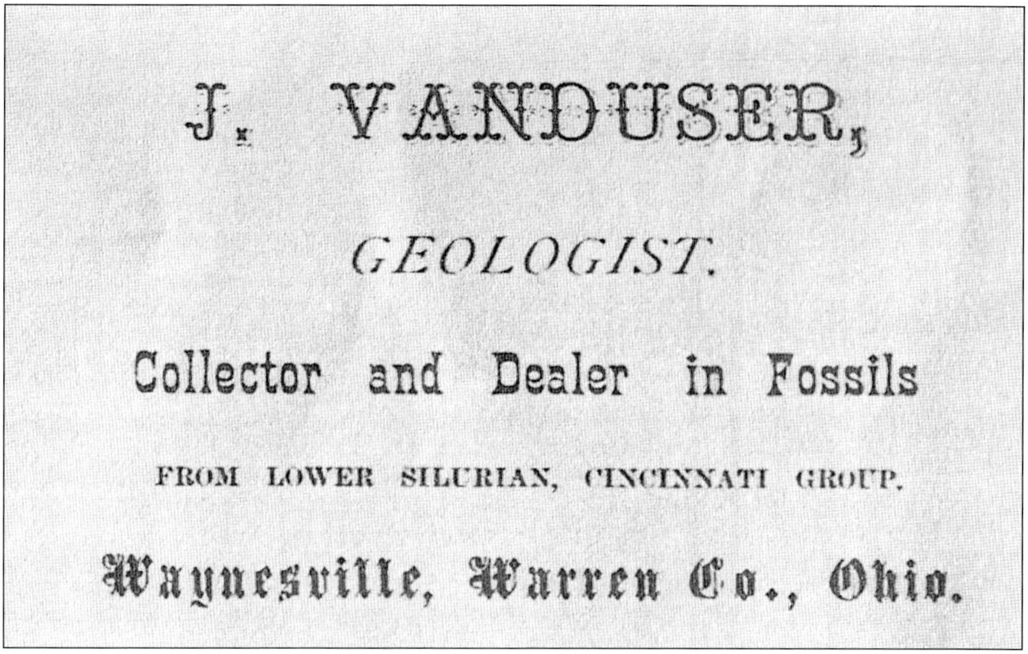

J. VANDUSER,

GEOLOGIST.

Collector and Dealer in Fossils

FROM LOWER SILURIAN, CINCINNATI GROUP.

Waynesville, Warren Co., Ohio.

The 1870 business card of Corwin geologist Jesse Van Duser is shown in this photograph. Van Duser was the buying agent for I.H. Harris's Little Miami Pearl Fisheries, Inc., at Waynesville. He discovered the world-renowned Kohinoor agatized freshwater pearl in the Little Miami River in 1879. (Courtesy of Suzanne Harlan Andrews.)

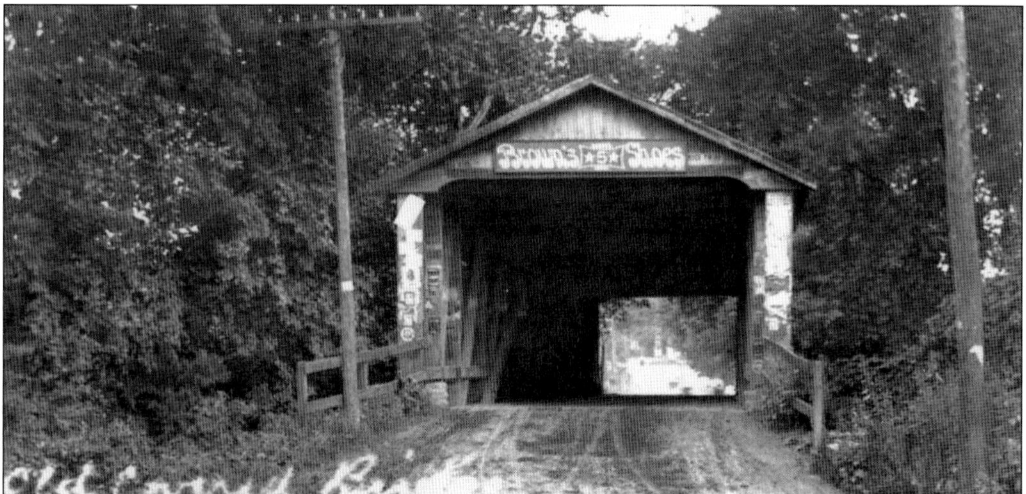

The covered bridge over the Little Miami River on Waynesville-Corwin Avenue is shown in this 1905 photograph. The bridge was constructed in 1859. It replaced a smaller bridge built in 1825. A sign on the bridge once read, "$5.00 fine for driving faster than a walk over this bridge." The structure was replaced in 1929 by an iron and concrete bridge installed by the Oregonia Bridge Company. The iron bridge was later removed. (Author's.)

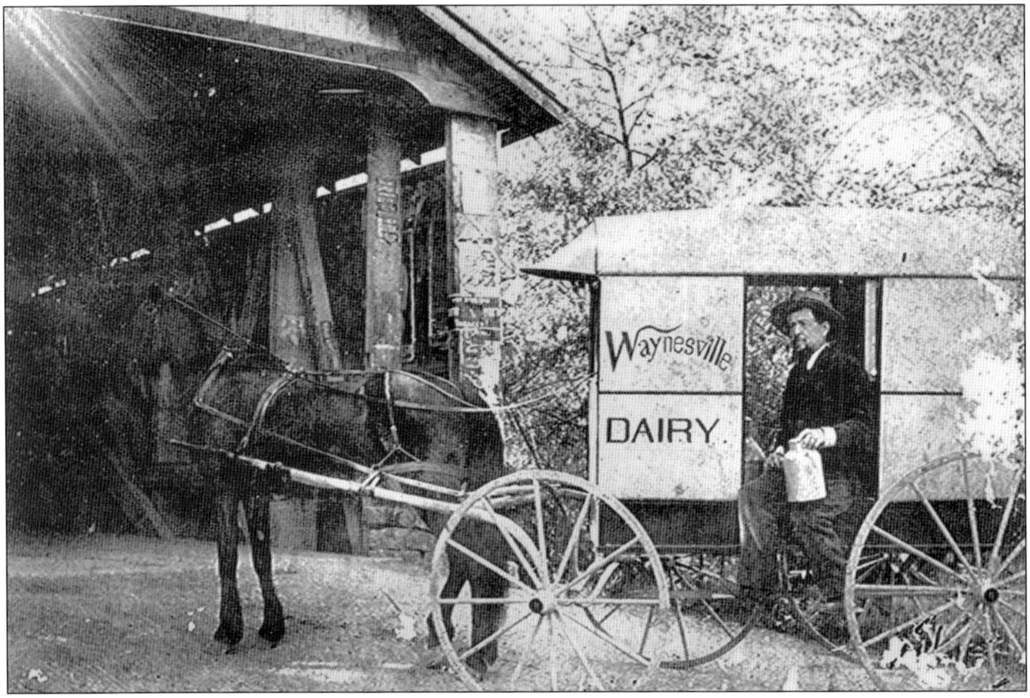

The Waynesville Dairy deliveryman pauses on Waynesville-Corwin Avenue at the covered bridge over the Little Miami River in this 1904 photograph. The dairy was owned and operated by the Stokes family on Lower Springboro Road. (Courtesy of Mary L. Cook Public Library.)

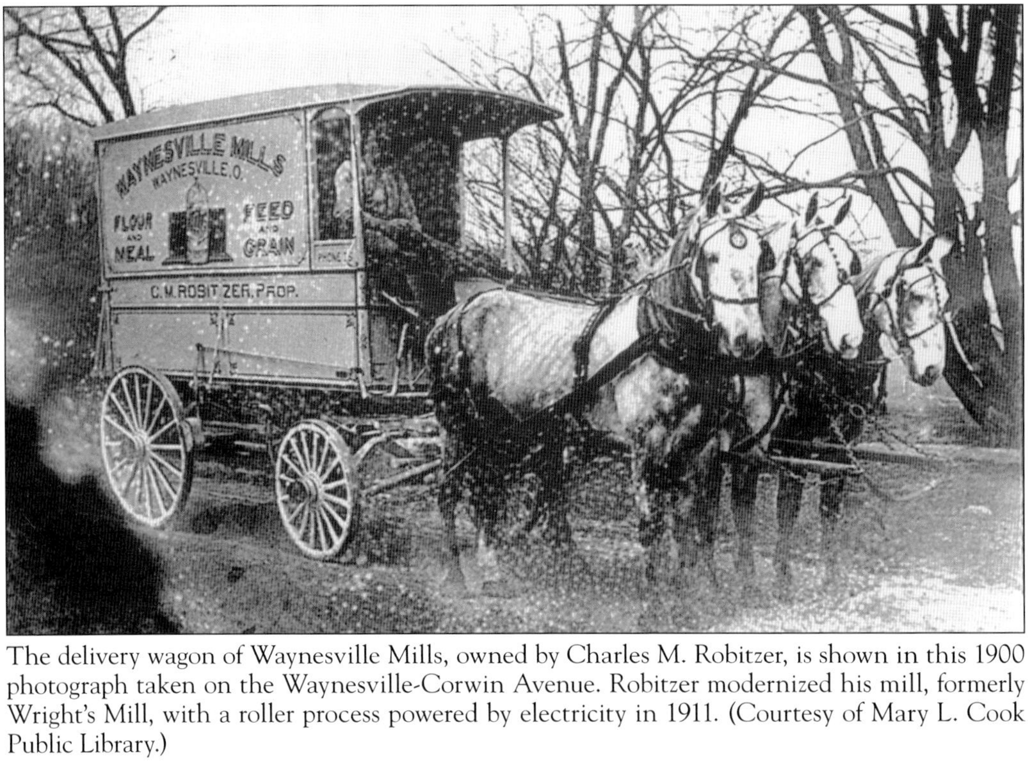

The delivery wagon of Waynesville Mills, owned by Charles M. Robitzer, is shown in this 1900 photograph taken on the Waynesville-Corwin Avenue. Robitzer modernized his mill, formerly Wright's Mill, with a roller process powered by electricity in 1911. (Courtesy of Mary L. Cook Public Library.)

Barclay Grimes, left, and Robert Adams of Corwin are shown in this c. 1928 photograph. They are holding sacks of flour from Charles Robitzer's Waynesville Mills. (Author's.)

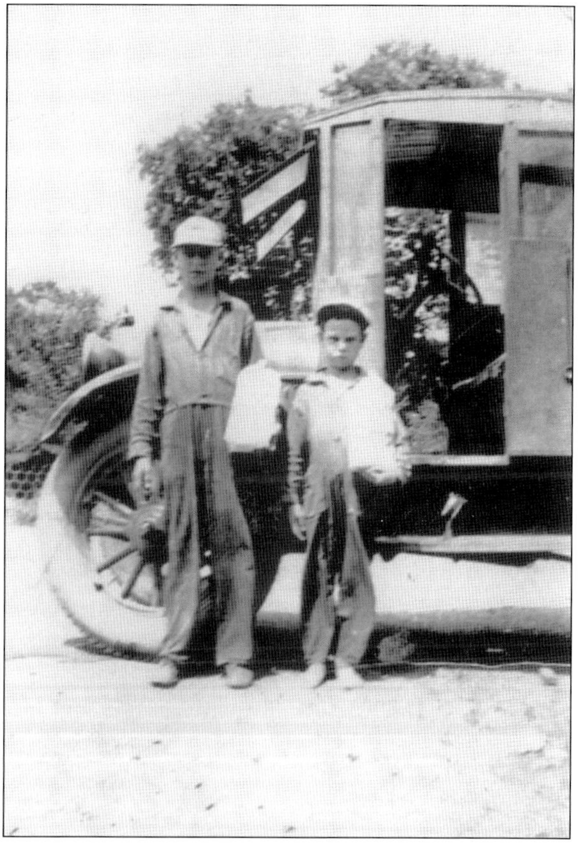

The two-room Corwin School was built in 1869. There was one room for elementary school classes and one room for high school. The school consolidated with Waynesville in 1917. Pupils are shown here in 1915. Fifth from left on the first row is Ernest Adams. Rachel Davis is the girl with the hair bow second from right on the second row. (Courtesy of Mary L. Cook Public Library.)

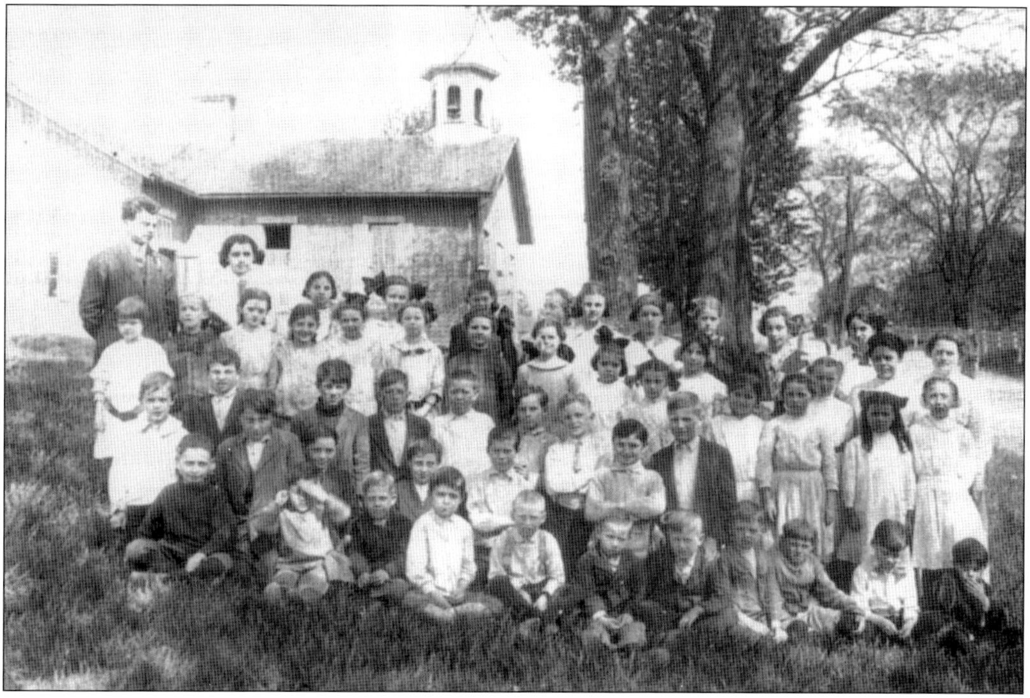

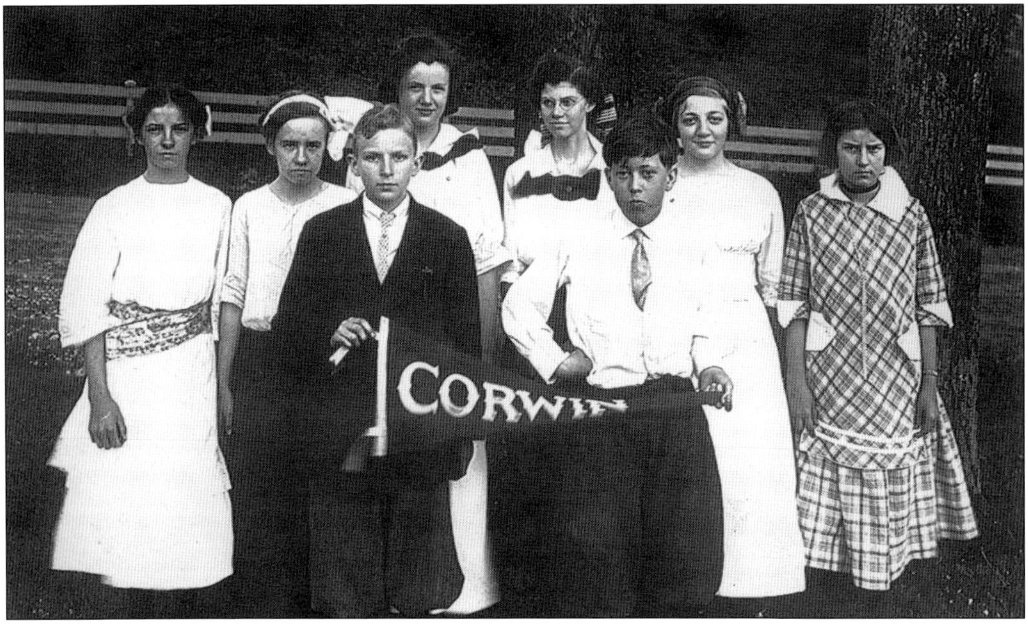

The high school class of Corwin School is shown in this 1905 photograph. The fence of Miami Cemetery across the road can be seen in the background. Corwin School was consolidated with Waynesville schools in 1917. Parts of the original building that was leveled by a fire in 1961 remain as well as the original bell, which is displayed on the site. (Courtesy of Mary L. Cook Public Library.)

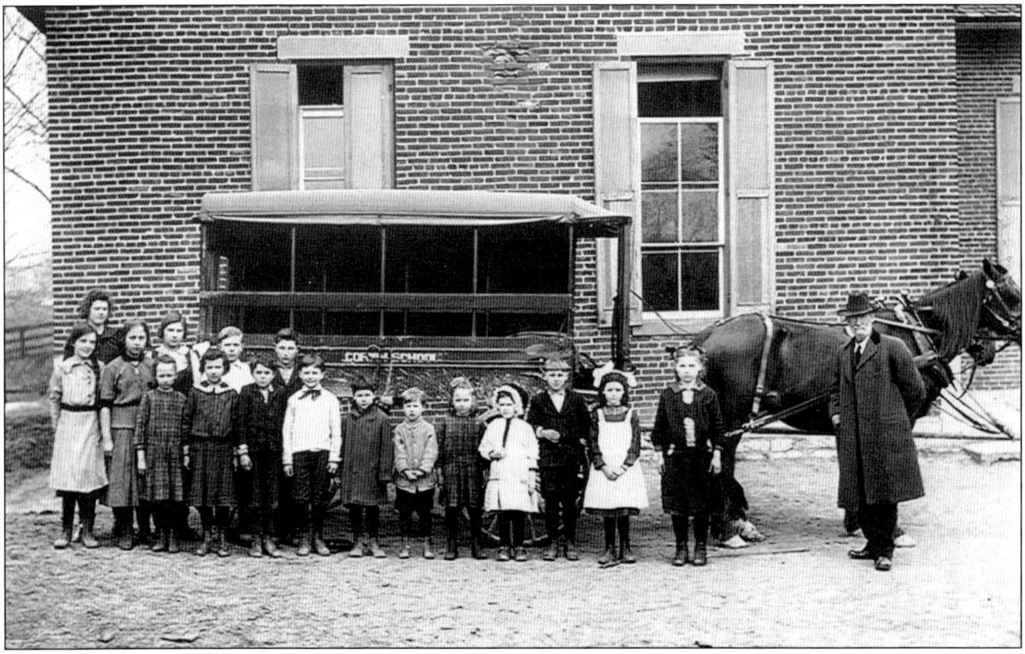

John Zell, at right in this 1906 photograph of Corwin School, is shown with students and a horse-drawn school bus. Corwin did not get motorized school buses until Rev. James P. Lamb convinced the Wayne Township School Board that Corwin schoolchildren deserved to be transported to Waynesville. (Courtesy of Mary L. Cook Public Library.)

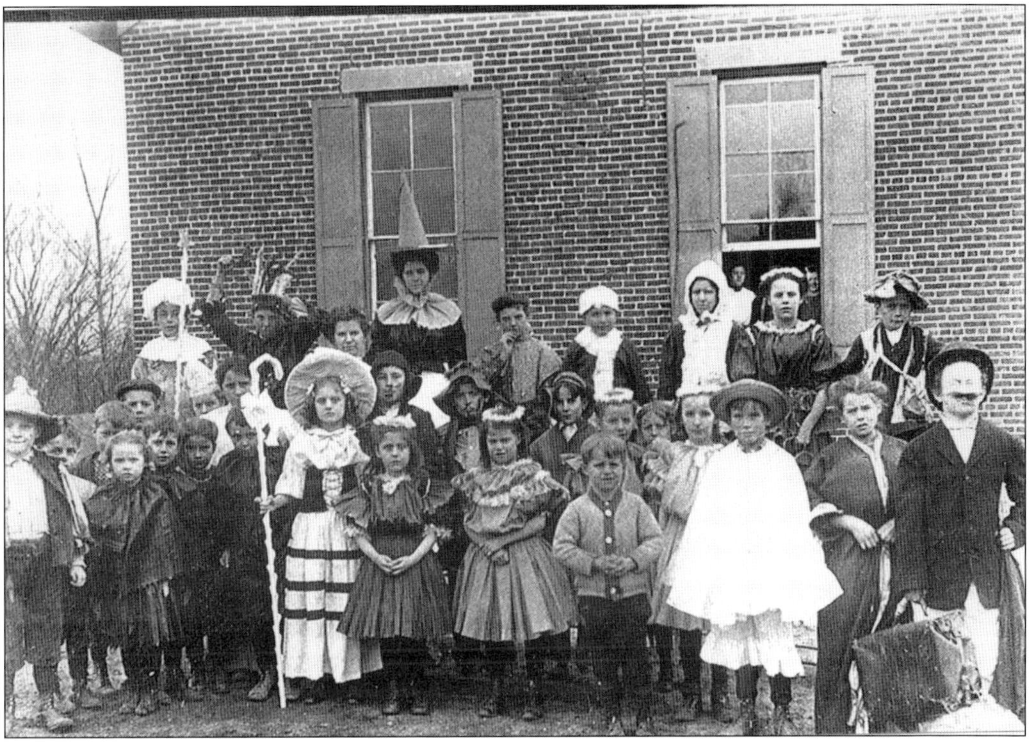

Corwin School students are shown in this 1910 photograph dressed in costume for a historical storybook play. The unidentified school pupils are from various grades. (Courtesy of Mary L. Cook Public Library.)

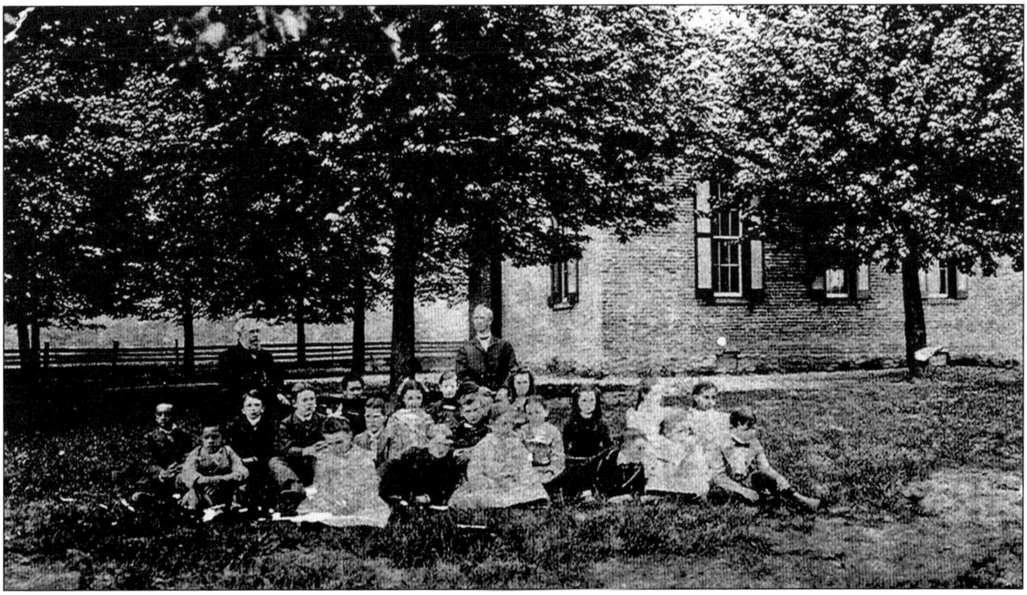

A Corwin School class is shown on the lawn at the rear of the school in this photograph, taken around 1876. There are three African American children among the unidentified students and faculty. The village had an antislavery society in 1853 and an African American school in 1869. (Courtesy of Mary L. Cook Public Library.)

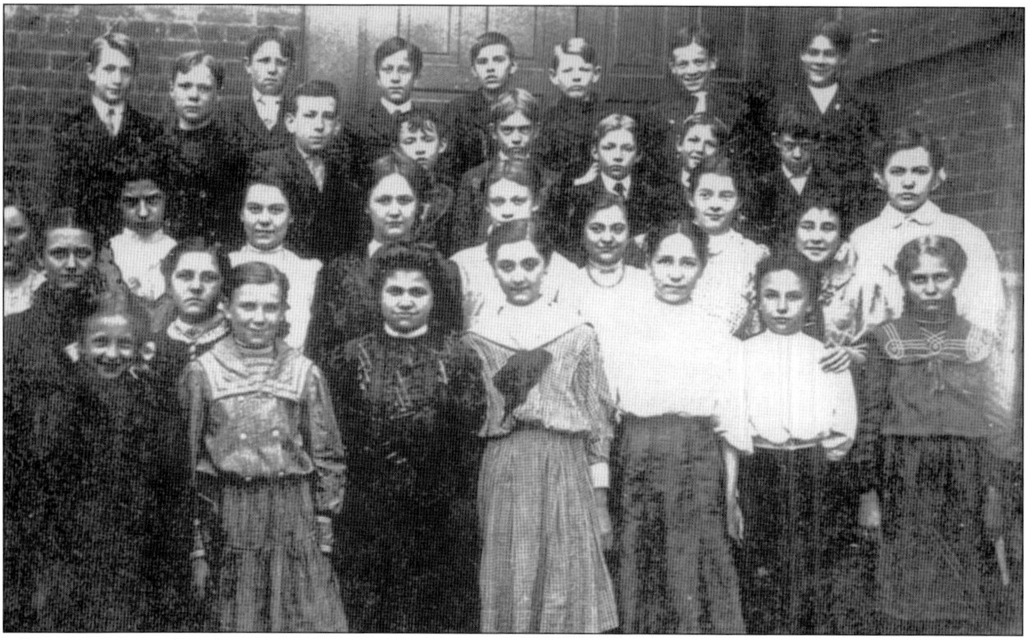

The Corwin School is shown in this photograph, taken around 1880. There are two African American girls in the class. Corwin supported stations on the Underground Railroad from 1846 until 1863. (Courtesy of Mary L. Cook Public Library.)

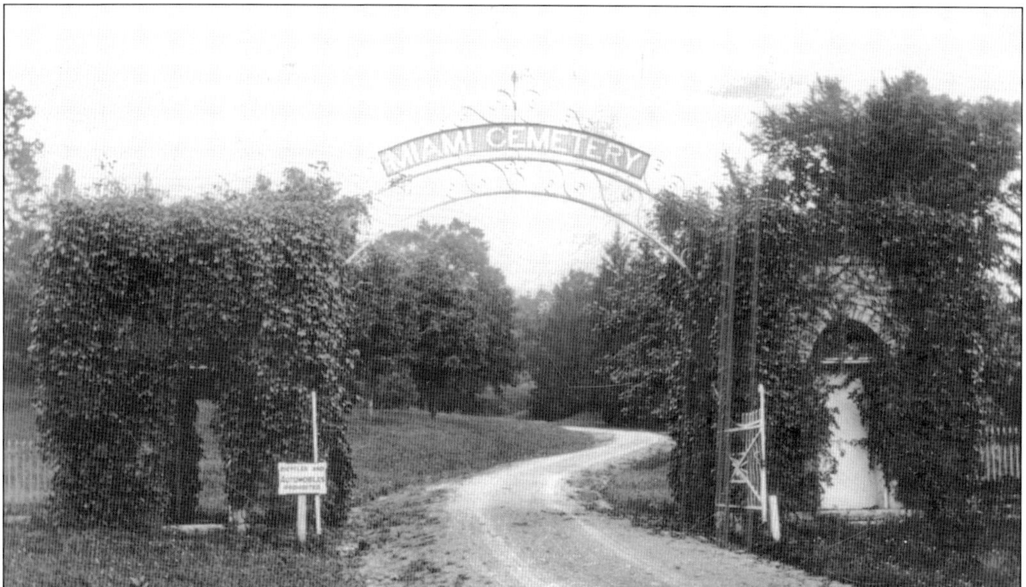

The sign and gates to Miami Cemetery at Corwin, Ohio, were new when this photograph was taken in 1907. Established in 1867 around a private cemetery on the farm of Gaines Goode, the grounds were landscaped by Leo Weltz, gardener to the emperor of Germany and the czar of Russia. Coates Kinney, Ohio's noted poet, is buried here as well as relatives of George Washington, Betsy Ross, Benjamin Scott (Yankee Doodle), Thomas Jefferson, Tennessee Williams, Daniel Boone, John B. Stetson, Gov. Simon Bradstreet, Ezra Cornell, Abraham Lincoln, and Annie Oakley. (Courtesy of Mary Cook Public Library.)

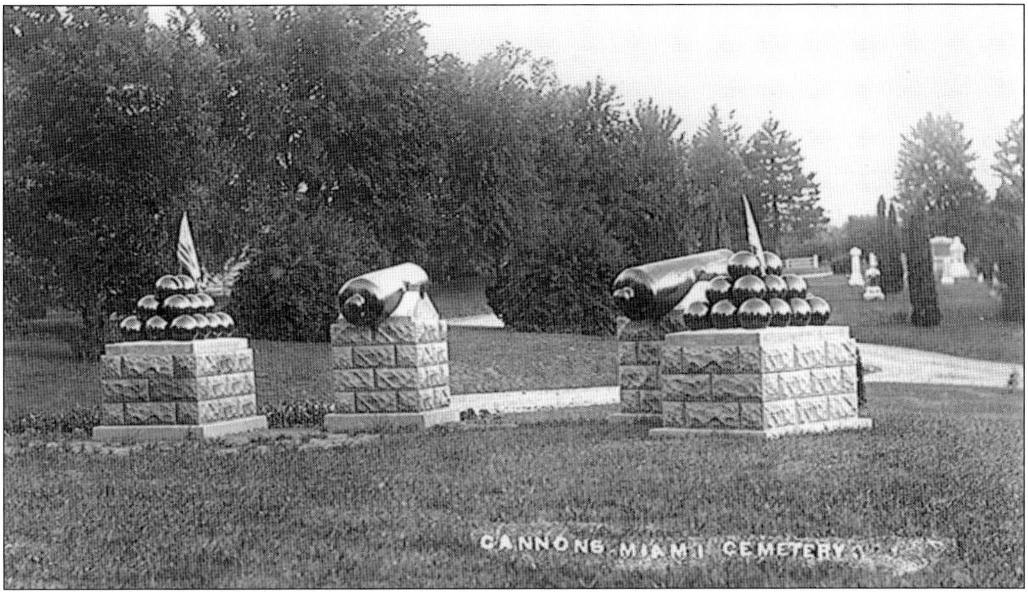

Civil War cannons and cannonballs were once the focal point of Miami Cemetery's Soldiers' Monument. The cannons and cannonballs, shown in 1907, were scrapped during World War II. Capt. William R. Hoel, who was an Ohio and Mississippi riverboat hero during the Civil War, gave the Civil War relics. Captain Hoel was one of the founders of St. Mary's Episcopal Church in Waynesville. He resided on Kildere Farm on Clarksville Road near Corwin. (Courtesy of Mary L. Cook Public Library.)

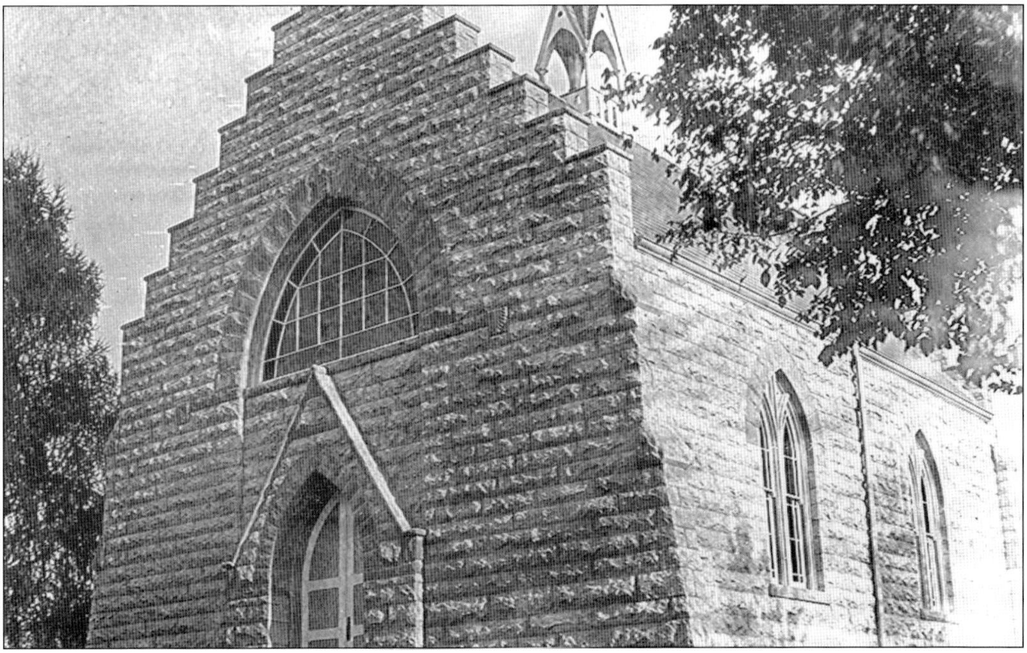

The funeral chapel of Miami Cemetery at Corwin is shown in this 1906 photograph. The building was constructed with a bell tower in 1894. The belfry was removed some time before 1930. The limestone construction features Egyptian-type architectural aspects. It has been restored and given additional usage for weddings and church services. (Courtesy of Mary L. Cook Public Library.)

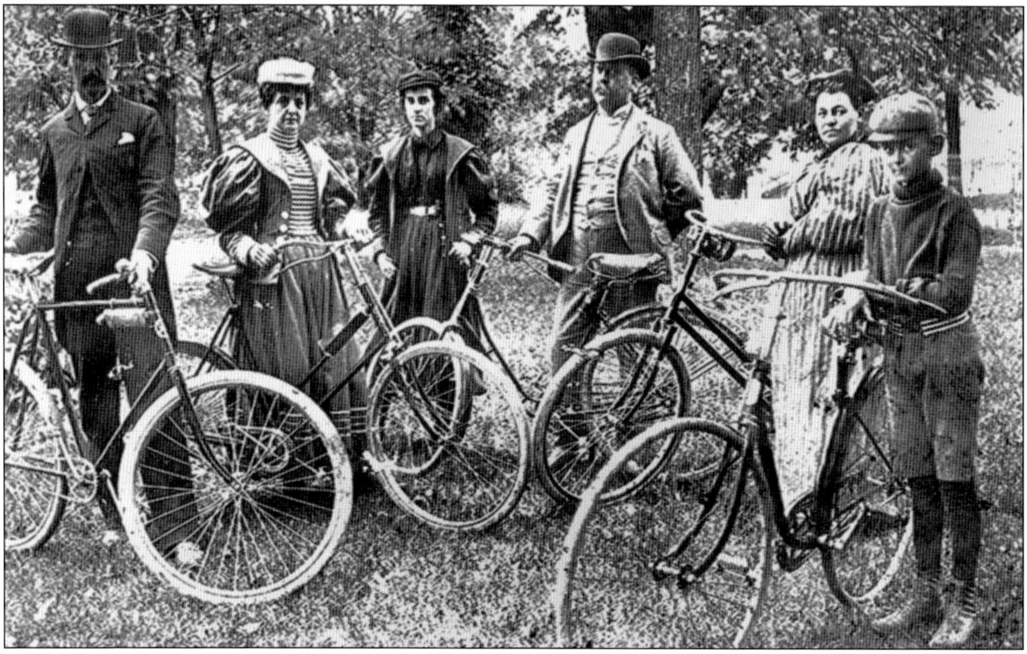

Bicycling was a fashionable pastime in Edwardian-era Corwin and Waynesville, Ohio. The group in this 1905 photograph prepares for an afternoon outing dressed in style. In 1905, it was against the law in Waynesville to ride a bicycle faster than five miles per hour down Main Street. The offense was punished with a $1 fine. (Courtesy of Mary L. Cook Public Library.)

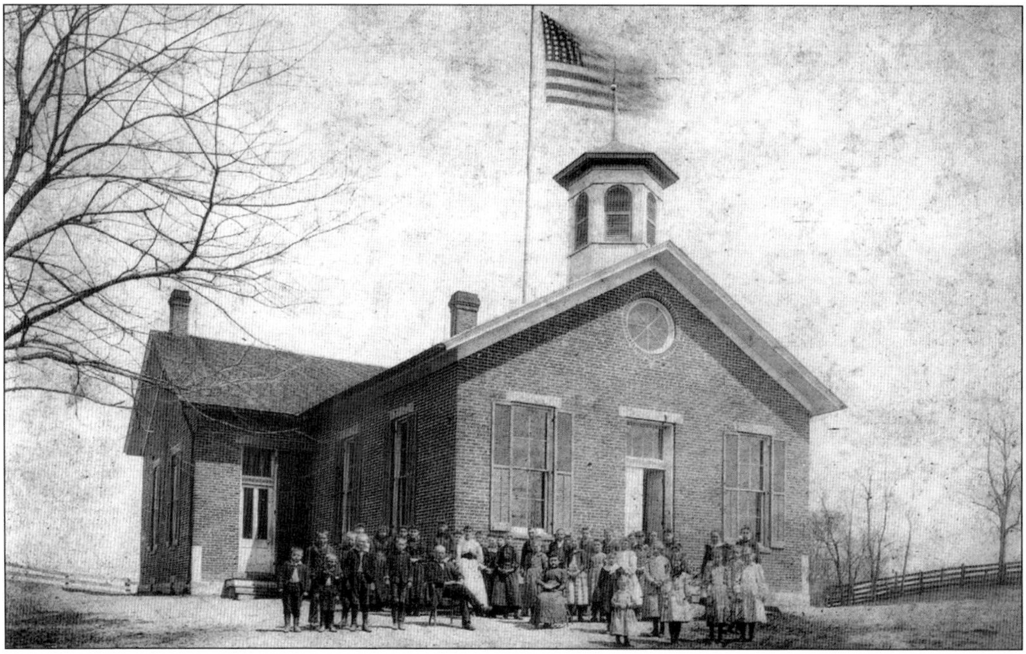

Corwin's two-room school was built in 1870 at the top of the hill on old State Highway 73 across from the Miami Cemetery. This photograph was taken in 1889. The entire school, consisting of both elementary and high school students and teachers, is shown in front of the building. The American flag has 40 stars. (Courtesy of Mary L. Cook Public Library.)

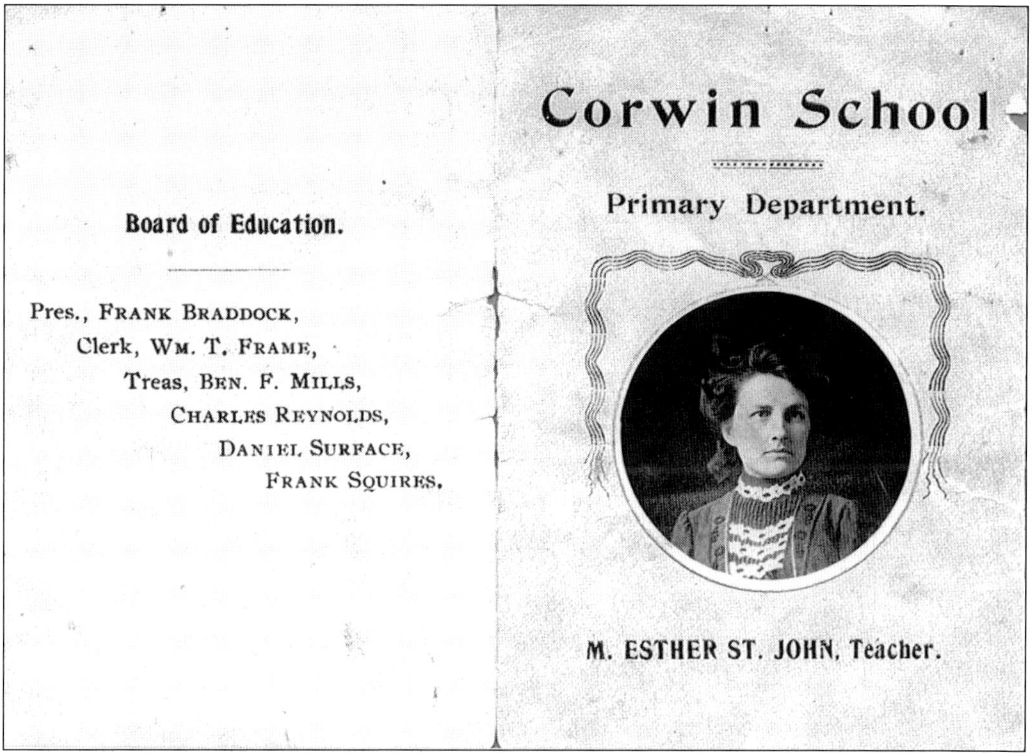

Board of Education.

Pres., Frank Braddock,
Clerk, Wm. T. Frame,
Treas, Ben. F. Mills,
Charles Reynolds,
Daniel Surface,
Frank Squires.

Corwin School

Primary Department.

M. ESTHER ST. JOHN, Teacher.

This photograph is of an Corwin School Primary Department pamphlet, printed in 1902. The Corwin School closed in 1917 and merged with Wayne Local School in Waynesville. (Courtesy of Mary L. Cook Public Library.)

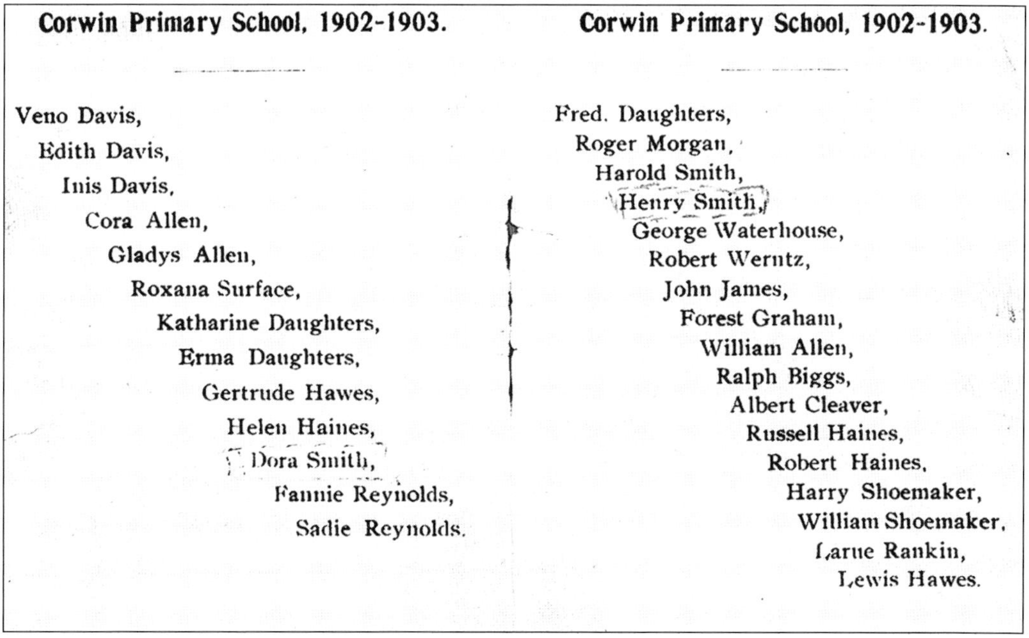

Corwin Primary School, 1902-1903.

Veno Davis,
Edith Davis,
Inis Davis,
Cora Allen,
Gladys Allen,
Roxana Surface,
Katharine Daughters,
Erma Daughters,
Gertrude Hawes,
Helen Haines,
Dora Smith,
Fannie Reynolds,
Sadie Reynolds.

Corwin Primary School, 1902-1903.

Fred. Daughters,
Roger Morgan,
Harold Smith,
Henry Smith,
George Waterhouse,
Robert Werntz,
John James,
Forest Graham,
William Allen,
Ralph Biggs,
Albert Cleaver,
Russell Haines,
Robert Haines,
Harry Shoemaker,
William Shoemaker,
Larue Rankin,
Lewis Hawes.

The 1902–1903 Corwin Primary School was made up of just 30 students of various grade levels. Many familiar names are found on this program. (Courtesy of Mary L. Cook Public Library.)

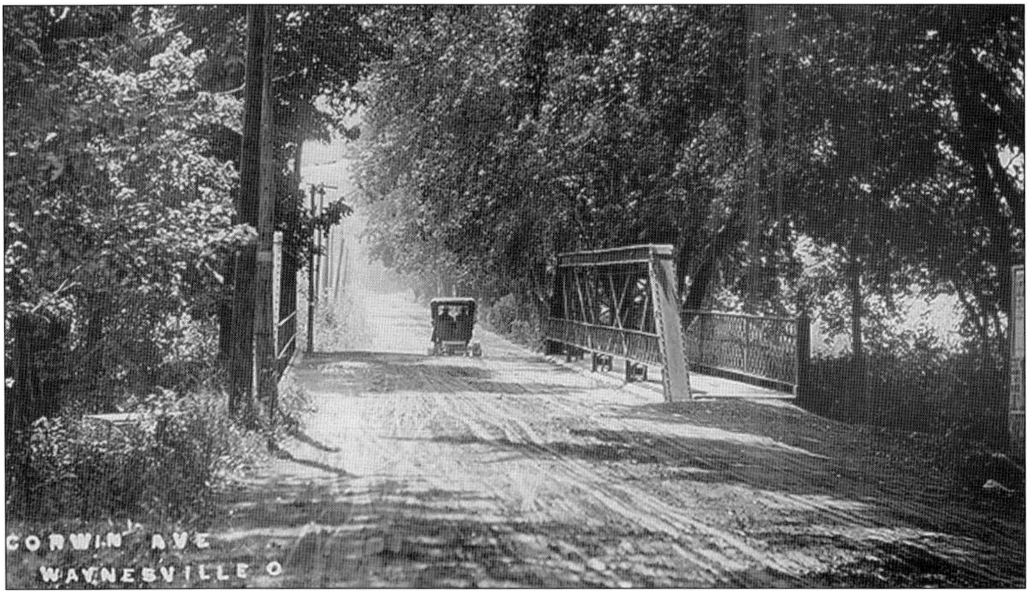

Corwin Avenue is shown in this photograph, taken in 1912 looking east to Corwin from Waynesville. The bridge over the west branch of the Little Miami River is shown in the center. From the early 1900s, the "Avenue" was favored for afternoon strolls between the villages and especially for parades to Miami Cemetery at Corwin on Decoration Day. (Courtesy of Mary L. Cook Public Library.)

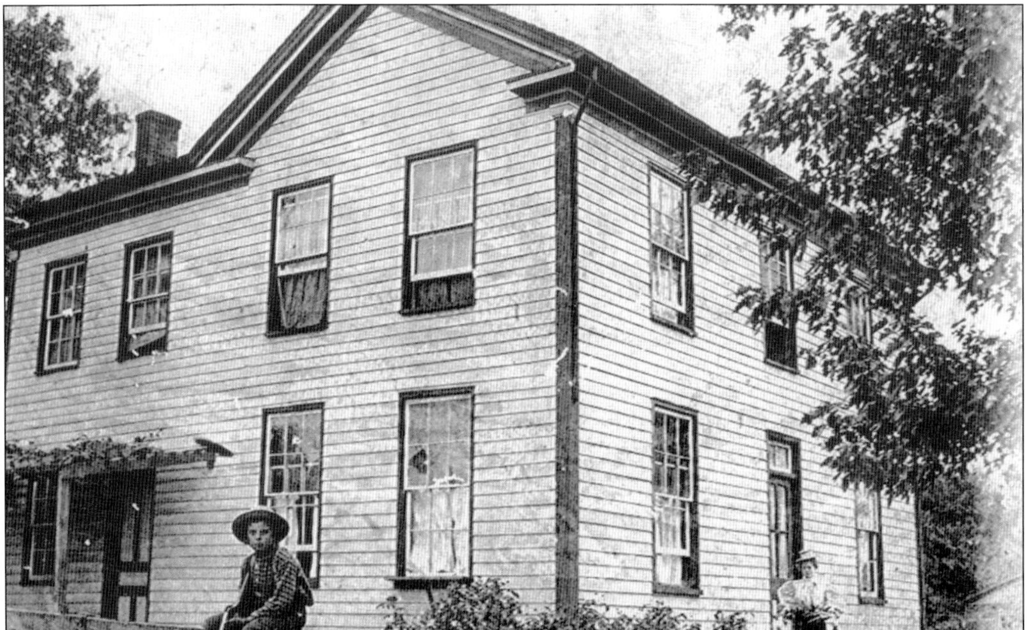

The Benjamin Mills residence at Corwin was built on North Main Street in 1871. Two unidentified Corwin residents are shown in this photograph, taken in 1905. The woman at the right is standing behind a bicycle; riding was a popular pastime. In nearby Waynesville, a person could be fined $1 for riding a bicycle down Main Street faster than five miles per hour. (Courtesy of Mary L. Cook Public Library.)

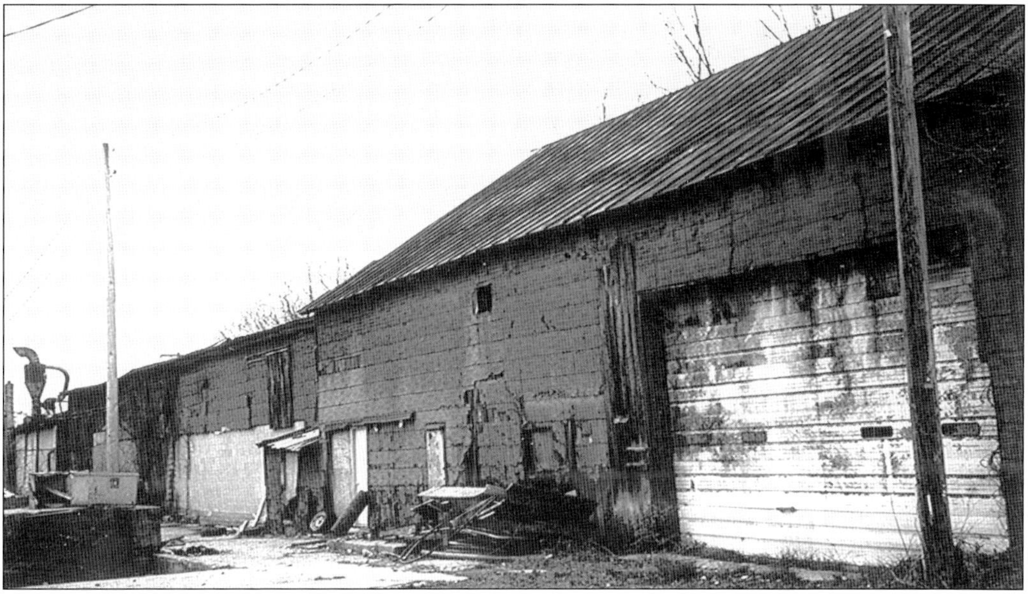

The ruins of the Waynesville Canning Company at Corwin are shown in this photograph, taken in 2002. The company was organized in 1904 primarily for the canning of sweet corn. The factory also canned tomatoes and later produced Churned Gold Margarine the winter. In 1905, when the building was new, the boiler operator fell asleep, and the steam pressure blew through the roof and high into the sky, with corn raining all over Corwin. The plant concluded operation in the early 1970s, when it was canning dog food. (Courtesy of Mary L. Cook Public Library.)

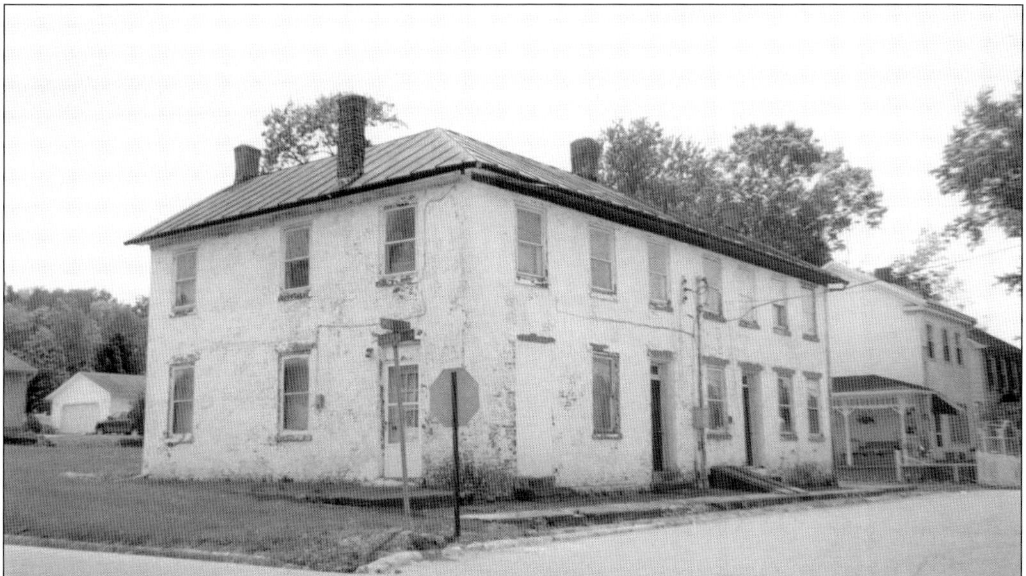

Israel Woodruff constructed the Woodruff House Hotel in Corwin in 1845 on the southeast corner of Main Street and Corwin Avenue. The brick inn accommodated both stagecoach and railroad passengers. The hotel was gutted by fire in November 1914. The first floor was rebuilt as it originally looked, but the second floor was made into fewer rooms. The hotel, which in the 1860s and 1870s accommodated vacationing Cincinnati opera stars, originally had 13 rooms. (Author's.)

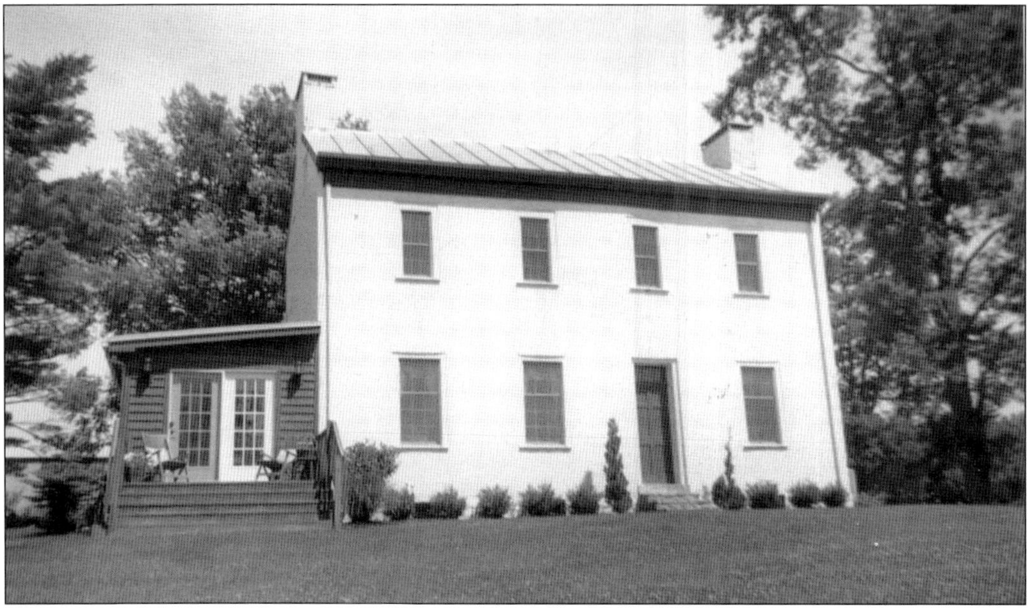

The Charles Hartshorn residence, on Corwin Road, is seen in this 2012 photograph. It was built in 1820 by Elizabeth Smith, widow of the founder of Waynesville Methodist Church, Rev. James Smith. The church was founded in 1807 in a log building on the same property. Just a few yards east of the house on the hillside was an early cemetery of the Smith family. The graves were all moved to Miami Cemetery at Corwin in 1867. (Author's.)

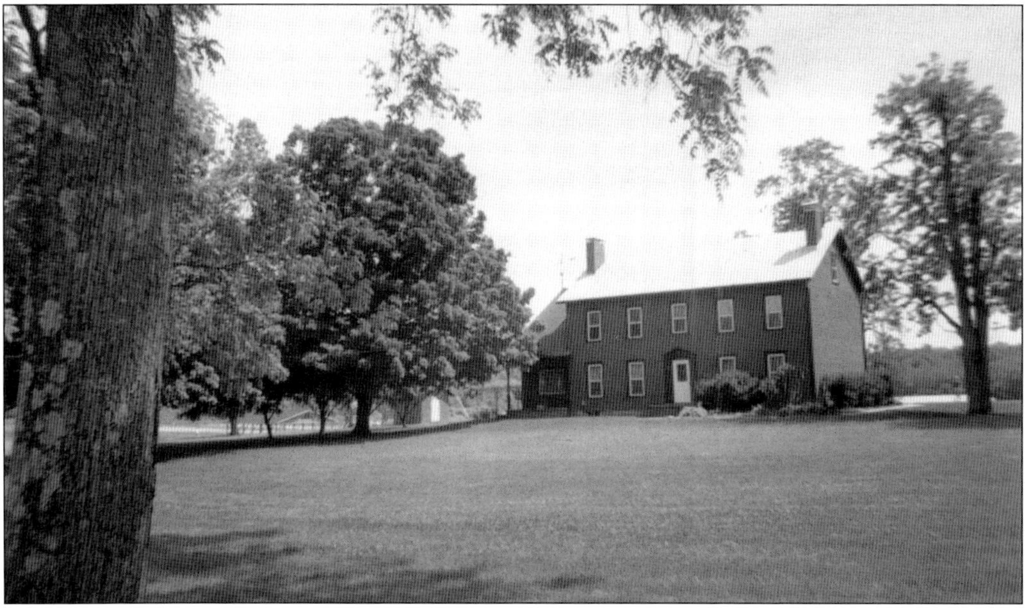

The Warren County Parks District has preserved the Hisey homestead, located at the intersection of Middletown and Corwin Roads near Corwin. The house, which shows evidence of being constructed in two parts, dates from about 1840. Corwin's first postmaster, Jacob R. Hisey, was born in the house in 1850. Historical records hint that the house was once a station on the Underground Railroad. John Curtis Hisey, Jacob's son, was a mail deliveryman for many years in Wayne Township. This photograph of the Hisey farmhouse was taken in 2012. (Author's.)

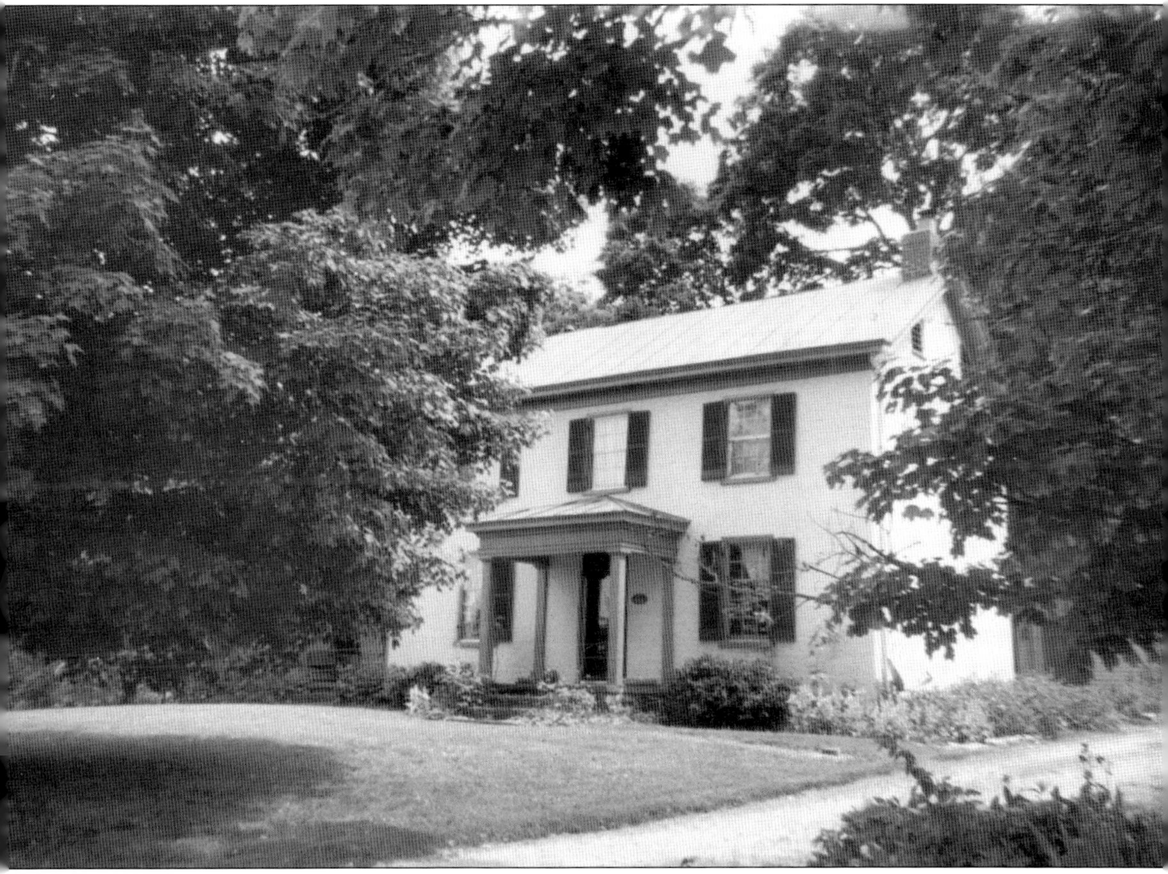

The current owner, Howard Doster, a direct descendant of the builder, took this photograph of the Moses McKay house, on New Burlington Road near Corwin, in 2012 showing preservation improvements. McKay built the house in 1818 with the help of 22 freed slaves after the family moved to the site from Virginia. A two-story addition was made to the house by McKay's son Jonas T. McKay about 1830. The house was a station on the Underground Railroad. The hiding place was a secret room under kitchen fireplace hearth. (Author's.)

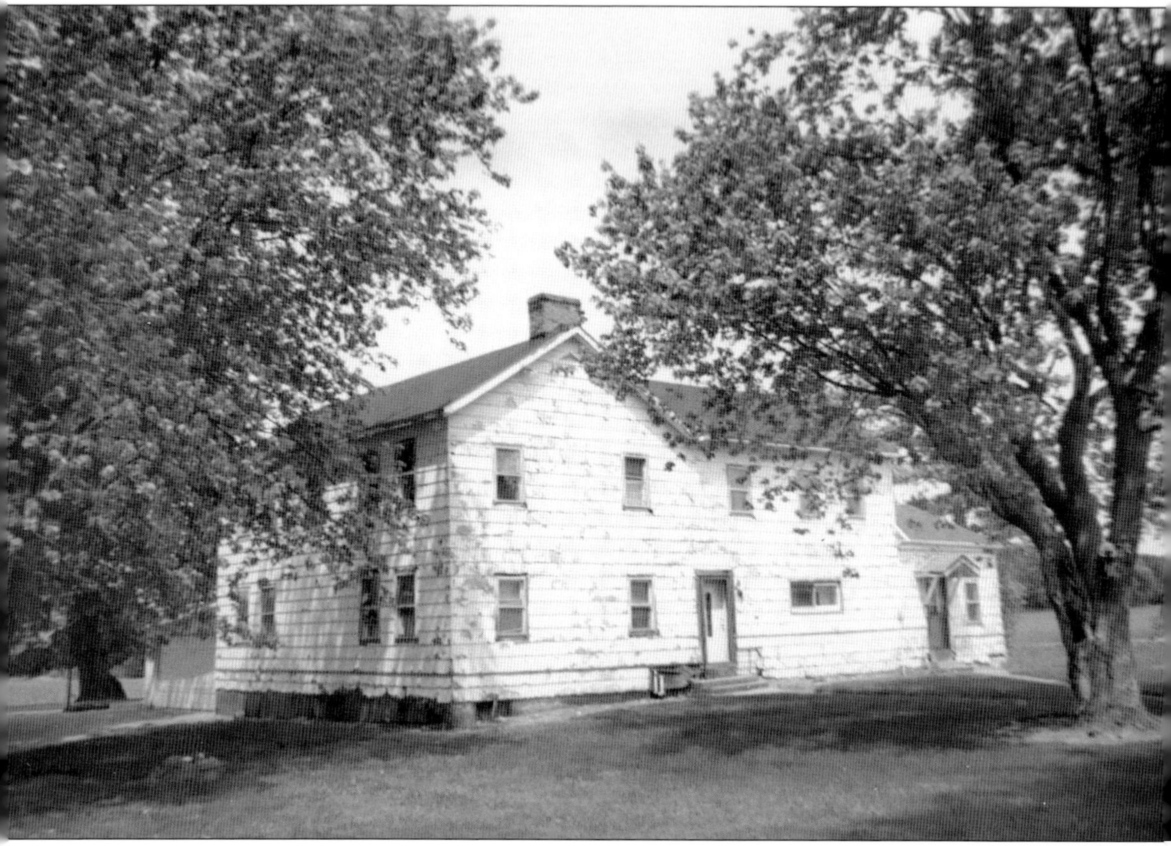

One of the earliest Quaker houses in Wayne Township is the Maria Compton farmhouse on historic Canby Town Road off New Burlington Road near Corwin. This photograph, taken in 2012, shows the house's stages of construction. When a new door was installed near the center of the east side, workers cut through log construction. Part of the farmhouse is a two-room log house built by the ancestors of Maria Compton in 1804. (Author's.)

Seven

Mount Holly and Lytle

Jacob Pearson settled Mount Holly, Ohio, in 1833. As early as 1816, a handful of settlers had already built a log Methodist church and established a cemetery. The place at the southern fringe of what is now the village was Bethel Church. Mount Holly was named after the origin of its settlers, Mount Holly, New Jersey. In its prime, it bustled with activity, including the stagecoach, which carried Charles Dickens through the village in 1842. Its early businesses included gristmills and sawmills, distilleries, taverns, a general store, a blacksmith, and a pottery maker.

In Mount Holly in 1860 at any of the distilleries, a customer could buy a gallon of whiskey for 10¢ if he brought his own jug.

There were settlers near Lytle before it was officially settled. Parts of what is now the Lytle-Ferry Road were built and in use by 1804. Well established by 1836, the road was called the Pinckney and Raysville Road. The route brought early settlers, including the Burnet family in 1804 and Alexander Ray, its initial namesake, by 1806. The Surface family pioneered into the vicinity in 1796.

The village changed names three times before Lytle stuck. Alexander Ray was considered the founder, and the town was called Raysville. The name continued through the platting by Mahlon Mills in 1855. For a short time starting in 1866, it was humorously nicknamed "Minktown" after a large mink roundup under a village bridge. Local citizens loafing at the village's general store one day decided to give the town a lasting name that would set it apart. Plucking a box of Lytle brand shoes from a shelf, Charles Surface declared a new name, Lytle. Lytle apparently got its official name when its post office was opened on June 5, 1882. The *Miami Gazette* newspaper of Waynesville reported the event and claimed that the village was named for Civil War hero Gen. William H. Lytle of Cincinnati. During its heyday, Lytle was known for making pottery and the manufacturing of drainage tile as well as tavern keeping and tobacco farming. It had the largest tobacco warehouse in Warren County in 1908. Grain and feed milling also became business staples.

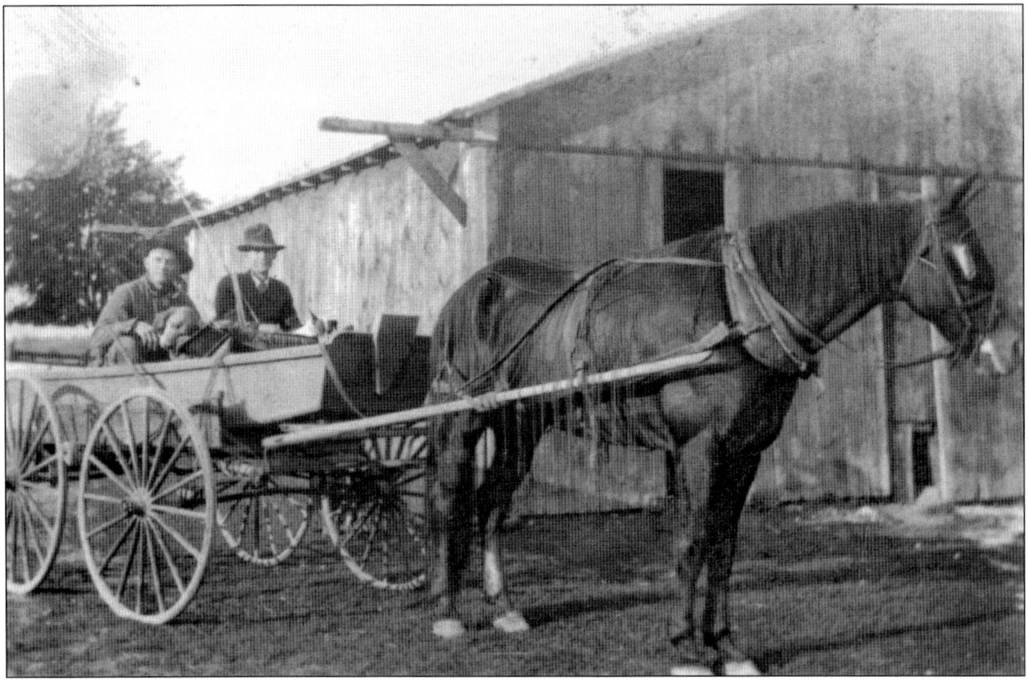

The Surface and Elwood families were among Lytle's most prosperous farmers. In this 1898 photograph, Warren Surface, left, and William Elwood are shown in front of the implement shed on the Surface farm. (Courtesy of Wilma Surface Coyan.)

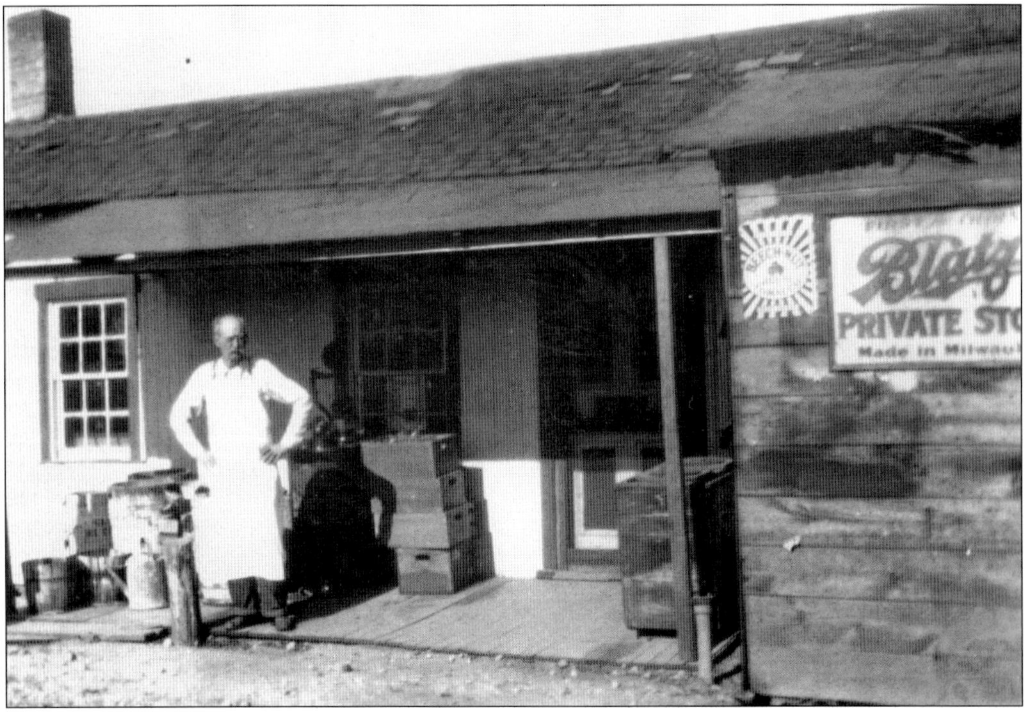

This 1928 photograph shows Bill Grimes in front of his store, located on the Lytle-Waynesville Road. The Robert Campbell residence is now on the site. (Courtesy of Wilma Surface Coyan.)

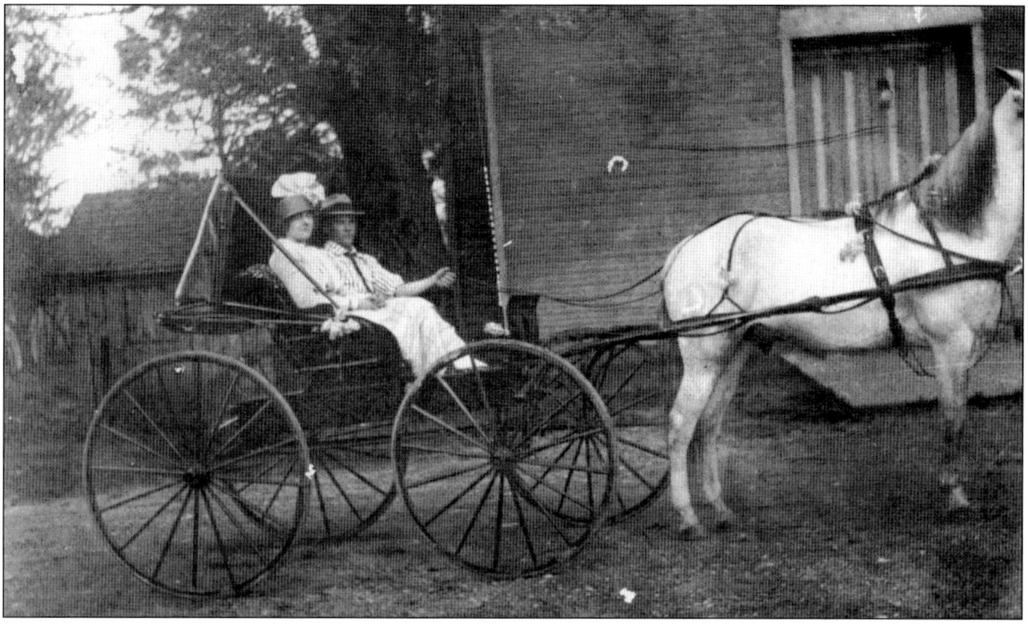

Afternoon buggy rides were still popular in rural villages like Lytle, Ohio, as late as the 1920s. This c. 1920 photograph shows Eva Mae Penewit and Bill Duke in front of the Lytle Methodist Church. (Courtesy of Wilma Surface Coyan.)

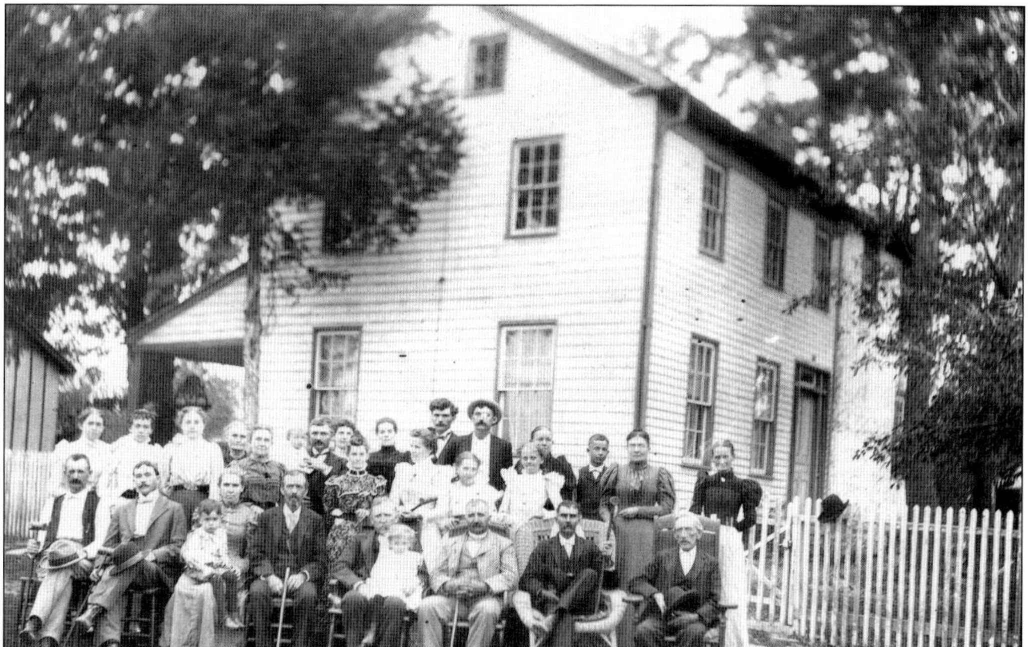

The Surface family settled in Wayne Township in 1796. Members of the Eyer-Surface families are shown in this c. 1890 photograph during a croquet party at the Surface farm. The brick portion at the back of the house was built by Surface pioneers in 1805. (Courtesy of Wilma Surface Coyan.)

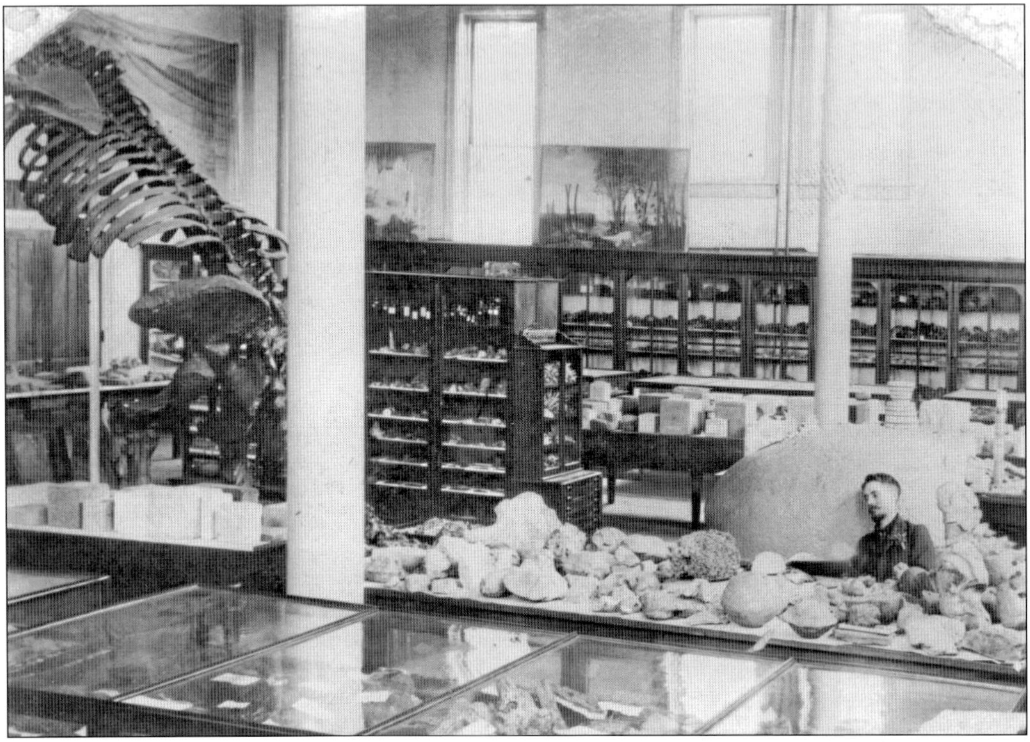

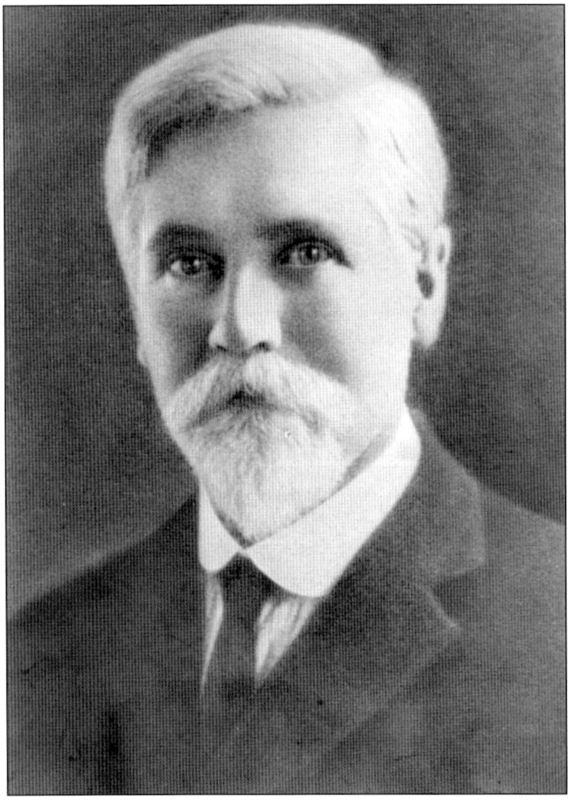

Harvey Adam Surface is shown in this photograph taken in the spring of 1892 at the Ohio State University Geological Museum. Harvey was the son of Daniel and Maria Surface of Lytle, Ohio. He was once director of the US Fish and Game Commission. Harvey was also a member of the Pennsylvania House of Representatives and taught at Cornell and Stanford Universities. (Courtesy of Wilma Surface Coyan.)

Harvey Adam Surface, whose ancestors settled near Lytle in 1796, is shown in this photograph in his later years. The photograph was taken around 1922. Harvey is one of many prestigious Americans with Wayne Township roots. (Courtesy of Wilma Surface Coyan.)

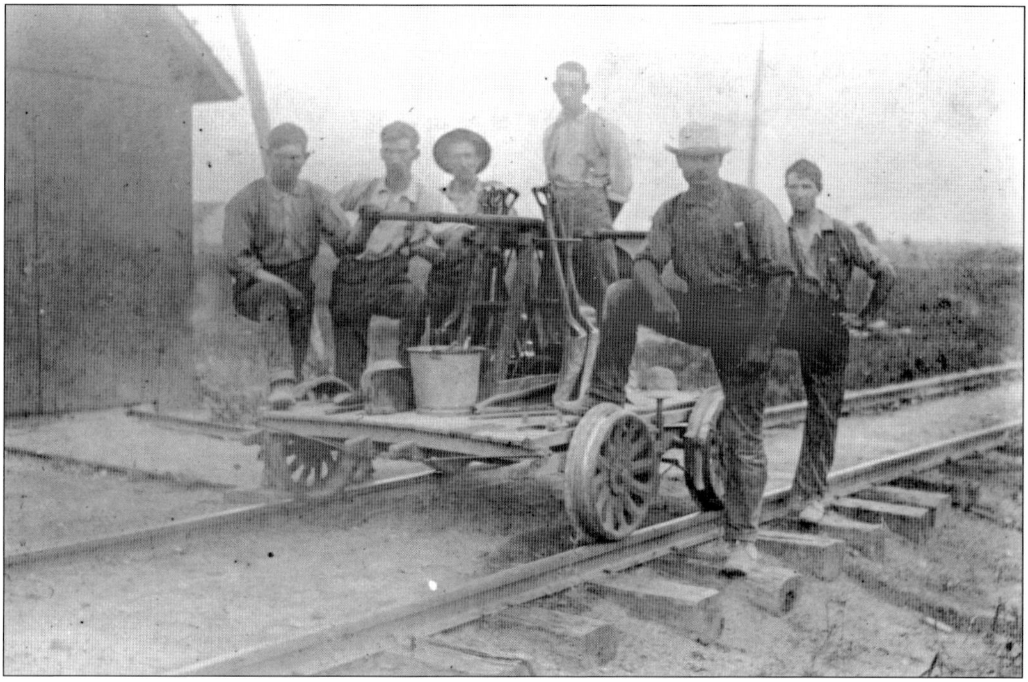

A crew of Dayton, Lebanon & Cincinnati Railroad (DL&C) workers is shown at Lytle in this photograph. Locals called the DL&C the "Damn Long Comin'." The railroad was an important passenger and freight link. (Courtesy of Wilma Surface Coyan.)

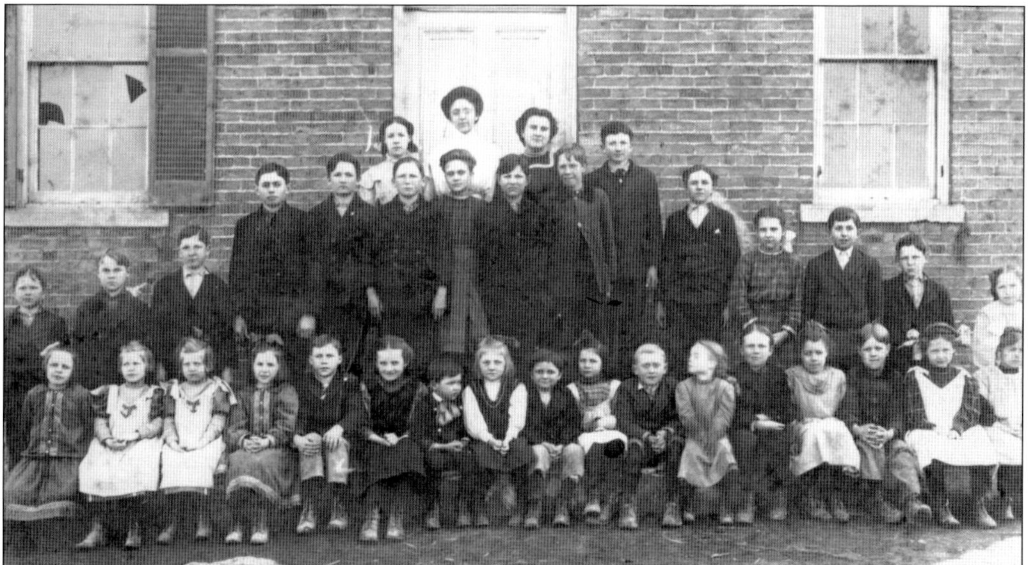

The teacher and students of Wayne School No. 9 are shown in this 1898 photograph. Located at the west edge of Lytle, only two can be identified. The sixth person from the left in the first row is Mildred Burnet. The fourth from the left in the second row is Oral Surface. The township schoolhouse was on Lytle Road. (Courtesy of Wilma Surface Coyan.)

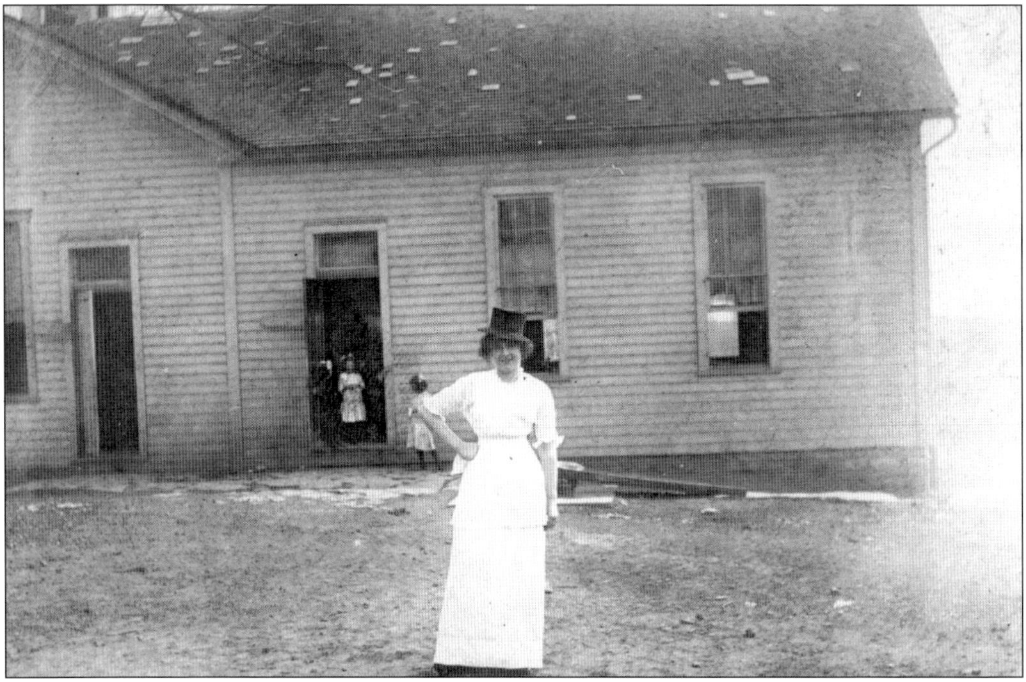

Ethel Graham is shown in this 1915 photograph in front of Lytle's two-room school on East Lytle Road. The school was consolidated with Waynesville schools in 1917, and the building was remodeled into a house, which still exists. (Courtesy of Wilma Surface Coyan.)

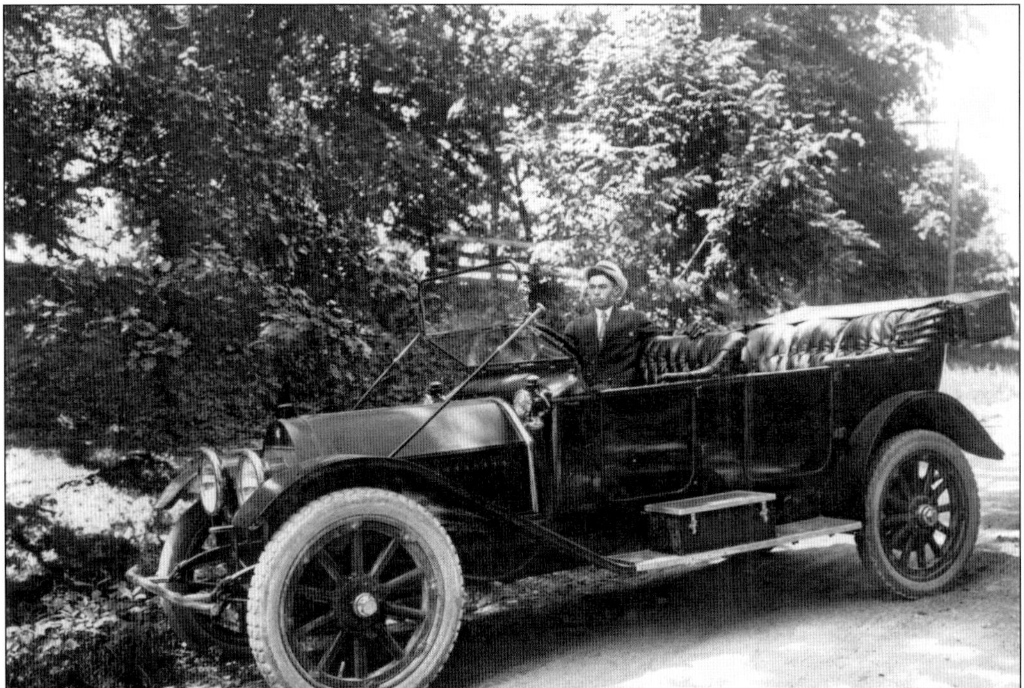

Oral Surface of Lytle is shown here in his new Allis-Chalmers touring car. The photograph was taken at Mason Springs near Waynesville, Ohio, in 1912. (Courtesy of Wilma Surface Coyan.)

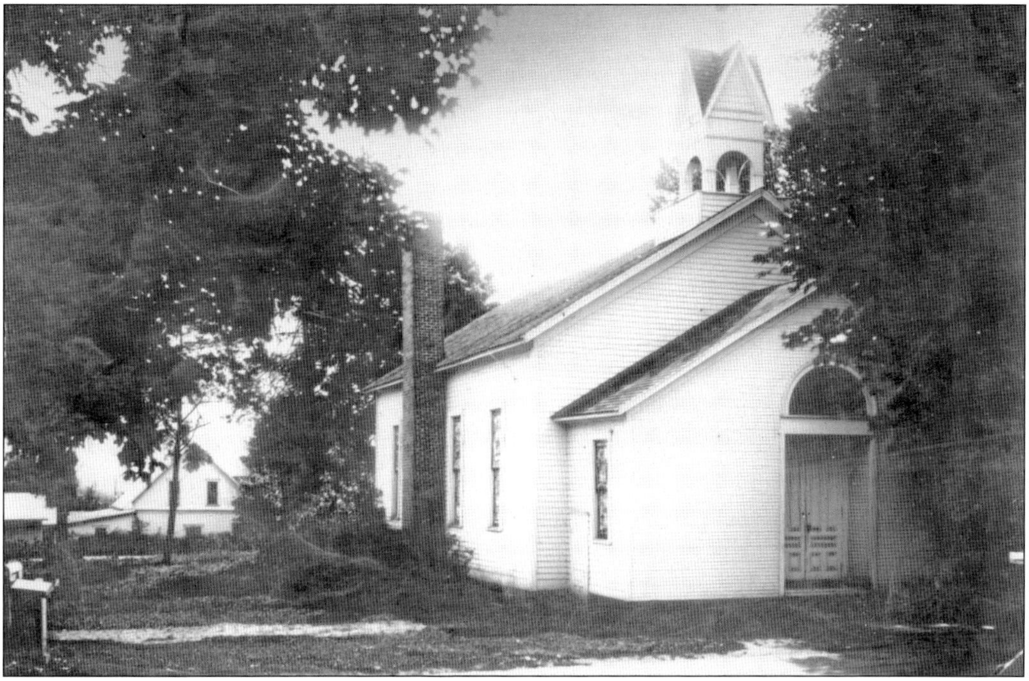

The Lytle Methodist Church was established early in the village's history. The church was constructed in 1852, replacing an earlier structure. This photograph was taken by moonlight by Horace Faulks in 1930. (Courtesy of Wilma Surface Coyan.)

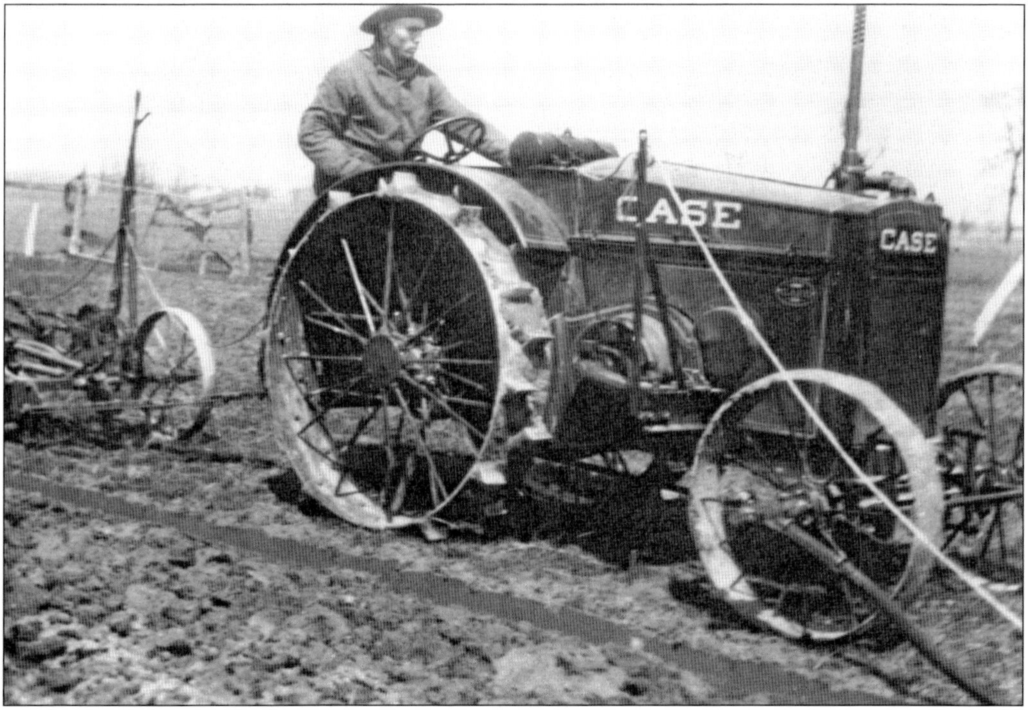

Lytle's rich soil attracted farmers as early as 1805. Oral Surface is shown in this 1930s photograph on his new Case tractor. (Courtesy of Wilma Surface Coyan.)

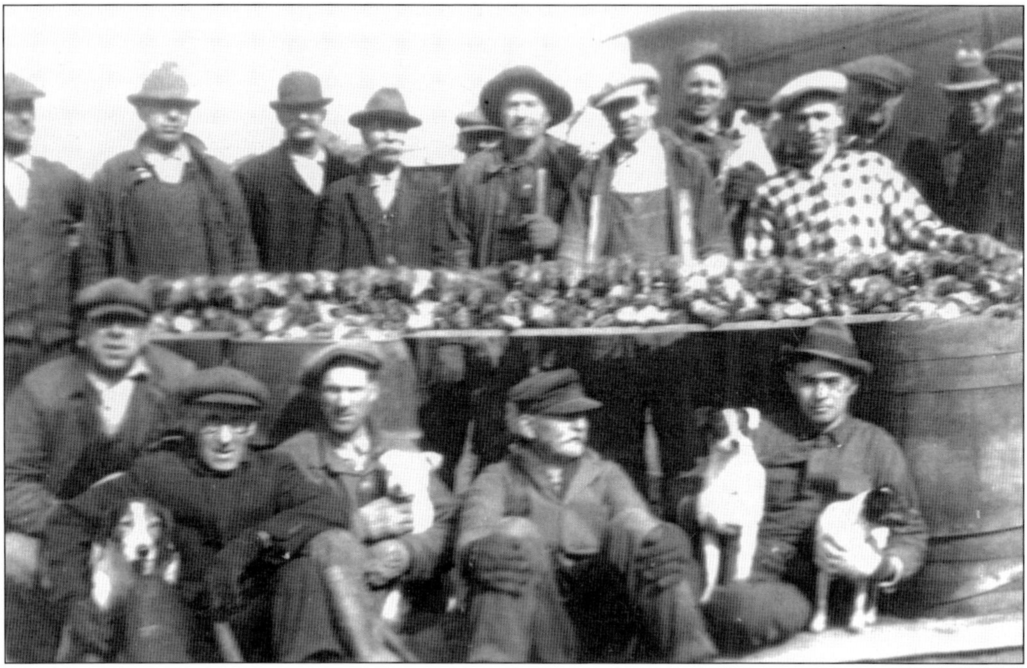

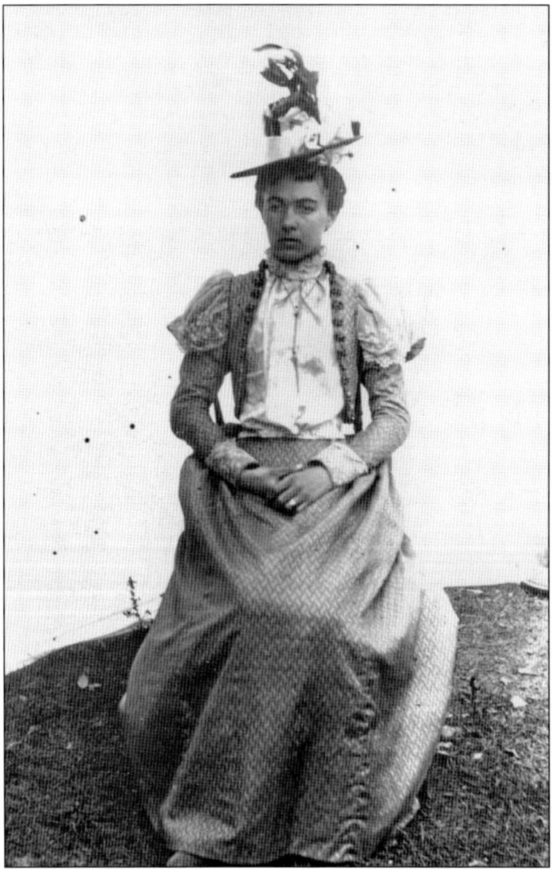

The Great Lytle Rat Hunt is shown in this photograph taken in 1922. Farms were rid of rats by hunting parties like this one, which cleared corncribs and barns. Pictured are, from left to right, (first row) Ben Hawk, three unidentified men, and Oral Surface with his dogs Buggs and Beans; (second row) unidentified, Herman Smith, Burt Stacey, Bill Burgdall, unidentified, Warren Surface, Frank Kerfiss, unidentified, Hick Wharton, Calvin Longacre, unidentified, Everett Early, and unidentified. In 1877, the Great Rat Hunt was initiated at Waynesville. So many rodents were shot at one country school at Waynesville that it was called Rat Tail School. (Courtesy of Wilma Surface Coyan.)

Claudia Ellen Eyer Surface poses for a fashionable photograph taken by a travelling photographer in 1899. The photograph was set up in front of a bed sheet thrown over a clothesline in the Surface farmyard in Lytle. (Courtesy of Wilma Surface Coyan.)

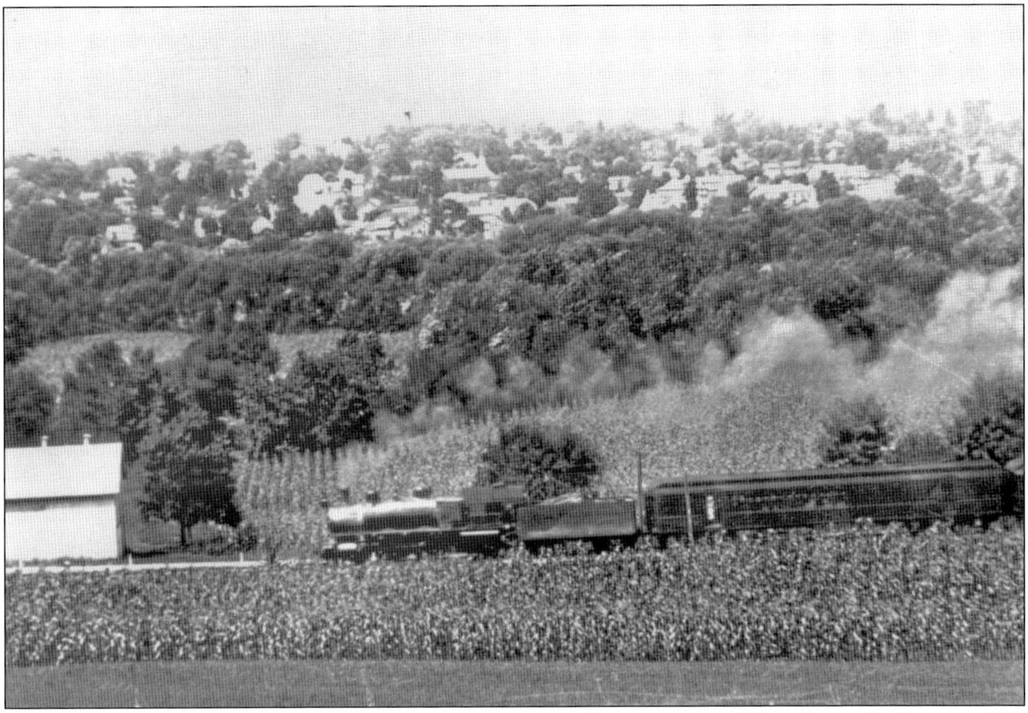

The Little Miami and Pennsylvania Railroads brought many notables through Corwin. US president Abraham Lincoln made a whistle-stop speech in Corwin in 1861. US president Theodore Roosevelt stopped and greeted the public in 1905. Waynesville's mayor failed to meet and greet former US president Ulysses S. Grant on October 12, 1879, and Grant refused to stop and rode straight through to Cincinnati. This photograph shows a train headed south around 1910. On the hillside in the background is Waynesville. (Courtesy of Mary L. Cook Public Library.)

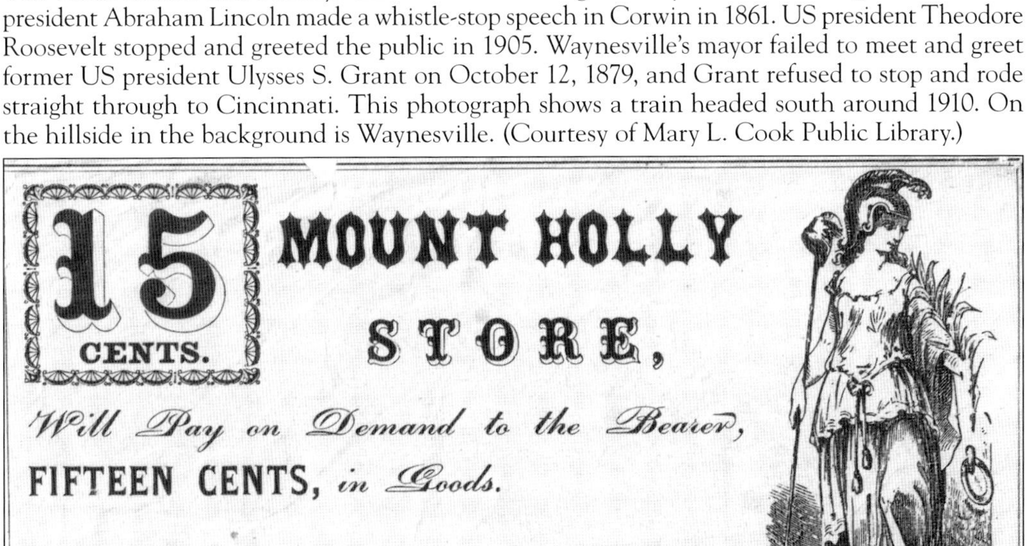

This 1860s coupon from the Mount Holly Store represented big savings for shoppers. The village, which was settled in 1833, had many flourishing businesses along its Main Street, which was once deemed the oldest main street in continuous use in the Little Miami River Valley. (Courtesy of Mary L. Cook Public Library.)

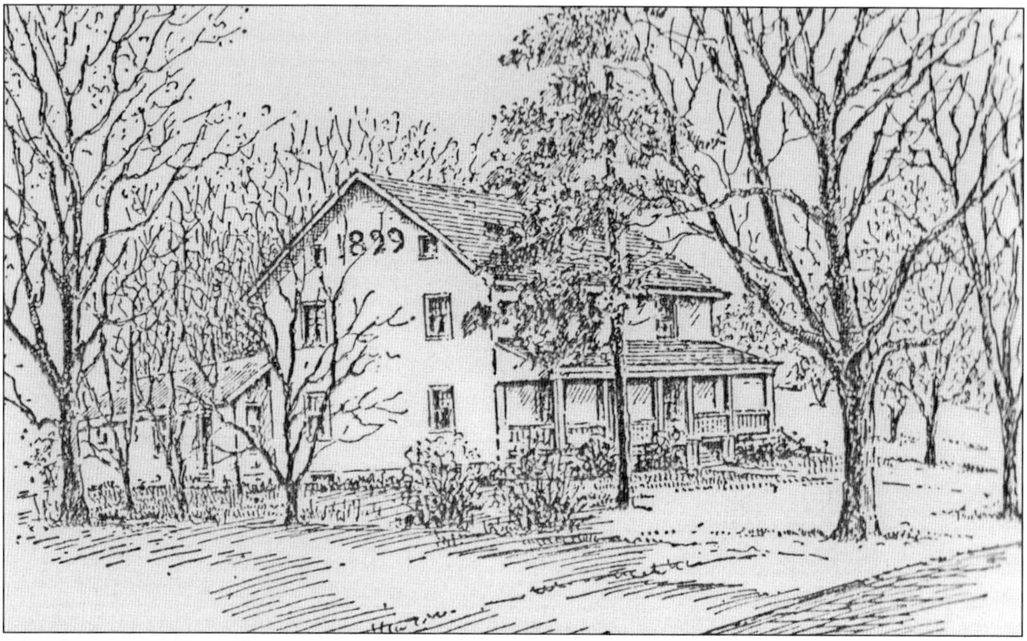

This drawing of the William Hartsock house, on Ohio Route 42 near Mount Holly, was done around 1960. George Sims built the brick house in 1829. Charles Dickens and party passed by this home on April 22, 1842, during his first American tour. (Courtesy of Mary L. Cook Public Library.)

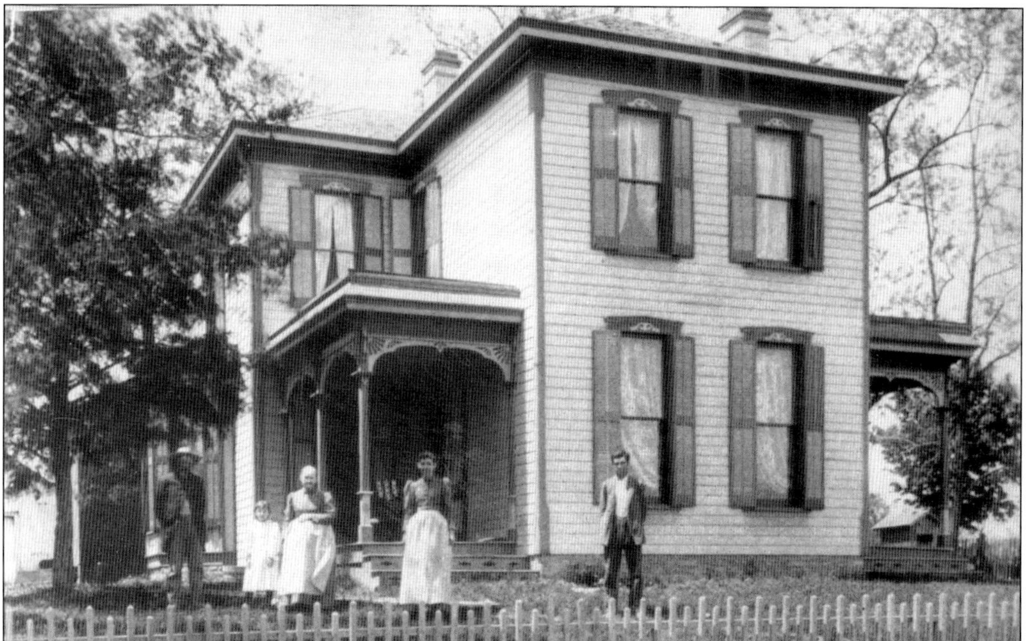

The Harry A. Cornell home, on State Route 42 at the north edge of Waynesville, is shown in this 1910 photograph. The Cornell family members, all cousins of Ezra Cornell, founder of Cornell University, are posed on the lawn. (Courtesy of Mary L. Cook Public Library.)

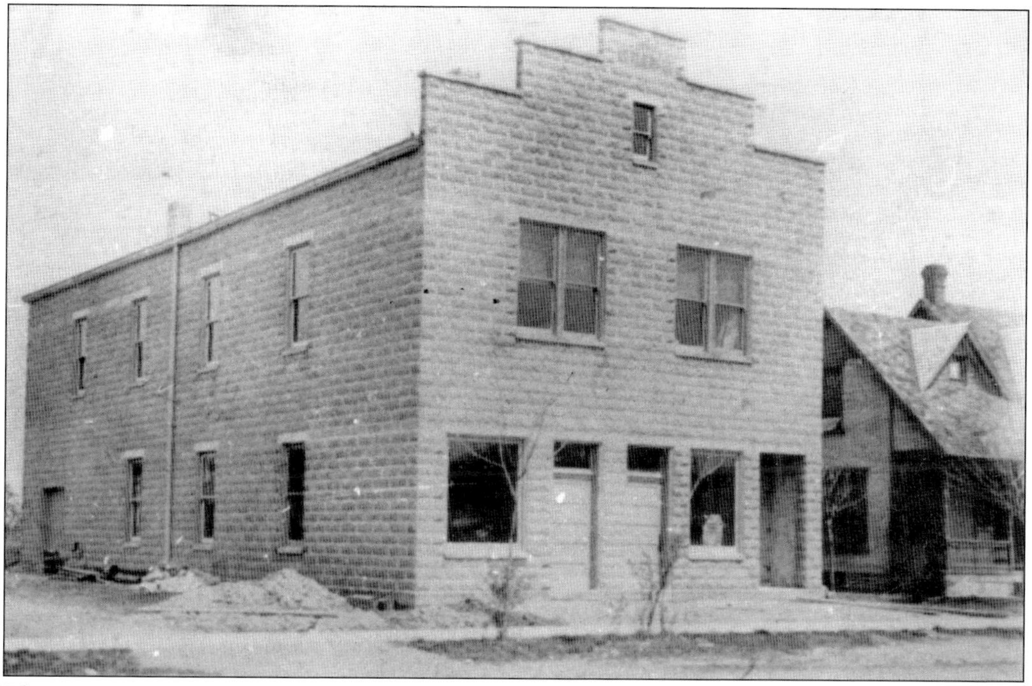

The construction of Lytle Hall had just been completed when this photograph was taken in 1907. Village businesses and offices were located on the first floor, and on the second floor, there was a village meeting room that was used for various community events, including theatrical programs. (Courtesy of WCHS Museum.)

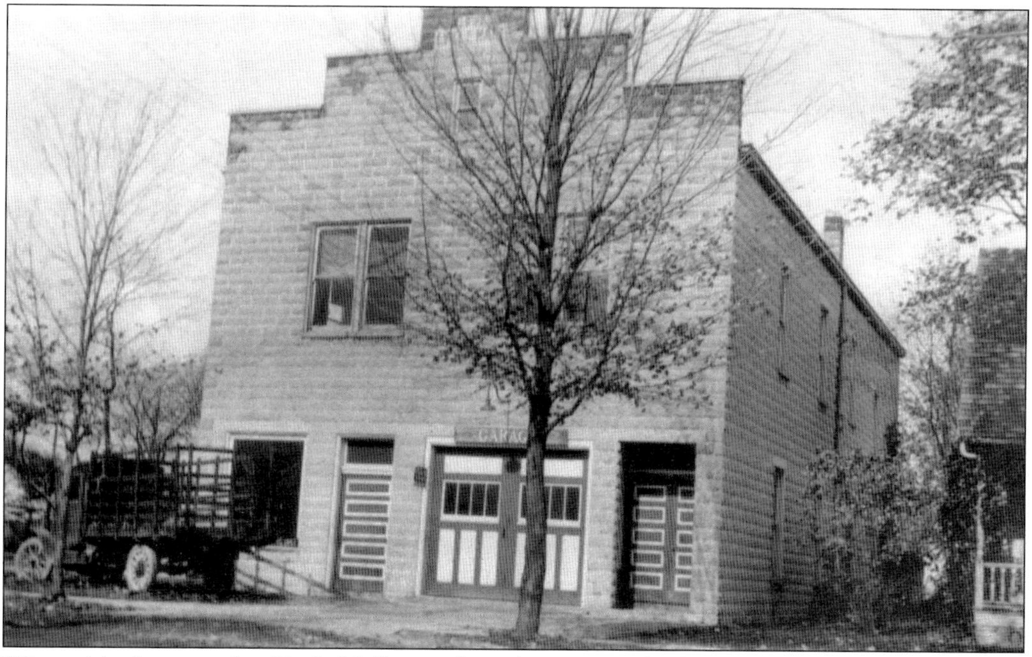

When this photograph of Lytle Hall was taken about 1930, the first floor had been converted for Routzahn's Garage. In its heyday, the village hall hosted many cultural and theatrical entertainments. (Courtesy of WCHS Museum.)

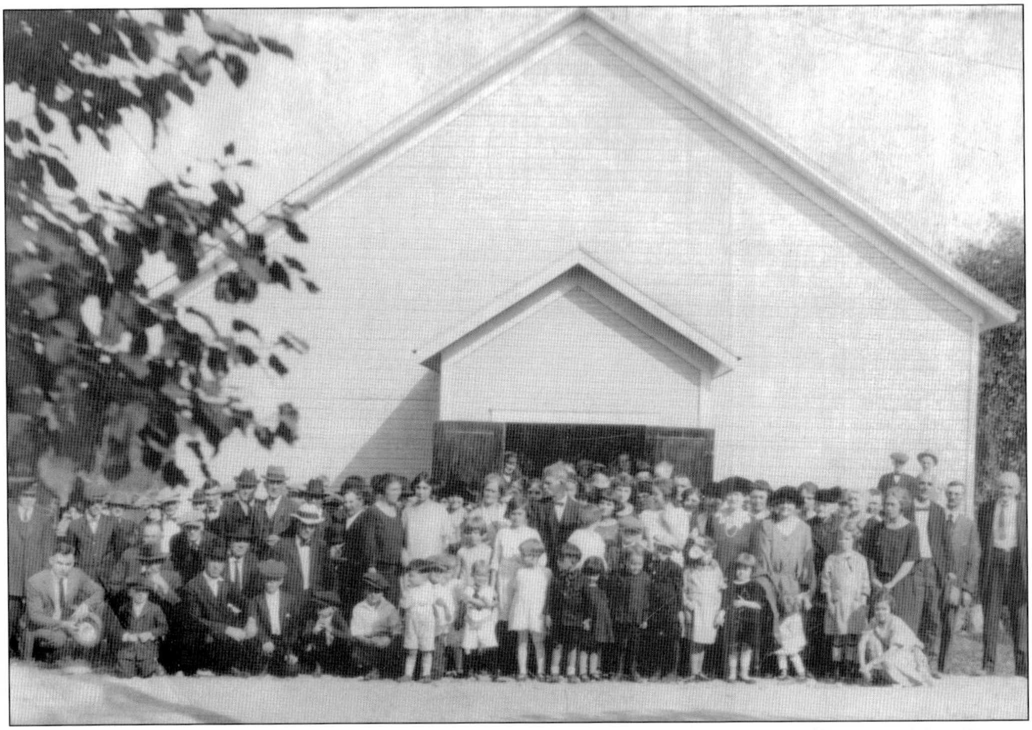

Mount Holly Methodist Church was for many years the heart of the tiny village on Ohio Route 42 four miles north of Waynesville. This photograph, taken in 1924, shows the congregation during a homecoming. The church was founded in 1816 in a log building at the southern edge of the village. (Courtesy of WCHS Museum.)

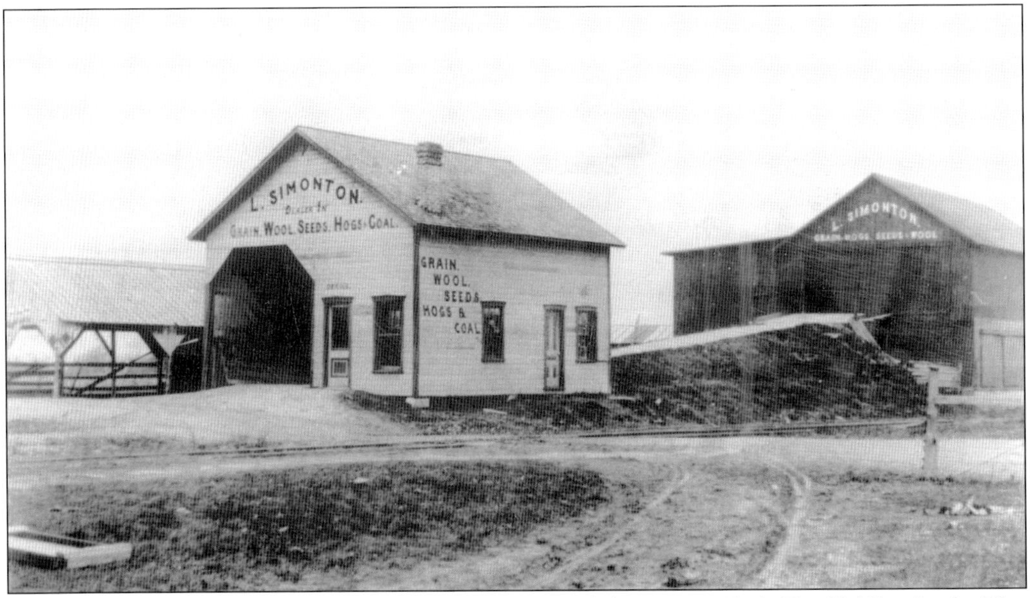

The L. Simonton grain dealership was the forerunner of the Everett Early Feed Mill at Lytle. The business, which sold grain, wool, seeds, hogs, and coal, was located beside the Dayton, Lebanon & Cincinnati Railroad. This photograph was taken around 1910. (Courtesy of WCHS Museum.)

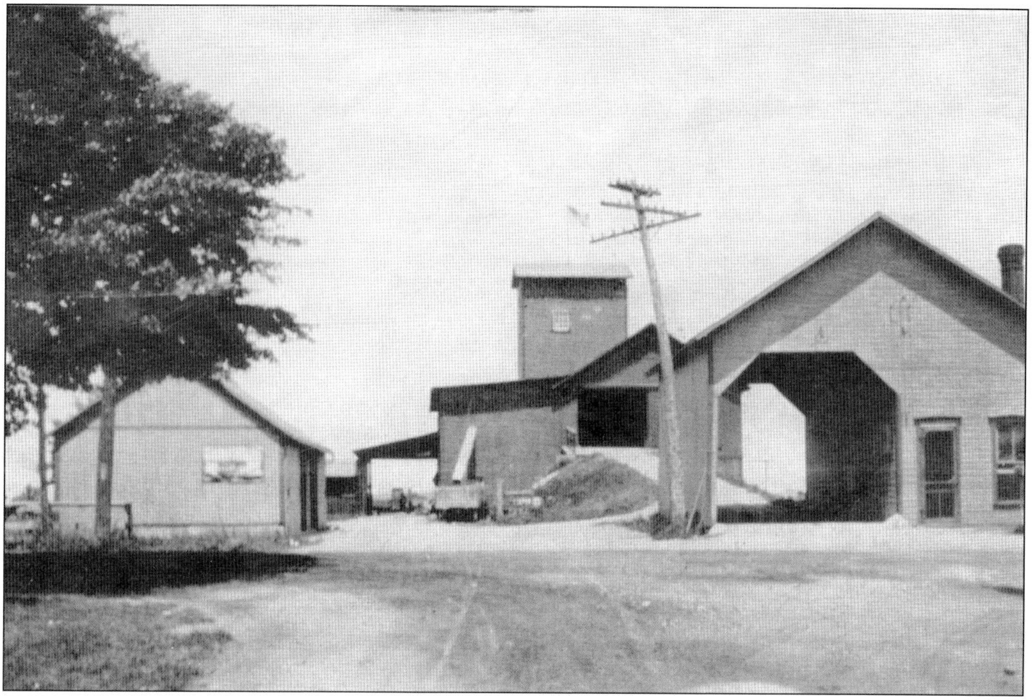

Everett Early, Inc., added a feed mill to the former Simonton property in Lytle. Early sold grain, feed, and coal and advertised "Most Of The Best For The Least." The Early mill was a Lytle landmark that still remains today. This photograph was taken about 1930. (Courtesy of WCHS Museum.)

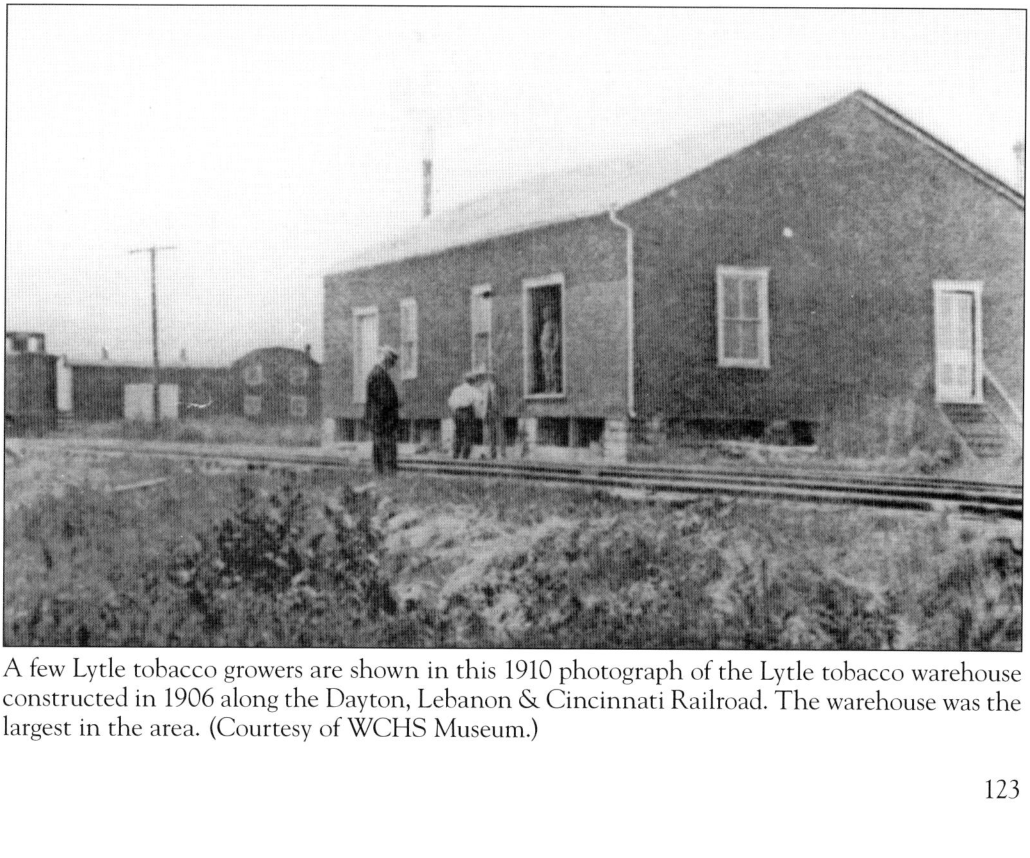

A few Lytle tobacco growers are shown in this 1910 photograph of the Lytle tobacco warehouse constructed in 1906 along the Dayton, Lebanon & Cincinnati Railroad. The warehouse was the largest in the area. (Courtesy of WCHS Museum.)

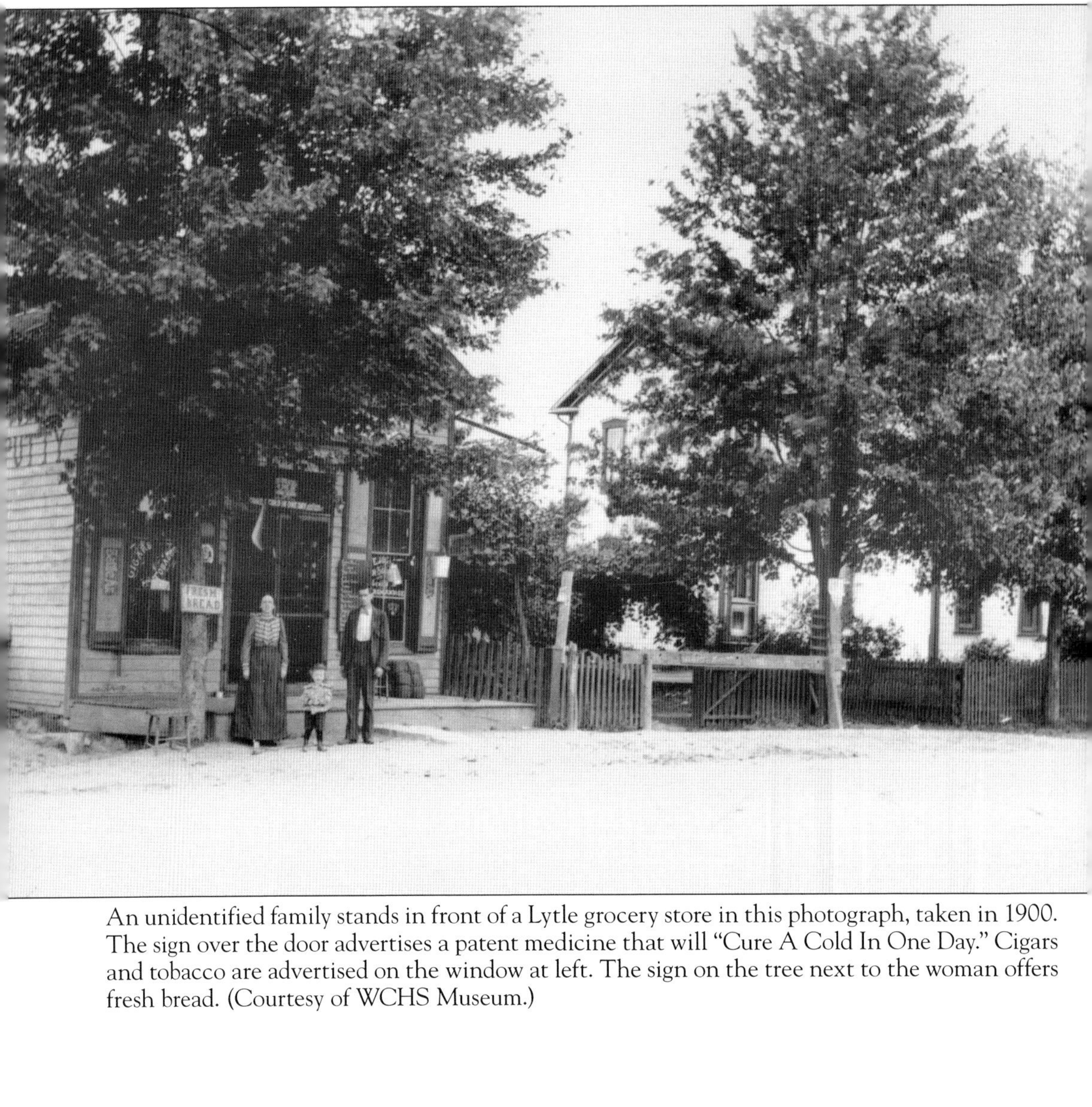

An unidentified family stands in front of a Lytle grocery store in this photograph, taken in 1900. The sign over the door advertises a patent medicine that will "Cure A Cold In One Day." Cigars and tobacco are advertised on the window at left. The sign on the tree next to the woman offers fresh bread. (Courtesy of WCHS Museum.)

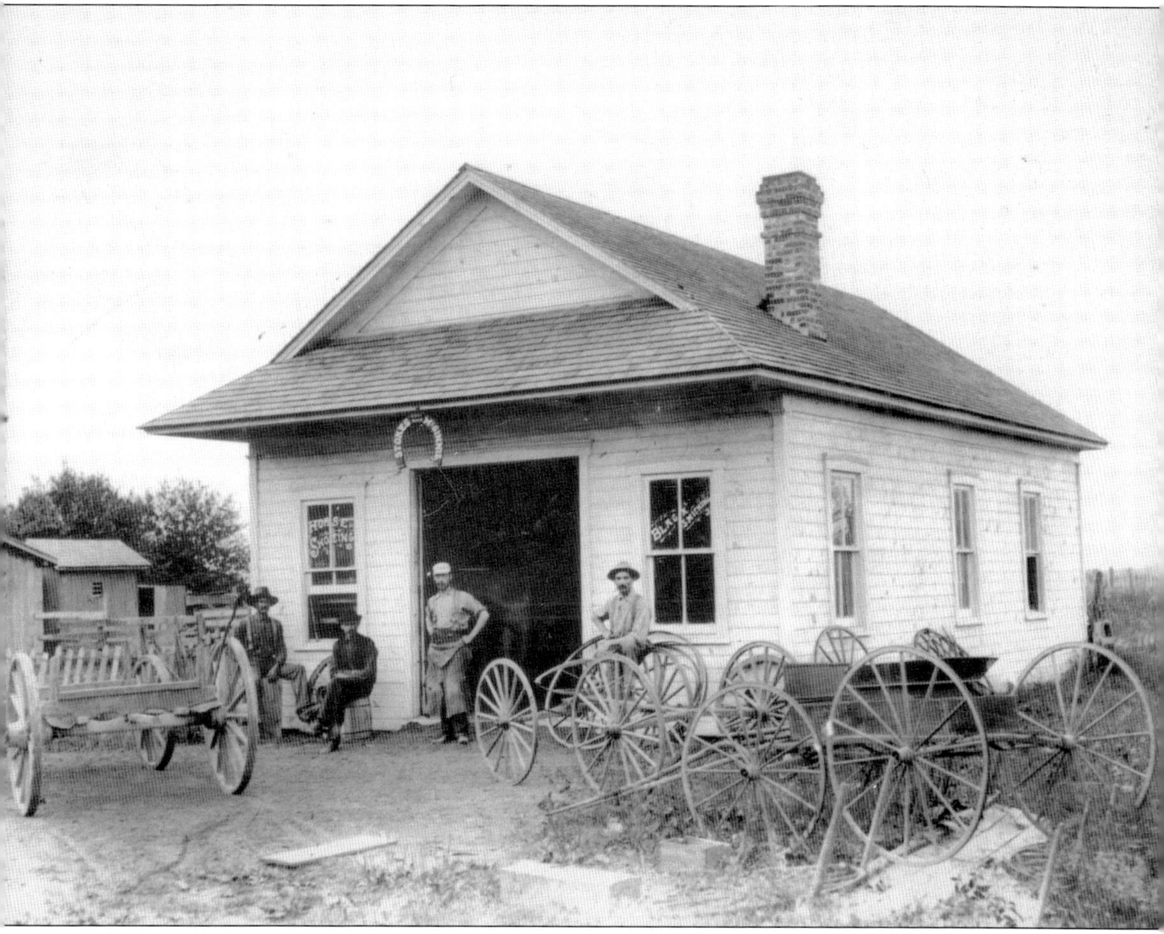

Four unidentified men are shown with the blacksmith in the door at the Stokes and McGinnis Blacksmith Shop in Lytle in this photograph, taken in 1900. The shop's name is painted on the wooden horseshoe-shaped sign over the door. (Courtesy of WCHS Museum.)

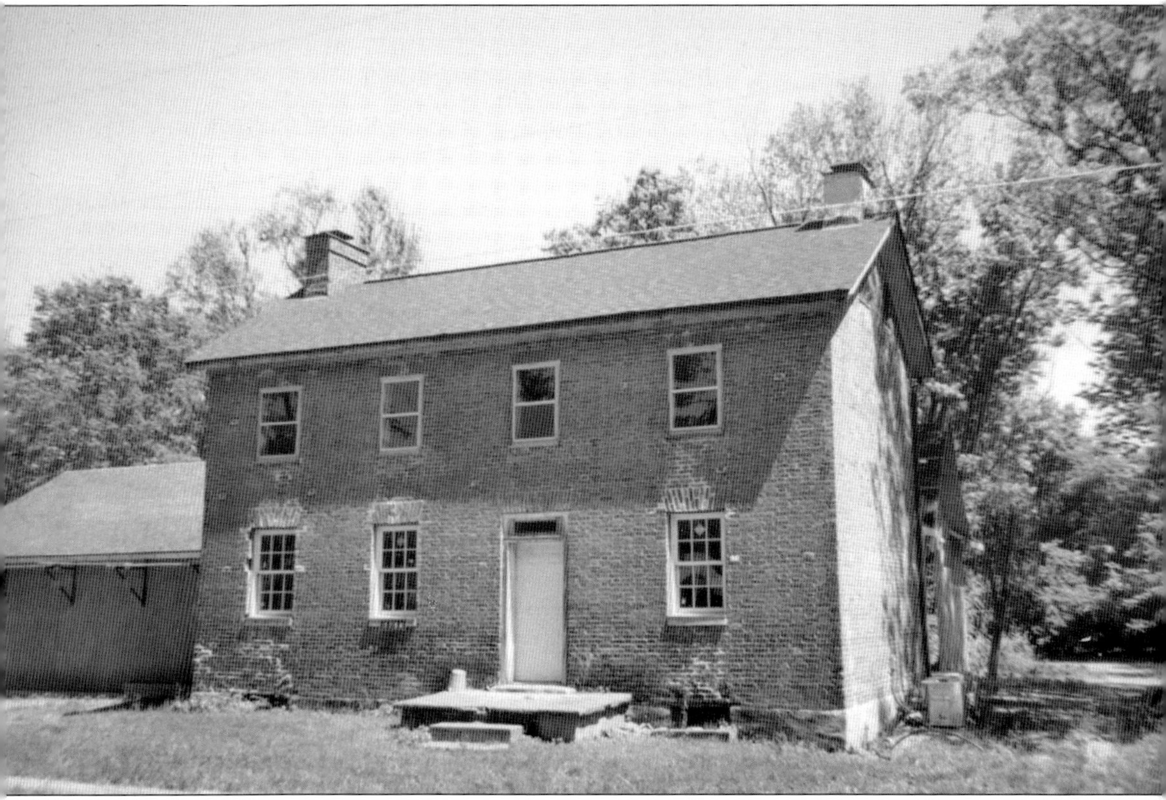

The cornerstone of Crosswicks is a two-story brick home now being renovated and preserved, as shown in this photograph taken in 2012. The residence is believed to have been built in 1814 by James Jennings, who surveyed and laid out the village of Crosswicks in 1821. The Howard Shutts family wired the house with electricity when they moved into it in 1935. For several years, this was the home of Marjorie Shutts and was co-owned by her brother, Robert Shutts. (Author's.)

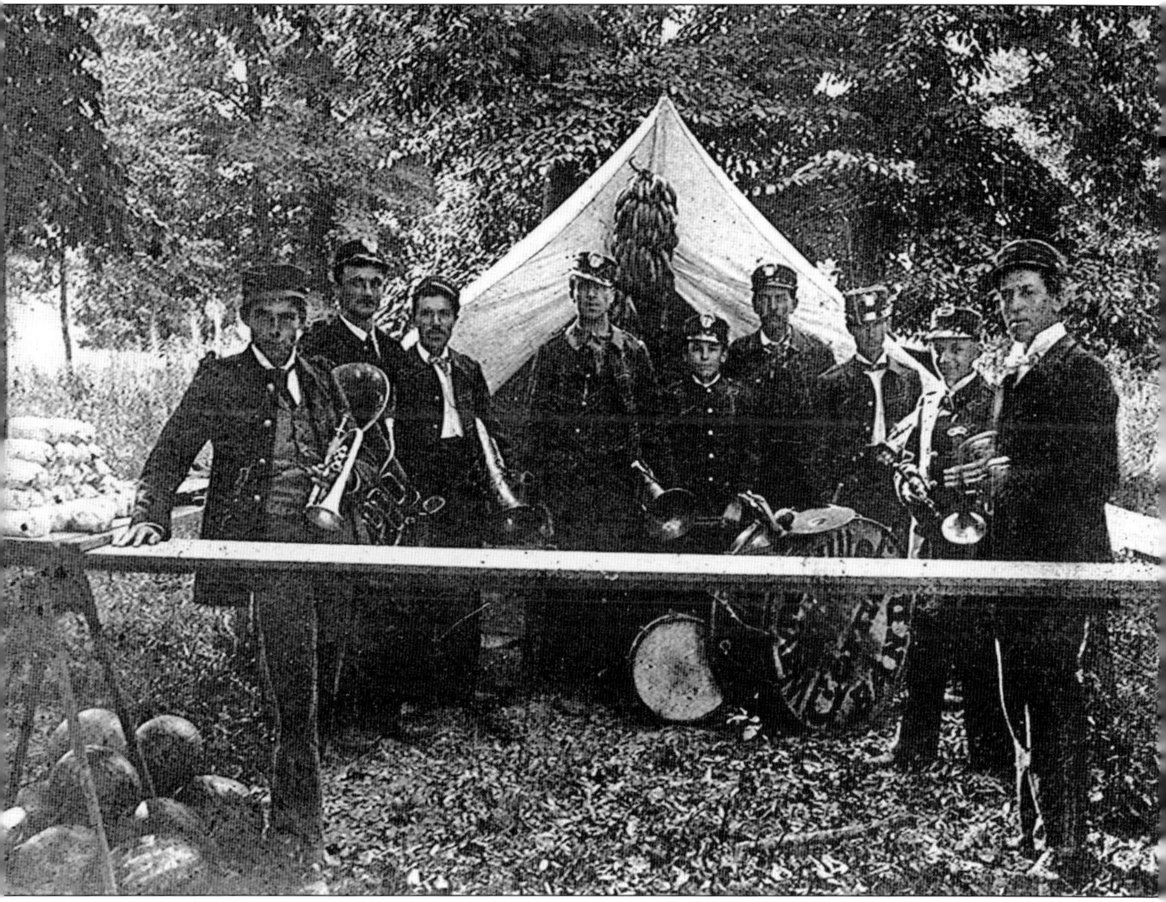

The Waynesville Cornet Band is shown in this c. 1880 photograph. The band was raising funds by selling sandwiches, watermelons, and bananas at a community picnic. (Courtesy of Mary L. Cook Public Library.)